Refiguring *Huckleberry Finn*

Refiguring *Huckleberry Finn*

CARL F. WIECK

The University of Georgia Press

Athens and London

Mark Twain's previously unpublished words are © 2000 by Richard A. Watson
and Chase Manhattan Bank as Trustees of the Mark Twain Foundation, which
reserves all reproduction or dramatization rights in every medium. Quotation
is made with the permission of Richard A. Watson, the University of California
Press, and Robert H. Hirst, General Editor of the Mark Twain Project. Subsequent quotations from previously unpublished words by Mark Twain are also
© 2000 and are signaled by an asterisk (*) in their citation.

Set in Janson by G & S Typesetters
Printed and bound by Thomson-Shore
The paper in this book meets the guidelines for permanence and durability
of the Committee on Production Guidelines for Book Longevity
of the Council on Library Resources.

Printed in the United States of America

04   03   02   01   00   C   5   4   3   2   1

Library of Congress Cataloging-in-Publication Data

Wieck, Carl F., 1937–
Refiguring Huckleberry Finn / Carl F. Wieck.
p.   cm.
Includes bibliographical references and index.
ISBN 0-8203-2238-5 (alk. paper)
1. Twain, Mark, 1835–1910. Adventures of Huckleberry Finn.
2. Literature and society—United States—History—19th century.
3. Twain, Mark, 1835–1910—Political and social views.   I. Title.
PS1305.W54   2000
813'.4—dc21   00-029912

British Library Cataloging-in-Publication Data available

To my parents,

Herman and Jean Wieck,

for sharing the miracle of wonder.

CONTENTS

PREFACE

During that time the most important book I read was *Tom Sawyer* and *Huckleberry Finn*—they were both in the same volume . . . It ruined me for the rest of the Third Reich. My mind was always with Jim and the Mississippi River. It was so special to me, had such an impact on me. It was such a different world than the one I knew, the Indians, everything. It seemed strange but wonderful. I read it at nine and I still remember it clearly. I had a good imagination, and could see the scenes very well. I would rather have been there than in Berlin.—Quoted in Gerald Posner, *Hitler's Children: Inside the Families of the Third Reich*

This statement by Norman Frank, taken from an interview given many years after World War II, is not greatly surprising when we consider that his father was Hans Frank, the notorious governor-general of Poland executed at Nuremberg for crimes committed against humanity under the Hitler regime. While young Norman's father was ascending the ladder of success within the National Socialist system and his mother was spending more and more time at official functions, the boy—who rubbed shoulders with Goebbels, Göring, Himmler, and Mussolini at times—lived a privileged but isolated existence, looking to books as a bulwark against loneliness.[1] As he observes: "Instead of going into the war I would have preferred going down the Mississippi with Huckleberry Finn."[2]

Several years later and an ocean away, my own father, a Berliner who had managed to immigrate to the United States ahead of the rising storm, made me a gift of the same two works in which Norman Frank had found a world to which he could flee when the Berlin of his young days became too barren and meaningless. Those books meant a great deal to this young American, whose father had served in the armed forces of his adopted country in order to help bring to a halt the actions of men like Hans Frank. I was grateful for the books but remember being much more grateful for the fact that my father had returned from the war and was able to give them to me personally.

The books revealed the joy of a special kind of world that did not seem all that strange to a boy growing up in the South along the Ohio River. Yet wonder was there, and Twain worked his magic, as only he can do. Over the years and in several countries I have tried to share that magic with students of various cultures and backgrounds, and I have found that Twain rarely fails to ignite something special that continues to glow long after the lights of the classroom have dimmed. The world Norman Frank found so receptive and bracing continues to live and offer respite as well as inspiration to those willing to open and roam through Twain's pages with Huck, Jim, and Tom.

I therefore harbor the hope that the reader of this collection will discover ideas, feelings, and perceptions that can kindle enthusiasm for the enlivening experience that the hours spent with *Huckleberry Finn* can provide. Should this occur, the sustenance found in Mark Twain's work by Norman Frank and myself, sons of fathers for whom the words "humanity" and "humane" have had profoundly different meanings, will have once again nurtured a vital human echo.

ACKNOWLEDGMENTS

The following pages have furnished me the princely privilege of skipping along for a space with the sprightly Mark Twain, and I am grateful to him for sharing so much with us all. In attempting to better understand him and *Huck*, however, I would not have been able to indulge myself nearly as freely had I not been royally indulged by many a friend, relation, colleague, or professional lover of books. Of necessity, I will fail in the effort to express adequate appreciation to those who have facilitated my work in some way; and, as I write this, many acts of kindness and generosity come to mind that will go unmentioned but not unremembered. Nonetheless, I wish to call attention to a few.

First of all, the members of my family deserve profound thanks for the strength of their support; I could not have essayed what I have without it, nor would the work have advanced apace and been as much fun. Others who have undergirded this endeavor include Bernth Lindfors, Jan Nordby Gretlund, Helmuth Joel, and Rose Vandewalle.

Superb service has been rendered by the Library of Congress, the Mark Twain Project at Berkeley, the Buffalo and Erie County Public Library, the Gannett-Tripp Library of Elmira College, the University of Louisville Library, the University of Tampere Library, the Mark Twain House in Hartford, Connecticut, the Henry W. and Albert A. Berg Collection at the New York Public Library, the Illinois State Historical Library, the Houghton Library of Harvard University, and the Chemung County Historical Society. In particular, I wish to acknowledge the generous and perceptive assistance accorded by Carmen Embry, Robert H. Hirst, William H. Loos, Kathleen C. McDonough, E. Cheryl Schnirring, and Mark Woodhouse.

A fruitful stay at the Elmira College Center for Mark Twain Studies also contributed to this work, and gratitude for making the experience a rich one goes especially to Gretchen Sharlow, Karen Ernhout, and Mark Connell.

To my students, colleagues, and friends at the University of Louisville, Morehouse College, the University of Abidjan, Joensuu University, and the

University of Tampere I recognize a debt directly related to *Huck* and would like to assure them that their succor over the years is reflected in this book. I also wish to recognize David E. E. Sloane, David Nye, Christine Raguet-Bouvart, Gayle Wurst, M. Thomas Inge, Victor A. Doyno, James S. Leonard, Gregg Camfield, Thomas A. Tenney, and Orvokki Hellsten, all of whom have favored me with aid and interest. In addition, I extend special thanks to the anonymous readers of the manuscript for their beneficial suggestions.

I am particularly grateful to all those associated with the University of Georgia Press who have bestowed thoughtful, subtle care on this book. Karen K. Orchard, Barbara Ras, David E. Des Jardines, Marlene Allen, Alison Klapthor, and Mary M. Hill have been in the forefront of an even more extensive phalanx that also earns my thanks and respect.

A deep bow and a wide sweep of the hat go to Ralf Norrman, Louis J. Budd, and Deba P. Patnaik, each of whom contributed selflessly to improvement of the following pages at sensitive stages of development. Their assistance was welcome, far more than requested, and essential. Much of what I feel is valuable here is tinged with their colors. In the same breath, I also want to honor those other scholars who have blazed paths and dedicated themselves to holding high a banner of mental rigor and rational, humane values. I wish their spirit to permeate this work, for I owe them much. Two whose memory warms me are George Brodschi and Richard Bjornson.

Last but most, a simple word of thanks to my brother Clifford, whose commitment to this undertaking touches every page and has been unflagging. Without him this book would not exist.

INTRODUCTION

Adventures of Huckleberry Finn is the focus of this book, but the reader will find the chapters linked by much more than the understandable bond of the novel itself. They underscore the unifying sense of humanity and rationality Mark Twain felt necessary to civilized social interaction, as well as the significance he accorded to an open-minded, unbiased perception of the wellsprings of the American spirit. In his efforts to speak to and about America, Twain stretched backward in history and forward into the future to indicate the kinds of values that needed to come to the fore. This aspect of the book is reflected in many of the chapters, and they are arranged in an order that allows the reader to first become acquainted with some unexplored historical features of Twain's novel before being introduced to examples of the author's skills in other domains. In addition, Twain conscripted humor to serve in the causes he took up with the writing of *Huckleberry Finn*, and the reader will find here some indications of the innovative ways he employed that tool to work toward a vision of a society where decency, equality, and freedom could be the norm rather than the exception. Even as he lashed out against society's failures, however, he was aware that his weapon was two-edged, and the satirical, sometimes ambiguous approach he employed can lead at times to producing an ambivalent reaction on the part of the reader. In that ambivalence may nevertheless be found a burgeoning of the tolerance that contributes so much to saving Twain and *Huckleberry Finn* from self-righteous preachments. I return frequently to that inescapable need for tolerance and to Twain's struggle to help America develop into more than it had yet become. The following brief summary suggests other themes and motifs that unite these chapters.

In responding to the query "What piece of imaginative writing best expresses the spirit of America?" the scholar and historian Arthur Schlesinger Jr. came to the decision that "a strong case can be made for Herman Melville's *Moby-Dick*, for Walt Whitman's *Leaves of Grass*, for Nathaniel Hawthorne's *The Scarlet Letter*. But in the end one is compelled to go for *Huck*

Finn." [1] Schlesinger is not the first to have drawn this conclusion, and critics have often wrestled with the problem of determining why Twain's book is considered to be quintessentially "American." In "A New Birth of Freedom: Jefferson, Lincoln, and *Huckleberry Finn*," I offer an answer to that question through revealing the distinct and shaping influence on Twain's novel of language and concepts formulated by Thomas Jefferson and Abraham Lincoln. This feature of the book has, until now, escaped the attention of scholars but contributes to providing an explanation as to why William Dean Howells sensed instinctively that Twain was the "Lincoln of our literature." [2]

I also deal with the uniquely American quality of Twain's novel in several other chapters. In "Frederick Douglass in *Huckleberry Finn*," for example, I investigate specific ways in which Douglass's influence appears to be manifested in the work. I present evidence to support the thesis that many of Douglass's astute observations regarding the American slave system find analogues and parallels in *Huckleberry Finn*. On the basis of that evidence, it seems probable that whereas Twain on at least one occasion proffered aid to the outspoken abolitionist, he was, without acknowledging it or necessarily realizing it, the recipient of as much if not a great deal more than he gave.

Douglass's finely honed sense of justice is just one of the qualities that may be reflected in Twain's novel, but that understanding of fair play bears directly on the chapter "'Right' in *Huckleberry Finn*," in which several of Twain's approaches to the notion of "rights," as well as to the word itself, are considered. While the author asks us to stretch our conception of "right" far beyond usual boundaries, we are furnished no directions for sorting out the seemingly arbitrary paths on which he often takes us. We are made to realize that in this critical area of human interaction we are very much "innocents abroad." Yet Twain himself seems to have betrayed similar innocence when undertaking and completing the writing of his novel. In "Finishing *Huckleberry Finn*" I contemplate ways in which the period during which the book was being crafted defined what kind of work *could* be written. I ask, moreover, whether the final failure of Reconstruction did not serve an embarrassingly beneficial function for the author through lifting a certain moral weight from his shoulders, thereby helping him bring his narrative to a frantic, but relieving and relieved, close.

In "Huck and Jim on the Mississippi: Going with the Flow?" features of the book are examined that depend on the rarely referred to fact that neither Twain nor Huck and Jim seem to have actually intended to go down the river. The concern of this chapter is to comprehend the limitations that that one-way river ultimately imposes on the author and his leading characters, as well as to fathom their response to its constrictive flow. That their response so frequently places them in opposition to that flow suggests that Twain swiftly seized on the rich potential inherent in the change of plan for his novel. The imposing force of the Mississippi again makes its presence felt in "Reflections on *Huckleberry Finn*'s Floating House," in which my aim is to twitch the veil from Twain's wildly humorous treatment of the Walpurgis Night events connected with the scene where pap's body is discovered. When Huck and Jim clamber through the window of the house the morning after they find it, a little daylight is also allowed to shine onto the involved web the author weaves in order to make the entire incident tightly integrated with, and pivotal to, the rest of the novel.

Two chapters—"The Figure Forty in *Huckleberry Finn*" and "The End, Yours Truly Mark Twain"—offer speculative conclusions regarding some of Twain's hitherto unremarked expertise in employing repeated numbers for the purpose of producing subliminal effects in the reader. The figures "forty" and "two" represent the key props for Mark Twain's dazzling display of personally and historically pertinent legerdemain, during which the reader is introduced to unsuspected aspects of his ingenuity. A further example of the author's dexterity is foregrounded in the chapter "On Black and White in *Huckleberry Finn*," where Twain's achievement in reversing simplistic notions concerning black and white races and "black" and "white" values is explored. I argue that in *Huckleberry Finn* Twain was taking a subtle but uncompromising stand on the issue of racism in a manner that would cause his revolutionary message to tend to be read and subconsciously absorbed long before—if ever—it became consciously perceived.

In contrast to the convoluted method to which Twain resorted in treating the subject of black and white, it is generally understood that at the beginning of his novel he was openly joshing the reader with introductory comments concerning, for instance, the possible fate awaiting anyone who dared look for a motive, a moral, or a plot. In "'I Never Seen Anybody but Lied One Time or Another,'" I demonstrate that this playful "warning" must be seen as part of a broader and more intricately developed pattern that reveals Twain to have been waging humorous but unrelenting guerrilla warfare on an old but honored tradition among fiction writers: the practice of claiming works of fiction to be the unvarnished truth. The accent in this case is on illustrating what role the prefatory material for *Huckleberry Finn* occupied in a still grander "game" Twain was playing.

As a counterweight to the treatment of Twain's aggressive attack on prefatory formulae, I reflect in the closing chapter, "Knowledge and Knowing in *Huckleberry Finn*," on the manner in which Twain grapples constructively with a broad range of considerations linked with the acquisition and nature of knowledge. I undertake to establish that the author's often profoundly complex approach to epistemological questions creates a parti-colored and insightful commentary on education and its processes, while his blade of irony is unsheathed primarily in order to pierce bubbles of presumption that arise from the very human belief that the whole truth concerning "reality" can be *known*.

From these inklings it should be apparent that the chapters cover a broad range of topics in an effort to increase appreciation of new dimensions of Mark Twain's artistry and thought. My intention is to stretch beyond existing scholarship—which in the case of *Huck* furnishes an imposing structure of support to which I am gratefully indebted—in order to examine aspects of Twain's genius that seem either to have been neglected or to have gone unnoticed. The reader may observe that I seek to contribute to a "refiguring," in several senses of that word, of a novel whose depths continue to offer the stimulus of unanswered questions. The fascination of following the often elusive author into some of those depths in order to unearth answers to some of those questions will, with any luck, rub off on all those who share this adventure.

CHAPTER ONE

A New Birth of Freedom:
Jefferson, Lincoln, and *Huckleberry Finn*

Adventures of Huckleberry Finn is considered today to be one of the most important works of American literature.[1] Whether or not one agrees with Ernest Hemingway's pronouncement that all modern American literature is beholden to Mark Twain's masterpiece, the book seems to be one that Americans can relate to strongly and more often than not with warmth.[2] Suggested reasons for this have touched upon such themes as the deep humanity of the book, evidenced in the relationship between Huck and Jim; the humor in the novel that seems always ready to bubble forth, even at the least likely moments; the relationship to nature, natural beauty, and natural behavior that Twain displays; the absence of religious and societal restrictions found in living on a free-floating raft drifting along the most important river in the land; and the freedom from formal language constraints that Twain pioneered in using the vernacular to make the characters of his novel easier for the ordinary American to relate to.

Although the novel contains enough violence, cruelty, death, and other "adult" features to have placed it off-limits to children from its first appearance (if only adults had realized just how much it differed from its more innocent predecessor, *The Adventures of Tom Sawyer*),[3] Twain was careful to ensure that the book would at least appear to be one that could be read by children.[4] His efforts resulted in allowing him to slip the book into the "youth market" while at the same time appealing to those adults who could appreciate the work on other levels. From the outset, then, *Huckleberry Finn* has occupied the enviable position of a book ostensibly suitable both for young people as well as adults and open to more than one reading by

1

the same audience, a book also capable of influencing the thinking of readers at different stages of their lives.

If read at an early age, the high adventure, the snakes, the fascination of the river, the friendship of Jim and Huck, the fears and dangers, and Tom Sawyer's high jinks are among the aspects that remain in a reader's memory long after the novel is closed. Subconsciously, however, one has probably absorbed much more. The fact that people of different races can be true and equal friends may be one of the more significant of the enduring images,[5] but other principles that Americans hold to be important are also dealt with by Twain. The ideas that it is possible to escape from an intolerable situation, such as the cruelty of a parent, that religion is not always holy, that one's own conscience—although perhaps dissenting from what one has been taught—has a right to be heard *and* respected, and that even scoundrels are, after all, human and can be seen in a humane light, despite their misdeeds, are all facets of the book that have the potential for leaving lasting traces in the mind of a youthful reader. All of these aspects have to do with the development of humane values, and all can give a young mind serious questions to ponder over in shaping a personal moral code.

The adult reader may be even more aware of the irony and wit Twain employs to emphasize his points, will probably be alert to more of the features of the novel that have reference to the periods about and during which it was written, and, hence, can comprehend the wider historical context of the book. Nonetheless, the values stressed remain the same and are, perhaps, only more *consciously* perceived by the adult reader. The result, however, is that in the lives of many readers Twain is permitted to make his points at least twice.

Is it, therefore, primarily repeated exposure to the book and the fact that the reading public is open to being doubly influenced by the spirit and values portrayed in the novel that make *Huckleberry Finn* so widely loved and often considered to be the most American of American novels?[6] Is the reason to be found in a combination of any or all of the various aspects of the book so far mentioned? Or should we expand our search?

There are, of course, many qualities and features of *Huckleberry Finn* that have not been alluded to here, such as the need of Americans for change, the movement west, the *Bildungsroman* aspect of Huck's growth toward responsible manhood within the confused and confusing American society—

to list but a few. None of these, however, seems to offer sufficient promise for a broadly based answer to the questions posed above.

I would therefore like to suggest that, at least in part, the specifically American quality often attributed to *Huckleberry Finn* lies elsewhere. To find a deeper unity and a wider meaning for Twain's novel,[7] we need to turn to the ideas and ideals promoted by Thomas Jefferson and expanded and underscored by Abraham Lincoln.

For Jefferson, as the author of the Declaration of Independence, it was a "self-evident" truth that "all men are created equal, that they are endowed by their Creator with certain inalienable rights; that among these rights are life, liberty and the pursuit of happiness; that to secure these rights, governments are instituted among men, deriving their just powers from the consent of the governed."[8] Jefferson's Declaration was overtly aimed at the despotism of a king and reflected the general mistrust of the kind of royal power from which so many of the early settlers had fled. It was also clear to Jefferson that if one believed in the equality of *all*, then slavery must perforce be wrong. This man, a slaveholder himself, thus wrote into the Declaration an extended passage condemning slavery, only to have it excised by the other members of the congressional committee responsible for the final version.[9]

In *Huckleberry Finn* Mark Twain clearly follows Jefferson's lead. Little by little it becomes evident that Jim and Huck, despite their difference in color, are equal as human beings; that they both should have the right to life, liberty, and the pursuit of happiness; that as long as a government does not respect these rights for all of its subjects it does not have the consent of all of the governed; that royalty—whether it takes the form of slaveholders or bogus kings and dukes—can never treat as equal those who are condemned to uphold and serve it; and that slavery in any guise is unjust and morally unacceptable.

When seen in this light, Twain's work represents a statement, albeit in a more lively form, of many of the principles held sacred by those men who in 1776 realized full well that they were placing at risk their lives and their fortunes but, insofar as they were faithful to their principles and to each other, *not* their sacred honor. These principles, and the rights to which the authors of the document referred, became part of what might be called

America's soul. And we find Twain's attitude toward that soul expressed during his first stay in Philadelphia at the early age of seventeen upon visiting the "old State House in Chestnut street," where, in his words, "the mighty Declaration of Independence was passed by Congress, July 4th, 1776." [10] We also know from a letter Twain sent to William Dean Howells on 9 August 1876 that he appears to have begun the writing of *Huckleberry Finn* somewhere around early July of that year,[11] at the height of the five-month American Centennial celebration in Philadelphia of the signing of the Declaration of Independence and the symbolic founding of the country. Given these circumstances, it would be difficult to conceive of his being insensitive to the significance this event held for Americans.

Although Twain had informed Mrs. Abel Fairbanks in a letter of 3 June that "I have decided to remain away from the Centennial altogether," [12] it seems quite possible that it was conscious awareness of the Centennial that in fact gave him the impetus to begin work on *Huckleberry Finn*. In a letter of 8 June of that year, Howells mentions to Twain having "written a mighty long account of the Centennial in the July number," [13] and, according to Henry Nash Smith and William M. Gibson, "In a communication now lost Mark Twain apparently asked Howells whether he was planning to attend the Congress of Authors arranged for 1 July in connection with the Philadelphia Centennial." [14] Twain himself contributed a eulogy of the American patriot Francis Lightfoot Lee to the Congress,[15] and that he did indeed attend the centennial is confirmed in a letter he sent Mrs. Fairbanks on 14 September: "I went there in July, & staid nearly a whole day; then I got discouraged & returned home. I became satisfied that it would take me two, or possibly 3 days, to examine such an array of articles with anything like just care & deliberation." [16]

Considering that Twain attests to having attended the Philadelphia centennial and begun *Huckleberry Finn* in the same month of July 1876, it would not seem unexpected to find his awareness of the importance of Jefferson and the Declaration of Independence reflected in specific as well as general terms in his novel. One example of this occurs when the author gives the names of two signers of the Declaration, as well as one of the most important figures in the early life of the country, to one of the Phelps children, whom he humorously christens Thomas Franklin Benjamin Jefferson Elexander (329).[17] Jefferson's Declaration is also alluded to, seemingly in

passing, when Twain has Huck offer the following explanation to Jim during some imaginative commentary on "Henry the Eight": "Well, Henry
he takes a notion he wants to get up some trouble with this country. How
does he go at it—give notice?—give the country a show? No. All of a sudden he heaves all the tea in Boston harbor overboard, and whacks out a
declaration of independence, and dares them to come on" (199). As may be
noted, Henry's "declaration" is actually that of an Englishman and by being
uncapitalized and accorded only an indefinite article loses any claim to being unique. At an American Society dinner given on 4 July in London many
years later, Twain would express the view that Jefferson's own Declaration
was also one of several spiritual equals, written, moreover, by an Englishman, since, at the time Jefferson penned the document, the United States
had not as yet formally become a nation.[18]

   In a more direct reference to the Declaration, Twain has Huck relate that
in the home of the slaveholding Grangerfords "they had pictures hung on
the walls—mainly Washingtons and Lafayettes, and battles, and Highland
Marys, and one called 'Signing the Declaration'" (137). There is obvious
situational irony involved in having a picture celebrating freedom and
equality for "all men" located in a home where the occupants are clearly
committed to living in direct conflict with such a philosophy. And the irony
is further heightened by having *Signing the Declaration* mentioned last on
the list, in throwaway-punchline style, as well as by providing this particular picture with a definite title while all the others are granted only
generic labels. Huck also takes time to draw our attention to what both he
and the Grangerfords consider to be an awe-inspiring table cover "made
out of beautiful oil-cloth, with a red and blue spread-eagle painted on it,
and a painted border all around. It come all the way from Philadelphia, they
said" (137).

   Twain again employs the Fourth of July date in the scene in which the
youngest Wilks sister, Joanna, inquires as to whether the English don't
treat their servants "better'n we treat our niggers?" After Huck tells her
"*No!* A servant ain't nobody, there. They treat them worse than dogs," she
asks, "Don't they give 'em holidays, the way we do, Christmas, and New
Year's week, and fourth of July?" (223). Twain's irony is unmistakable, but
it acquires added sting when we consider that the Wilkses' "servants" are
not hired help but slaves. The situation is further complicated a few lines

later when Huck is cornered by Joanna into realizing that he, too, is pretending to be the king's "servant," a fact that bespeaks an unequal status
and links the boy to the comparison with the Wilkses' "niggers."

In answering Joanna, Huck explains that English servants "never see a
holiday from year's end to year's end; never go to the circus, nor theatre,
nor nigger shows, nor nowheres" (223). While not sparing the English and
their treatment of menials, Twain utilizes Huck's general ignorance about
England in order to criticize America, since one might well ask how often
Southern slaves were allowed to attend either a circus or a theater performance. And even if they *were* actually allowed to attend a "nigger show," it
would be astonishing if chattel slaves would find it the most uplifting or
liberating of experiences. A similar attitude among these noncitizens, allowed almost no human rights, might also be predicted with regard to their
philosophical "appreciation" of an Independence Day "holiday" that, despite its welcome respite, would carry only hypothetical rather than personally felt, practical grounds for celebration.[19] Additional proof of the fact
that Twain was consciously aware of the 4 July date and was considering at
least one further possibility involving its use can also be found in his working notes for *Huckleberry Finn*, in which he indicates that if he had carried
out one of his plans for the book, we would have seen Huck "join Sunday
School before 4th July."[20]

Less direct but of equal importance in Twain's novel are the abundant
examples of expressed or implied declarations of independence. Huck and
Jim find themselves continually in conflict with the world around them and
frequently are forced to remove themselves from situations that threaten
their independence of thought or action. We see Huck gradually reject the
ways of the widow and Miss Watson, Tom, pap, the king and the duke, and
finally Southern "sivilization" itself, while Jim takes the ultimate step of
carrying out his belief that he should be independent of his "owner." To
find more congenial worlds, both characters most often allow their actions
to express their independence through "lighting out." Indeed, the entire
work evinces a continual tension between subjection and freedom, with
flight the most usual solution. Given the omnipresence of this pivotal
theme, it is not surprising to find Clifton Fadiman affirming: "Just as the
Declaration of Independence . . . contains in embryo our whole future history as a nation, so the language of *Huckleberry Finn* (another declaration

of independence) expresses our popular character, our humor, our slant."[21] But it was more than the innovative language that was a declaration of independence from what had gone before; it was Huck's book itself.

Thomas Jefferson thus contributes to the novel a unique spirit that reveals Twain to have found essential inspiration in the words of that founding father. The many ways in which *Huckleberry Finn* reflects that spirit permit the book to offer subtle support to the humane concepts expressed in the Declaration of Independence and to speak unobtrusively to Americans of their roots in a brave revolutionary past. Huck and Jim in their turn serve to make Jefferson's ideals contemporary through actually attempting against all obstacles to put them into practice. But as essential to the book as Jefferson may be, it should be realized that he was not the only important American to have had an influence on the novel.

Abraham Lincoln, like Twain, was born a Southerner but moved to the North. Both Lincoln and Twain were consummate storytellers who employed humor to penetrate to the heart of a problem, and both were masters of the English language who used the vernacular to render their ideas accessible to the common people. Both, as transplanted Southerners, were forced to come to grips with the violent changes wrought by the Civil War and the freedom granted to black Americans. And both were richly complicated men who wrestled with their own divisive, private demons while simultaneously serving as cynosures in the life of their times.

Possibly it was Twain's nephew, Samuel E. Moffett, who first drew the comparison with Lincoln in 1899 after Twain, claiming that it was at his wife's urging, wrote a "skeleton" autobiographical sketch that was then submitted to, fleshed out by, and subsequently attributed to Moffett.[22] In the sketch, which was returned to Twain for final revision and approval,[23] Moffett suggested that Twain's "humor is as irrepressible as Lincoln's, and like that, it bubbles out on the most solemn occasions; but still, again like Lincoln's, it has a way of seeming, in spite of the surface incongruity, to belong there."[24] The parallel between Lincoln and Twain also found favor with Howells, who expanded on the idea in 1910 on the occasion of Twain's death, stating that his old friend was the "sole incomparable, the Lincoln of our literature."[25]

In addition to the similarities of background, perspective, and attitude, there existed yet another interesting connection between Lincoln and Twain. Both had a close personal relationship with John M. Hay, a man not particularly well known today but who in his own lifetime played a strategic role on the world stage as the author of the Open Door Policy as well as of the treaty leading to the Panama Canal.[26] Hay also served as secretary of state to both William McKinley and Theodore Roosevelt and, to Mark Twain's chagrin, presided over the acquisition of the Philippines.[27]

According to Twain, his own friendship with Hay began in 1867 and endured thirty-eight years until his friend's death.[28] The relationship was so close at one point that when Twain considered founding, along with Howells, what he christened "The Modest Club," John Hay was the first person on the list of likely members.[29] Hay was an appropriate choice by these two literary men since he was both an editor and an author, and his book of poetry, *Pike County Ballads*, published in 1871, was well known in its day. In his poems, Hay employed the Pike County dialect Twain would also use in *Huckleberry Finn*,[30] and Mark Twain was a staunch defender of the view that Hay preceded Bret Harte in publishing poems in the vernacular.[31]

For Abraham Lincoln, on the other hand, John Hay's talents were employed in quite a different manner. It was as private secretary to the president of the United States that Hay served his country during the American Civil War. Since this was the period during which Lincoln was shaping a concept of America that would permit a revitalization of the country through a "new birth of freedom," it would seem reasonable to assume that when Hay and Twain became friends within a year after Lincoln's death, Hay's past was not a mystery to Twain and that there was sympathy on the part of both men for the goals toward which Lincoln had striven.[32]

It may also be of significance to the novel Twain commenced writing in July 1876 that on 14 April of that same year—the eleventh anniversary of the assassination of the fallen leader John Hay had served so well—a memorial to Lincoln was dedicated in the nation's capital. To commemorate the event, Frederick Douglass, the widely known abolitionist, former slave, and critic and supporter of Lincoln, was chosen to address an audience that included "the President of the United States and his Cabinet, Judges of the Supreme Court, the Senate and House of Representatives, and many thousands of citizens."[33] They had come together in Lincoln Park to witness the unveiling of a monument erected by the "colored people of the United States" in honor of the man who had done so much to secure a "new birth of freedom" for the nation.[34] Mark Twain, a friend to Douglass as well as Hay,[35] would almost certainly have been conscious of and sensitive to the potentially far-reaching implications for the country of that solemn occasion.

During his debates with Stephen Douglas prior to the Civil War, Abraham Lincoln frequently denied that the black man was fully equal to the white man.[36] The point was a crucial one, and Douglas more than once obliged Lincoln to take a public stand on this issue. Despite Lincoln's seemingly unambiguous position,[37] however, he would make what to many of his supporters appeared to be a serious change of course in November 1863 when he delivered what has come to be known as the Gettysburg Address.[38] Though employing a mere 272 words,[39] Lincoln, in the expression of one historian, "remade America" with that one short speech.[40]

In his brief statement at the dedication of the cemetery created for the soldiers who had died at the Battle of Gettysburg, Lincoln incorporated from the Declaration of Independence Jefferson's words "all men are created equal" into the following sentence: "Four score and seven years ago our fathers brought forth on this continent a new nation, conceived in Liberty, and dedicated to the proposition that all men are created equal." By echoing Jefferson's words and thought in this fashion, Lincoln could imply that they possessed the legal force of the laws set forth in the Constitution, something the Declaration of Independence had never pretended to claim.[41] The fathers of the country had not written into the Constitution a statement concerning equality. Lincoln, however, took Jefferson's principle into his own hands and, in effect, made equality the law of the land.

At Gettysburg, Lincoln spoke in the vernacular, used the word "that" as repetitiously as Jefferson had,[42] and refrained from qualifying the word "equal" in any manner. He frequently employed terms connected with birth such as "conceive" and "create,"[43] and he concluded his speech with the hope that the country might have "a new birth of freedom, and that government of the people, by the people, for the people shall not perish from the earth." Lincoln mentioned neither slaves nor slavery, but the simple fact that he failed to exclude any group or race was sufficient to change the course of American history.[44]

Lincoln's use of the Gettysburg Address to confer upon some of Jefferson's most cherished ideas the status of constitutional law caused a sea of change in America, and the waves have yet to subside. For it is in the terms of Jefferson and of Lincoln that many of today's arguments regarding varying interpretations of equality are ultimately expressed. It is also apparent from the writings of these men that both realized that in creating the positive possibilities that could flow from failing to limit equality or rights to any race or group, they were opening a Pandora's box of problems for future generations. That they did not flinch from drawing the conclusions inherent in their logic, despite their own personal difficulties in dealing fairly and objectively with the "peculiar institution," represents an impressive display of courage, conviction, and faith in the power of reason.

When Mark Twain began the writing of *Huckleberry Finn* in that centennial year of 1876, he chose to place his work in a time frame preceding the Civil War—and Gettysburg.[45] This allowed him to draw a distinct contrast between, on the one hand, pap's benighted attitude toward blacks, as seen in his violent tirade against even an almost white and highly educated representative of the race, and, on the other hand, Huck's growth toward the realization about his friend Jim late in the book that "I knowed he was white inside" (341).[46] The change of attitude that takes place within the ignorant Finn family represents a transformation of a magnitude similar to that which Lincoln himself, and no doubt Twain, had to go through within a painfully short time span.

Twain is also careful to have Huck fake his own death on precisely the same day that Jim runs away from his owner. When Huck and Jim compare their arrival times at Jackson's Island, it is easy for the reader to fail to notice that both had run away the same evening, for Jim informs Huck that he arrived "the night arter you's killed" (51), and Huck tells Jim a few lines later that *he* arrived "the night I was killed" (52). A close examination of the subsequent pages, however, reveals that Jim actually ran away the same night as Huck but was forced by circumstances to spend that first night as well as the following day hidden "under de shavins," where he heard people talking about Huck's "death" (53). The almost simultaneous departure times receive further confirmation when Judith Loftus, unaware of Huck's true identity, innocently explains to him that his "killer" is assumed to have been "the nigger" because "he hadn't ben seen sence ten o'clock the night the murder was done" (69).

Both Huck and Jim thus die to the constraints of the old life and receive a "new birth of freedom" at exactly the same moment in time. They begin their new lives together as outcasts from the old; and, as numerous interpreters of the novel have noted, the theme of death followed by the opportunity for renewal embodied in the idea of rebirth is repeated often throughout the novel. Frequently this occurs in association with the idea of release from enslavement to some more powerful, always unreasonable force, and, no less frequently, in connection with that ever-available source of connotative meaning, the river.

Huck's "new birth of freedom" actually begins to take tangible shape prior to the boy's flight from pap, when he starts his formal education and learns to "spell, and read, and write just a little, and . . . say the multiplication table up to six times seven is thirty-five" (18).[47] Upon discovering this, pap jealously points out that Huck has surpassed the educational achievements of all members of the family up to that point and tears up the paper Huck has received for doing well at school. Pap is too late, however; Huck's new knowledge is not circumscribed by a piece of paper. Education is irreversible, and the boy has begun the incremental process that will make him a free individual, separating him from pap's ignorance forever.[48]

When pap deprives Huck of his liberty, treats him as property, keeps him locked in for days at a time, and threatens worse, Huck begins preparations for a flight to freedom. He is even symbolically ready to kill his father, if it should come to that, in order to preserve his own new-found life. Jefferson, we should not forget, listed life and liberty as primary rights, and Huck clearly comes to feel as Jefferson did. But pap, who continually harps on the subject of his own rights, seems completely oblivious to the possibility of Huck having any but those he, as a parent, might choose to bestow. For pap, the boy is merely a piece of white property whose position within the society does not differ to any great degree from Jim's or from what pap feels *should* be the position of the hated "white-shirted free nigger" (34). For Huck, the only effective escape route, short of murdering his father, thus appears to lie in feigning his own death in order to be reborn into freedom from what he terms "the old ways."

Prior to Huck's carefully staged "demise," however, Twain provides the

reader with a humorous treatment of the concept of "death" and renewal
in the riotous episode of pap's own short-lived "rebirth" into respectable
society. But there is more than being "born again" involved here. Pap's
supposed moral rebirth is preceded somewhat earlier in the book by a presumed physical death by drowning, and in both cases society turns out to
be in error, first about pap's "death" and then about his "rebirth." It is
Huck, standing in his own way outside of society, who alone perceives the
mistakes. This understanding of the gullibility of humanity concerning
death as well as rebirth allows Huck to realize the full potential for a rebirth of freedom from both pap and society that a false drowning-death
might offer.

The theme receives an even more elaborate treatment in the Grangerford-Shepherdson feud section when Twain indicates that the death of
young Buck Grangerford is actually a positive thing, in that Buck had im-
bibed hate and destructive ideas from the older generations of his family
and hence could be seen as someone who would only have contributed to
promoting those ideas down through the years. In contrast to Buck's fate,
Twain allows Harney Shepherdson and Sophia Grangerford to elope with
their lives to the other side of what can be seen as both a physical and a
symbolic river. By crossing that river, they succeed in taking with them into
the future the possibility of offering the generations of Americans who will
spring from their tolerance and new love a fresh freedom from the evils of
past intolerance and ancient hatreds. In their escape lies the hope for a new
birth of freedom from the limitations placed upon them by their own
births. In this respect, their story corresponds to what happens to Huck
and Jim. The characters make conscious decisions to break away completely from the restrictions placed upon them by the past, and, cost what
may, their choice is to risk the challenges involved in freeing themselves
from that past. It is not difficult to draw a parallel between them and all
those refugees who risked everything in crossing even larger water barriers
for the purpose of becoming citizens of a new world where they could be
free from the birth-imposed limits and intolerance of an older one.

This segment of the book ends with Jim saying to Huck, "I 'uz right
down sho' you's dead agin" (154), and with Huck, seeing immediately the
plus side of that false belief, replying, "All right—that's mighty good; they
won't find me, and they'll think I've been killed, and floated down the

river—there's something up there that'll help them to think so—so don't you lose no time, Jim, but just shove off for the big water as fast as ever you can" (154). Not until the raft is out in the river does Huck feel "free and safe once more" (154). A supposed death, with the body once again mistakenly assumed to be in the river, serves anew to permit a rebirth of freedom for Huck.

In the Grangerford-Shepherdson section, as elsewhere in the novel, Twain enriches his work through counterpointing successful and unsuccessful examples of rebirth. Huck, for instance, is "reborn" as "George Jackson" at the Grangerfords after he and Jim have their violent encounter with a steamboat. But the initially promising situation swiftly deteriorates, ultimately destroys any hopes Huck might have had, and results in a dreary emptiness signaled by the merging of Huck's existence under a false identity with the falsity of the values of the family in which he finds himself living. Hence, despite the fact that this rebirth occurs by the traditionally sanctifying element of water, it can offer only slavery to ancient griefs rather than genuine, new freedom. The escape back to the raft, however, allows the river to contribute in a positive manner to returning to Huck both his identity and his freedom within that identity. And, not long afterward, when he and Jim sit naked together on the sandy bottom of the river in its summer-warm water watching night turn into day, peaceful immersion provides a "clean" rebirth—this time without a loss of identity—into the full freedom of a moment that has all the richness of the First Morning.[49]

Twain seemed to enjoy playing with the possibilities that the theme of rebirth, linked not only to freedom but also to a new identity, offered, and we find him gently mocking the idea in the scene where Aunt Sally mistakes Huck for Tom Sawyer. Huck exclaims, "But if they was joyful, it warn't nothing to what I was; for it was like being born again, I was so glad to find out who I was" (282). Whether Huck actually finds out much about who he is can be considered open to debate, but here, as in the Grangerford section, Twain illustrates the conflicted importance that the intertwining of the idea of rebirth with the concept of a change of identity has so frequently had for Americans. It may be noted, in addition, that the religious overtones evident in this scene clearly connect the son's fraudulent rebirth to the earlier failed "conversion" of his father.

Huck is also slowly reborn in this novel to a new freedom in his perception of the blacks in his world. At each stage of his dawning awareness of Jim's humanity (for example, when Jim stands watch while Huck sleeps, reveals his feelings about his deaf daughter, expresses distaste for the "trashy" treatment he receives from Huck after the night in the fog, or offers humane arguments concerning the children of Sollermun), Huck seems to peel off a thin layer of the old pap-like prejudice. Although he continues to use such expressions as "Well, if ever I struck anything like it, I'm a nigger" (210), statements of this nature only contribute the additional emphasis of irony to the steadily increasing closeness developing between Huck and Jim.

Twain also shows Huck unconsciously becoming aware of equality between blacks and whites other than himself and Jim, as can be seen in the transition scene that occurs at his meeting with Aunt Sally toward the end of the book when a "nigger woman" saves him from a pack of hounds. Huck tells us:

> And behind the woman comes a little nigger girl and two little nigger boys, without anything on but tow-linen shirts, and they hung onto their mother's gown, and peeped out from behind her at me, bashful, the way they always do. And here comes the white woman running from the house, about forty-five or fifty year old, bare-headed, and her spinning-stick in her hand; and behind her comes her little white children, acting the same way the little niggers was doing. (277) [50]

For Huck, the comparison has been made; the conclusion concerning it must, however, await a less tense and exciting moment as well as the leisure required for reflection. That this will probably transpire may be inferred from Huck's reaction on an earlier occasion when, upon perceiving that telling the truth can be "safer" than telling a lie, he decides: "I must lay it by in my mind, and think it over some time or other, it's so kind of strange and unregular" (239).

Huck thus grows and sheds the skins of old beliefs and outworn attitudes in a manner similar to that of the ever-present snakes in the novel. And in a gesture of multilevel significance, he swears, as we may remember, never to touch another snake skin after the near-fatal trick he plays on Jim. These changes are outwardly reflected in the various kinds of clothing and different personas Huck experiments with and one by one sloughs off. A fact not lost on Huck is that society's mistake concerning pap's presumed drowning early in the book hinges on the clothing worn by the corpse, and this information seems to contribute throughout the remainder of the novel to the boy's understanding of just how to gull society. By showing Huck's attempts to protect his slowly developing individual identity through the use of continually changing surface disguises, Twain also depicts his young protagonist as constantly involved in a process of self-renewal and possessed of the imagination and initiative necessary to avoid being fenced in by convention.

Huck ultimately decides at the close of the book that he is not interested in going to "the Territory" for only "a couple of weeks or two," as Tom Sawyer first suggests, but, rather, for as long as fate will have it, and without his friend. In making this decision he indicates that, unlike Tom, he is ready to commit himself to whatever future rebirths might be required in a life too exciting and full to be limited by the "sivilizing" forces of Aunt Sally, Tom, or any others who live within the shackles of shore-slavery.

The tortuous and protracted ordeal that Huck—not to mention Jim—goes through in the closing chapters of the novel appears to gradually lead him to a clearer perception of the wider implications of the fact that, no matter how "bad" a situation might appear at first sight, the Tom Sawyers of this world can never truly identify with, much less steal, a real or even a metaphorical "nigger." This realization brings Huck, who, like Jefferson and Lincoln, experiences personal anguish in connection with the institution of slavery, to finally comprehend that he must cling tenaciously to the flexibility that will allow for continual change and serial rebirth, forever ready to depart "ahead of the rest" if he means to live differently.[51] Jefferson and Lincoln, despite their own individual difficulties with slavery, also came to slowly understand that they had to be a step "ahead of the rest" in venturing into new "territory." Considering that fact, one might ask whether these two men, both of whom agonized long over questions that carried import for a young nation of a different yet parallel nature to those that trouble Huck, would not have smiled comprehendingly at the bold but seemingly unavoidable decision this young man takes to maintain his new life open-ended.

Jim's final revelation about the true death of pap also occurs at the end of the novel, and it is one of the pleasures of this book that the newly freed slave, who was set free long before he knew of it, acts as the agent in setting Huck, his intended liberator, free—long after the actual event has taken place. Old pap, like young Buck Grangerford, proves incapable of growth or renewal in ideas and attitudes and therefore cannot be allowed to cast a permanent shadow over the lives of those, like Huck, for whom the potential for change and development is vital. The elimination of pap at the threshold of his son's new existence liberates Huck from a major threat to his independence for the first time since his birth, and at this point he feels truly reborn. He is now free of brutal father, superficial friend, and unfulfilling society, ready to strike out on his own.

Jim, too, is ready to depart. Tom's revelation about Jim's true condition occurs only shortly prior to Huck's obtaining his own freedom, and Twain clearly parallels the two liberations as well as the two deaths that make them possible. By linking the passing of pap and Miss Watson, two characters who in life were polar opposites in most ways other than their socially acceptable attitude toward slavery, Twain underscores the fact that their deaths allow for the demise of "old ways," while at the same time serving to give birth—in pap's case unwillingly, but in Miss Watson's, and to her credit, *will*ingly—to new freedoms for the human beings formerly subjected to the injustice and caprice of these "owners." Nor can it any longer be considered a coincidence that it turns out to be on exactly the same day—in a manner reminiscent of their earlier, almost simultaneous flight from society's grip—that Huck and Jim acquire a more complete freedom, not to mention equality, than either has previously known. Such parallel occurrences indicate an inescapable and necessary bond between what these two unlikely friends have shared in the past and what future freedom holds for each of them.

Twain also contributes to our sense of being able to look into the kind of future where freedom is the rule rather than the exception. By situating *Huckleberry Finn* in the pre–Civil War period, the author made it easy for postwar readers to see the conclusions reached by Huck's naive but humane moral conscience as the natural result of a logical development: the decisions come to by Huck's prewar conscience simply seem to prefigure postwar reality.[52] In this manner Twain causes the reader to tend to accept Jeffersonian and Lincolnian concepts, and the postwar changes stemming from those concepts, as the inevitable consequences of a logical process that even a little-educated, under-aged river-rat could come to understand when given time and freedom enough to follow his natural instincts.

It would appear, moreover, that Mark Twain was following not only *his* natural instincts in the writing of his novel but was, during his lifetime, highly conscious of and sensitive to the ideals of both Jefferson and Lincoln concerning equality and freedom for all human beings. Additional external evidence of this might, therefore, be examined here with profit.

In commenting on the French Revolution in a letter sent to Howells on 22 September 1889, only a few years following the publication of *Huckleberry Finn*, Twain explicitly indicates the importance he assigned to the Declaration of Independence by making the claim that "next to the 4th of July & its results, it was the noblest & the holiest thing & the most precious that ever happened in this earth."[53] And several years later in "The Stupendous Procession," one of Twain's Fables of man, we behold among the marchers "THE GETTYSBURG SPEECH—a noble figure, and mournful. Broken sentences, embroidered upon its robe, are vaguely legible: 'Our fathers brought forth a new nation, conceived in liberty and dedicated to the proposition that all men are created equal. . . . . Now we are . . . . . testing whether this nation, or any nation, so conceived and so dedicated, can long endure.'"[54] In the same selection, under the heading "THE PIRATE FLAG," we also find Twain directly mocking the imperfect implementation of the ideals of both Jefferson and Lincoln. The following sardonic pseudo-quotations leave little doubt as to his position:

"ALL WHITE MEN ARE BORN FREE AND EQUAL." *Declaration of Independence.*

"ALL WHITE MEN ARE AND OF RIGHT OUGHT TO BE FREE AND INDEPENDENT." *Ibid.*

14th AMENDMENT: "WHITE SLAVERY SHALL NO LONGER EXIST WHERE THE AMERICAN FLAG FLOATS."

> "Christ died to make men holy,
> *He* died to make white men free."
> (Battle Hymn of the Republic. "He" is Abraham Lincoln.)

"GOVERNMENTS DERIVE THEIR JUST POWERS FROM THE CONSENT OF THE GOVERNED WHITE MEN." *Declaration of Independence.*[55]

"The Stupendous Procession" concludes with the heading "SHADE OF LINCOLN" followed by a brief evocation of the former president as "towering vast and dim toward the sky, brooding with pained aspect over the far-reaching pageant."[56] It is important to realize, however, that Twain's original version closed with Lincoln's "shade" uttering considerably more revealing words: "These pigmy traitors will pass and perish, and be forgotten—they and their treasons. And I will say again, with the hope and conviction of that other day of darkness and peril, 'This nation, under God, shall have a new birth of freedom.'"[57]

That Mark Twain admired the ideas and concepts framed in Lincoln's persuasive prose is thus evident; and that this admiration could, a few years prior to the writing of these lines, have found expression in *Huckleberry Finn* would appear to be well within reason.[58] Since the author's initial impulse when bringing "The Stupendous Procession" to a close was apparently to recognize Lincoln's poetic phrasing as worthy of sharing the stage with even his own, it seems only logical to find him including the entire final sentence of the Gettysburg Address in his remarks at festivities held at Carnegie Hall on 11 February 1901 in honor of Lincoln's birthday.[59] And on 4 July 1907, at an Independence Day dinner given by the American Society in London, he praised Lincoln's Emancipation Proclamation, "which not only set the black slaves free, but set the white man free also. The owner was set free from the burden and offense, that sad condition of things where he was in so many instances a master and owner of slaves when he did not want to be."[60] Given the celebration and the sentiment, Thomas Jefferson is one such owner Twain may well have had in mind.

In *Adventures of Huckleberry Finn* Mark Twain appeals to principles and ideals advocated by Thomas Jefferson and Abraham Lincoln, thereby helping to crystallize for Americans what their own dreams, ideals, and philosophies can boil down to in practice. Jefferson and Lincoln, each in his own way and in his own day, struggled with the problems of defining basic guidelines for the people of a new country in its formative stages. Twain demonstrates what those guidelines can mean to the human beings who have to go through the difficulties required to make of them a living reality. And American dreams must be able to make allowance for growth, change, and renewal. While an immigrant to the United States may feel reborn upon receiving American citizenship, the freedom for rebirth must also exist for Americans already living within the country. Only this will permit the nation to develop a spirit that allows for growth toward its full potential—as Lincoln came to realize when faced with interpreting Jefferson's words and as Twain clearly indicates. In *Huckleberry Finn*, Mark Twain gives human dimensions to the humane ideals of Thomas Jefferson and Abraham Lincoln. In that we discover a fundamental reason why this work has so often been considered uniquely American, and why it has never ceased to speak a universally understood language.

CHAPTER TWO

Frederick Douglass in *Huckleberry Finn*

MARK TWAIN'S FUTURE father-in-law, Jervis Langdon, was known in Elmira, New York, as an active abolitionist and a "conductor" on the Underground Railroad who continued his efforts on behalf of freed slaves following the Civil War and until the end of his life.[1] One of those who benefited from his aid was the ex-slave Frederick Douglass,[2] and it was apparently in the Langdon home that Douglass first came to know Twain. Their initial meeting probably occurred somewhere between August 1868, when Twain first met Langdon's daughter, Olivia Louise Langdon, the woman who was to become his wife, and 15 and 16 December 1869, when he wrote to her of a chance encounter he had just had with the now-famous abolitionist.[3] The author was immediately impressed by Douglass: "Had a talk with Fred Douglass, to-day, who seemed exceedingly glad to see me—& I certainly was glad to see *him* for I do so admire his 'spunk.'"[4] This meeting occurred about six and a half years before Twain began the writing of *Adventures of Huckleberry Finn*. In 1881—almost four years before publishing his novel—Twain wrote to President James Garfield on behalf of Douglass, referring to him as a "personal friend of mine" and urging the president to "retain Mr. Douglass in his present office of Marshall of the District of Columbia . . . because I so honor this man's high and blemishless character and so admire his brave, long crusade for the liberties and elevation of his race."[5]

That Twain held Douglass in high esteem and did not hesitate to link his own name with that of the distinguished former slave in the highest circles of the land is thus evident. Given this level of respect, together with Douglass's key position in the ongoing civil rights struggle, it might therefore be anticipated that reflections of Twain's admiration could be found in a novel that satirizes benighted Southern concepts and ideas that were prevalent before as well as after the American Civil War. As *Huckleberry Finn* clearly exhibits this kind of satire, more than one critic has seen the possibility of linking Douglass with the "white-shirted, free nigger,"[6] described by pap in the novel as

> a free nigger there, from Ohio; a mulatter, most as white as a white man. He had the whitest shirt on you ever see, too, and the shiniest hat; and there ain't a man in that town that's got as fine clothes as what he had; and he had a gold watch and chain and a silver-headed cane—the awfulest old gray-headed nabob in the State. And what do you think? they said he was a p'fessor in a college, and could talk all kinds of languages, and knowed everything. (33–34)

Because Douglass was a free mulatto possessed of elegance, eloquence, and education who in later life became gray-haired and was, moreover, personally known to Twain, this association was a reasonable one to make.

There is, on the other hand, the possibility that since pap mentions that the man was from Ohio, worked as a professor, and spoke several languages, it was not Douglass at all but another man entirely who was in Twain's mind as he wrote. As the editors of the California edition of *Huckleberry Finn* point out,

> The learned black professor could hail from Ohio, because slavery had been banned there by the 1787 Northwest Ordinance long before Ohio became a state in 1803. Although it can only be conjectured that Clemens knew him, there was in fact such a professor in the 1860s: John G. Mitchell (1827–1900), a light skinned black, who earned his doctorate of divinity and became a professor of Greek, Latin, and mathematics at Wilberforce (Ohio) University. During the Civil War Mitchell raised funds for his university in Missouri.[7]

Yet whether in the end it was Douglass, the man from Ohio, a combination of the two (or more) men, or someone else altogether, the notion that Douglass might have had more than a superficial influence on Twain's novel would seem to merit further exploration.[8] And since Douglass's widely read and easily available autobiographical *Narrative of the Life of Frederick Douglass, Written by Himself,* first published in 1845, seems to present itself as the logical source for such influence, I shall examine the possibility that this particular work finds reverberations in *Huckleberry*

Finn.[9] I will also refer to Douglass's *My Bondage and My Freedom* (1855) and *Life and Times of Frederick Douglass* (1891–92) whenever I find that these later, expanded versions of the *Narrative* have something to add to the discussion.[10]

Adventures of Huckleberry Finn opens with the well-known lines "You don't know about me, without you have read a book by the name of 'The Adventures of Tom Sawyer,' but that ain't no matter. That book was made by Mr. Mark Twain, and he told the truth, mainly. There was things which he stretched, but mainly he told the truth" (1). The intricacy of Twain's playful beginning emphasizes that in order to be authorized as the author of the book the reader has just taken in hand, Huck must appeal to the authority of another book, one in which Huck himself appears as a fictional character and in which the truth has been stretched by an author who only "told the truth, mainly." The fun Twain enjoys creating is scintillating, but Huck's own position remains, at best, tenuous.

Frederick Douglass's *Narrative* receives somewhat similar treatment in being furnished with a preface written by William Lloyd Garrison and a letter from Wendell Phillips. Both men take it upon themselves to confirm the truth of the tale on which we are about to embark, although each formulates a declaration that can be read as less than an unreserved endorsement. Garrison carefully attests that "I am confident that it is essentially true in all its statements" (38), while Phillips expresses confidence that "every one who reads your book will feel, persuaded that you give them a fair specimen of the whole truth" (44).[11] The introductory testimony of Garrison and Phillips was necessary because, as Houston A. Baker informs us, "By 1844, [Douglass's] credibility as an abolitionist lecturer was under attack by those who insisted that he did not look, act, think, or speak like a man who had just recently escaped slavery."[12] Garrison consequently offers his assurance that "Mr. Douglass has very properly chosen to write his own Narrative, in his own style, and according to the best of his ability, rather than to employ some one else" (37–38). The result of such well-intentioned, if perhaps unconsciously condescending and seemingly tentative, support unfortunately makes it appear that, without the authorizing introductory assurance of a white writer-father figure, Douglass, like Huck, cannot be considered a fully authorized writer. Douglass's book, like Twain's, thus begins by placing its central figure in a position of dependence vis-à-vis an "outside" authority, and again, as with Twain's, truth as an indeterminate quantity somehow takes center stage. It cannot be unexpected, therefore, to find Douglass, ten years after publishing his *Narrative* and after people had come to "know about" him, omitting from *My Bondage and My Freedom* the earlier authorizing preface and letter, substituting instead an introduction by a prominent black medical professional.[13] Nor is it any wonder that twenty-six years later, for *Life and Times*, the thoroughly emancipated leader no longer deemed necessary any introductory comments at all. Huck, on the other hand, can never break free of Mr. Mark Twain's authorizing voice.

Another parallel between the two books can be seen when Jim and Huck engage in a debate concerning the wisdom of Solomon, during which the runaway slave feels free to oppose the young white boy's received interpretation of the tale and reject it as ridiculous. Jim fully understands that the dispute Solomon seeks to resolve is not about half a child but about a "whole chile" and thus about being considered completely human. Through an instinctive, common-sense approach to the problem, Jim manages to defeat Huck's more prosaic arguments and achieves his victory despite never having read the story he shows such skill in analyzing. For whereas pap's "free nigger" was highly literate, Twain leaves no doubt that Jim is not. When Huck reads about "kings, and dukes and earls," Jim exclaims, "I didn' know dey was so many un um. I hain't hearn 'bout none un um, skasely, but ole king Sollermun, onless you counts dem kings dat's in a pack er k'yards" (93–94). What the unschooled slave knows about royalty has therefore come either by word of mouth or from what he has gleaned from seeing the pictures on playing cards.

Twain has taken special care to point out that Jim cannot actually read the story of Solomon on which he comments. Unlike Huck and Tom, Jim has not been taught this useful skill, because, as the author was well aware, it was accepted gospel among slave masters that reading knowledge on the part of slaves could prove damaging to the entire slave system. Having been raised in a family that owned slaves, Twain fully understood that Jim's argument about Solomon represented a distinct challenge to the authority of a biblical story, and, by extension, to the Bible itself, including the passages to which slave owners appealed in order to justify slavery. That this idea possessed particular importance for Twain is revealed by the fact that the section in which the argument occurs was added to the book only in 1883,[14] as the novel was being brought to completion, and not long before it was published.

Jim's questioning of the wisdom of Solomon signals a threat to the Southern system of slavery by a man who dares, as did Frederick Douglass, to think for himself. The awareness by slave owners of the dangers that literacy on the part of slaves held for the "peculiar institution" may be explicitly seen in Douglass's book when a certain Mr. Auld, one of Douglass's slave masters, finds his wife, Sophia, teaching the young man to read. The former slave movingly describes how Auld explained to his wife:

> it was unlawful, as well as unsafe, to teach a slave to read. . . . "If you give a nigger an inch, he will take an ell. A nigger should know nothing but to obey his master—to do as he is told to do. Learning would *spoil* the best nigger in the world. Now," said he, "if you teach that nigger (speaking of myself) how to read, there would be no keeping him. It would forever unfit him to be a slave. He would at once become unmanageable, and of no value to his master. As to himself, it could do him no good, but a great deal of harm. It would make him discontented and unhappy." (78)

Douglass's description of his reaction to this statement indicates just how well Auld had perceived the danger:

> These words sank deep into my heart, stirred up sentiments within that lay slumbering, and called into existence an entirely new train of thought. It was a new and special revelation, explaining dark and mysterious things, with which my youthful understanding had struggled, but struggled in vain. I now understood what had been to me a most perplexing difficulty—to wit, the white man's power to enslave the black man. It was a grand achievement, and I prized it highly. From that moment, I understood the pathway from slavery to freedom. (78)

In *Huckleberry Finn*, Mark Twain has Huck react to Jim's hopes and plans for the freedom that will result from reaching Cairo in a spirit congruent with that of Mr. Auld, and, in addition, has Huck employ the identical expression "give a nigger an inch and he'll take an ell": "It most froze me to hear such talk. He wouldn't ever dared to talk such talk in his life before. Just see what a difference it made in him the minute he judged he was about free. It was according to the old saying, 'give a nigger an inch and he'll take an ell'" (124).[15]

When Tom hangs Jim's hat from a tree branch while the slave is sleeping and leaves a "five-center piece" in recompense for the candles he has taken, the "inch" in the form of a coin that Jim receives does not, however, lead him to steal an "ell." Rather, he shows a good head for the capitalist system and develops a small business on the basis of a story he makes up to explain the mysterious appearance of the coin. Huck, however, expresses the concern that "Jim was most ruined, for a servant" because of this, and the echoes of Auld's "learning would *spoil* the best nigger in the world" and "it would forever unfit him to be a slave" would not seem that far removed from this scene. Auld also makes clear that such a slave "would at once become unmanageable, and of no value to his master," and although Huck's "ruined, for a servant" glosses over Douglass's "slave" with the word "servant," the result for the owner is no different. Twain employs humor in the situation, but we must not forget, as the author manifestly did not, that Jim is not a hired or even an indentured "servant." He is a slave who can be sold, and he comes very close to being so somewhat later in the book when his owner, Miss Watson, takes quite seriously the offer of a slave buyer. Huck was no more mistaken about Jim than Auld about Douglass, and from the fact that Jim does not risk waiting to find out what Miss Watson's final decision will be before taking to his heels, it becomes apparent that he is truly "ruined, for a servant."

While the issue for Jim is not learning to read, as it is for Douglass, he is nonetheless "spoiled" by what he learns and by the advantages he gains from that knowledge. With Douglass it is literacy itself that is of primary importance; he, too, is "bewitched" by the possible advantages that "learning" seems to promise. And he is not to be deterred from striving to become literate by the fact that knowledge of such a crucial nature cannot be acquired without loss and difficulty. As Douglass explains, "Whilst I was saddened by the thought of losing the aid of my kind mistress, I was gladdened by the invaluable instruction which, by the merest accident, I had gained from my master. Though conscious of the difficulty of learning without a teacher, I set out with high hope, and fixed purpose, at whatever cost of trouble, to learn how to read" (78–79). (It warrants mentioning here that Douglass's initially "kind mistress," Sophia Auld—also referred to in

his later versions of the *Narrative* as Miss Sopha [*sic*] and "Miss" Sophia—
has a counterpart in Twain's "Miss Sophia" Grangerford with respect to
given name, kindness, and belonging to but in some manner quietly oppos-
ing a culture of brutality.) Douglass goes on to recount: "From this time I
was most narrowly watched. If I was in a separate room any considerable
length of time, I was sure to be suspected of having a book and was at once
called to give an account of myself. All this, however, was too late. The first
step had been taken. Mistress, in teaching me the alphabet, had given me
the *inch*, and no precaution could prevent me from taking the *ell*" (82).

Although Mark Twain does not seriously expand on the theme of Jim's
illiteracy in *Huckleberry Finn*, we learn from the author's working notes for
his book that the subject was one of which he was unquestionably conscious. Apparently feeling the need for Huck and Jim to be able to com-
municate over distance and realizing that this would require reading knowledge on Jim's part, Twain wrote: "Teaches Jim to read & write—then uses
dog-messenger. Had taught him a little before" (753).[16] (It is of interest in
this regard that Douglass was ultimately taught some of his own reading
skill by "little white boys whom I met in the street" [82].)[17] Had Twain
actually allowed Jim to learn to read, the results for the novel could easily
have been just as dramatic as learning to read ultimately proved for Douglass. But Twain, who spends considerable time and effort in providing
Huck with the ability to "spell, and to read and write *just a little*" (18, emphasis added) and who underscores the importance of those skills as a
source of power for Tom and other characters in the book, obviously came
to the conclusion that within the realm and time frame of his novel there
were some things that Jim simply could not be permitted to either know or
learn.

If at this point we leave Jim to his illiterate devices and return for a moment
to pap's diatribe against the "free nigger there, from Ohio; a mulatter, most
as white as a white man," we can note that pap in his fury labels the man
"a prowling, thieving, infernal, white-shirted free nigger" (34). Frederick
Douglass in his *Narrative* also describes a scene that is strikingly similar in
tone. The famous abolitionist relates that when he was apprehended with
two other slaves, Henry and John Harris, while on the point of attempting
an escape,

Betsy Freeland, mother of William Freeland [the man to whom Douglass had been hired out], came to the door with her hands full of biscuits, and divided them between Henry and John. She then delivered herself of a speech, to the following effect:—addressing herself to me, she said, "*You devil! You yellow devil!* it was you that put it into the heads of Henry and John to run away. But for you, you long-legged mulatto devil! Henry and John would never have thought of such a thing." (128)

Not only does Mrs. Freeland's wrath in this furious outburst match that of pap, but the emphasis on Douglass's mixed blood (Douglass has told us earlier he had a white father), as well as the woman's perception of him as a devil (having originated, therefore, in the same "infernal" regions mentioned by pap in connection with the despised "p'fessor"), reveal further distinct correlations with Twain's novel. A common feature in both cases is that the feeling that treachery has occurred seems aggravated by the fact that the claimed culprit is partially white and hence closer to the color of the aggrieved party while nevertheless remaining permanently on the wrong side of the color line.

Douglass was only too aware that the fury directed against him as a "yellow devil" had yet deeper roots. As he explains in his *Narrative:*

such slaves invariably suffer greater hardships, and have more to contend with, than others. They are, in the first place, a constant offence to their mistress. She is ever disposed to find fault with them; they can seldom do any thing to please her; she is never better pleased than when she sees them under the lash, especially when she suspects her husband of showing to his mulatto children favors which he withholds from his black slaves. (49)

Then, too, there was the menace to the system itself of which the mulatto was the visible reminder:

Every year brings with it multitudes of this class of slaves. It was doubtless in consequence of a knowledge of this fact, that one great statesman of the south predicted the downfall of slavery by the inevitable laws of population. Whether this prophecy is ever fulfilled or not, it is nevertheless plain that a very different-looking class of people are springing up at the south, and are now held in slavery from those originally brought to this country from Africa; and if their increase will do no other good, it will do away with the force of the argument, that God cursed Ham, and therefore American slavery is right. (50)

Douglass points here to the long-term threat that "black blood" would one day actually lead to the fall of slavery, and, in Twain's novel, pap expresses in his own way the possible future shift of power embodied by the representative mulatto he decries: "It was 'lection day, and I was just about to go and vote, myself, if I warn't too drunk to get there; but when they tole me there was a State in this country where they'd let that nigger vote, I drawed out. I says I'll never vote agin. Them's the very words I said; they all heard me and the country may rot for all me—I'll never vote agin as long as I live" (34). Pap's skewed vision is illustrated by the fact that he so easily and thoughtlessly discards a right crucial to maintaining white ascendancy, a right that he has been told the mulatto already possesses. In acceding to this reversal of rights, pap is already subordinating himself to future legal dominance by this hated, half-white human. And though violence toward the man is presently permitted to people like pap ("he wouldn't a give me the road if I hadn't shoved him out o' the way" [34]), the right to vote promises to one day render that, too, unacceptable.

Pap's unthinking dismissal of his right to vote might seem at first glance somewhat startling, but it is worth considering that William Lloyd Garrison, the white abolitionist and leader of the Anti-Slavery Society, chose to do precisely the same thing. His grounds were not the same as pap's (at the root of Garrison's decision was the conviction that the Constitution of the United States was racially biased), but the result was similar. Frederick Douglass was a strong supporter of Garrison and the Anti-Slavery Society's position for several years, only changing his mind and direction in 1851 after deciding that he could, after all, work within the political system and make use of his right to vote.[18] Mark Twain, through his friendship with Douglass and through his own political awareness, would have known of this schism, and it is not inconceivable that it is reflected in pap's ill-considered resolution. It would not have been beyond the mischievous Twain to make the violently proslavery Southern pap the vehicle for a teasing reference to a major Northern antislavery faction, with a talented mulatto ex-slave serving as an awkward linking element between the two.

Pap's attitude toward the gentlemanly mixed-blood college professor (who apparently did not respond with violence to pap's shove) also exhibits obvious envy as he criticizes the attributes of dress, appearance, and education possessed by the man. Pap's feelings were not atypical of the lower-

class white and, as Eric Sundquist indicates, represented, at the most profound level, fear of the mulatto menace:

> the imitation of white manners by blacks underscored the legal drive to
> prevent any true imitation of white rights. The danger that imitation might
> actually lead to the acquisition of political and social graces or to economic
> gains became uncanny in the figure of the mulatto . . . the light mulatto
> [was] an uncanny reminder that blackness both *was* and *was not* visible and
> whiteness both *was* and *was not* a form of property with legal significance.[19]

Less directly but just as emphatically, Twain also touches on the notion
of the imprecision involved in distinguishing by color through having
Huck twice refer to Jim's "whiteness" in emotionally charged moments in
the novel. When the two slave catchers ask if the man on the raft is black
or white, Huck is spiritually in mulatto country until he comes up with the
answer "white," and even then this answer becomes for him something he
will not be able to fully forget. Toward the end of the novel, when Jim aids
Tom and is described by Huck as "white inside," Huck is, without realizing it, once more on slippery ground as far as a clear distinction is concerned, but he is now surer than before that Jim is actually possessed of this
"quality."

An additional mulatto linkage between the works of Douglass and Twain
lies in the name William Wilks. Douglass makes brief mention in the *Narrative* of William Wilkes "the coach-driver" (61), then drops the *e* in *My
Bondage and My Freedom* and *Life and Times*,[20] while adding the information
that Wilks was a light-skinned, handsome man—widely assumed to be the
mulatto son of Col. Edward Lloyd—who eventually succeeded in the un-
heard-of feat of outbidding all other purchasers to buy himself out of slavery. In Twain's novel, William Wilks is the name of the deaf and dumb
brother of the late Peter Wilks. As will be recalled, however, Mark Twain's
William, in what would take considerable effort to regard as simple serendipity, is almost the exact opposite of Douglass's mixed-blood American
slave. He is free, white, and English. The question thus arises once again
as to whether in creating such a character the author might not have been
indulging in an impish private joke. Whatever the answer, had Twain not
been thoroughly familiar with the writings of Frederick Douglass, there is
little likelihood that William or any other Wilks—black, white, or mu-

latto—would have found his way under that surname into *Adventures of Huckleberry Finn*.[21]

A pivotal linking factor between the works of Douglass and Twain may also be discovered in their attitudes toward and treatment of darkness. In the following passage, Douglass explains why he would like to employ the ignorance of the slaveholder as a weapon in defense of the hunted against the dark designs of the hunter:

> I would keep the merciless slaveholder profoundly ignorant of the means of flight adopted by the slave. I would leave him to imagine himself surrounded by myriads of invisible tormentors, ever ready to snatch from his infernal grasp his trembling prey. Let him be left to feel his way in the dark; let darkness commensurate with his crime hover over him; and let him feel that at every step he takes, in pursuit of the flying bondman, he is running the frightful risk of having his hot brains dashed out by an invisible agency. Let us render the tyrant no aid; let us not hold the light by which he can trace the footprints of our flying brother. (138)

The situation Douglass conjures up is not merely one where nothing would be revealed that could harm an escaping slave but is one fraught with dread and unseen threats for the hunter. It is a scene where fears and roles are completely reversed. What is more, the dramatic potential of such a terrifying image of darkness may well have captured the attention of Mark Twain and made a strong enough impression to have been employed in the closing Evasion section of *Huckleberry Finn*. For, as Michael Egan observes:

> All the preparations for the evasion are carried out at night, and the climactic moments occur in a darkness so profound that even the three escapees, as they have become, are hidden from one another . . . The enveloping gloom now, however, is a mutual ally and no longer only an interposition between friends. It is the armed slave-owners, bent on murder to defend their crumbling system, who are lost in the darkness. They have chained Jim to a bed and sealed him in a wood-shed; now in the dark they fumble with its padlock and stumble over the furniture. Amazingly—the detail is so telling that it cannot be a mere oversight on Twain's part—they have failed to bring a lantern or a torch with them. They can see nothing.[22]

Despite their superior numbers they must nervously realize that any one of them can at any moment suddenly fall victim to having "his hot brains dashed out" from one swift blow by the cornered and terrified slave, that threatening but "invisible agency."

In Mark Twain's work of fiction, darkness thus plays precisely the role that Frederick Douglass hoped would be assigned to it in real life. The exact kind of dread and trepidation that Douglass hoped would be the result of such an unknown and unseen threat is generated at the Phelps plantation by Tom's "nonnamous letters," together with the fact that Tom and Huck stick "a picture which Tom drawed in blood, of a skull and crossbones, on the front door; and next night another one of a coffin, on the back door" (334). Huck affirms: "I never see a family in such a sweat. They couldn't a been worse scared if the place had a been full of ghosts laying for them behind everything and under the beds and shivering through the air" (334).

Douglass's *Narrative* describes how he was once under the control of two separate masters, the brothers Thomas and Hugh Auld. At different times we see him make the request of each of them that he be allowed to hire himself out for wages, and in the end Master Hugh permits what Master Thomas refuses. (Did Mark Twain find a hint here as to attitudes and names that could correspond to those of Huck and "Marse Tom"?) Douglass goes on to tell us that, in refusing his request, Master Thomas counsels him

> to content myself, and be obedient. He told me, if I would be happy, I must lay out no plans for the future. He said, if I behaved myself properly, he would take care of me. Indeed he advised me to complete thoughtlessness of the future, and taught me to depend solely upon him for happiness. He seemed to see fully the pressing necessity of setting aside my intellectual nature, in order to find contentment in slavery. But in spite of him, and even in spite of myself, I continued to think, and to think about the injustice of my enslavement, and the means of escape. (139–40)

In the Evasion section of *Huckleberry Finn* we find similar soothing advice being supplied by "Marse Tom" to another slave yearning for freedom. Huck observes that Jim

> was so glad to see us he most cried; and called us honey, and all the pet names he could think of; and was for having us hunt up a cold chisel to cut the chain off of his leg with, right away, and clearing out without losing any time. But Tom he showed him how unregular it would be, and set down and

told him all about our plans, and how we could alter them in a minute any time there was an alarm; and not to be the least afraid, because we would see he got away, *sure*. (309)

In both cases the slave wishes to be free while the master wishes to see only his own personal interest served; in both cases the slave is advised to abandon his autonomy to the wisdom and generosity of the white "master"; in both cases the slave is treated as an inferior who should not trouble himself to think so long as the "master" can do it for him. And although Huck reports that "Jim he couldn't see no sense in the most of it, but he allowed we was white folks and knowed better than him; so he was satisfied and said he would do it all just as Tom said" (309), it is evident that while Jim accepts the game as unavoidable for the time being, he continues to harbor doubts about Tom's plan in the manner of Douglass with Master Thomas. Such doubts are certainly well-founded, for Huck reveals that, in spite of reassuring words to Jim, Tom actually believes that "it was the best fun he ever had in his life, and the most intellectural; and said if he only could see his way to it we would keep it up all the rest of our lives and leave Jim to our children to get out; for he believed Jim would come to like it better and better the more he got used to it" (310).

Neither Jim nor Douglass would evidently be well-advised to accept the reassurance offered; neither Master Thomas nor "Marse Tom" is truly promising any serious immediate improvement of the slave's position, while both simply wish to exploit their fellow human for selfish ends. For dramatic effect, however, Twain waits until the end of his novel to deliver the "kicker": Tom knew Jim was free all the while he was advising him to patiently remain imprisoned. It should hardly need underlining that Frederick Douglass was a man whose personal experience made him particularly well qualified to appreciate the gravity of Tom's callous action and insensitivity and thus of Twain's achievement.

It should also be noted that during the chance meeting Twain had with Douglass in 1869, it was not merely Douglass's "spunk" that found favor with the novelist. According to Twain:

He told the history of his child's expulsion from Miss Tracy's school, & his simple language was very effective. Miss Tracy said the pupils did not want a colored child among them—which he did not believe, & challenged the proof. She put it at once to a vote of the school, and asked "How many of

you are willing to have this colored child be with you?" And they *all* held up
their hands! Douglass added: "The children's hearts were right." There was
pathos in the way he said it. I would so like to hear him make a speech. Has
a grand face.[23]

Twain's memory of this story and the effect it had on him may also have
had an effect on *Huckleberry Finn,* for not only do we see a Jim who has
spunk, but we hear a story that certainly produces pathos when Jim tells of
his remorse at slapping his child for not obeying him—not realizing she
has been made deaf and dumb by scarlet fever. Twain's working note for
this story indicates that it was one he had heard before and was adapting
for use in his novel.[24] The fact that he supplies Jim with names for his two
children ("po' little 'lizabeth" and "po' little Johnny") just prior to telling
this story permits him to pull on the reader's heartstrings in a manner impossible before those names appear, and we also find him mentioning a wife
(who remains forever anonymous) and two children twice in his working
notes.[25] The story Jim recounts is not the one Douglass tells, but Twain's
stance and strategy are similar, and we see Jim in the same light in which
Twain saw Douglass. Twain, however, was clearly precluded from using
Douglass's actual story, since during the period in which the novel is set
there would have been little chance of formal schooling for Jim's children
anywhere in the South, and a debate between black and white, such as the
one that occurred between Douglass and the schoolteacher, would have
been all but unthinkable.[26]

Twain did not need Douglass to show him how to wring sympathy from
an audience, but it is conceivable that in this instance the personal contact
between the two men nudged Twain toward bringing out Jim's humanity
in the way he did.

Another area of Douglass's influence on Twain may be found in the treatment of religion in the *Narrative.* Douglass states that "he who proclaims
it a religious duty to read the Bible denies me the right of learning to read
the name of the god who made me" (154). In the first chapter of *Huckleberry Finn,* Twain has the widow teach the white, uneducated Huck about
"Moses and the Bulrushers" while Miss Watson does her best to teach the
boy to spell and "all about the bad place." But Huck also reports that "by
and by they fetched the niggers in and had prayers, and then everybody was

off to bed" (4). Neither Huck nor anyone else expresses surprise that despite praying to the same god there is no attempt made to teach the "niggers" to spell the name of that god.

We learn from Douglass's *Narrative* that such evening prayer sessions for slaves were customary, though they were not always carried out. Douglass mentions a Mr. George Cookman whom the slaves believed to be "a good man" and relates that "when he was at our house, we were sure to be called in to prayers. When the others were there, we were sometimes called in and sometimes not" (98). Could it be that the ironic contrast between Huck's Bible lessons and the prayer session for the "niggers" was inspired by Frederick Douglass's own irony on the same subject?

Of direct significance to the present discussion is also Douglass's assertion that "revivals of religion and revivals of the slave-trade go hand in hand together" (154), as well as a statement he makes concerning "the overwhelming mass of professed Christians in America":

> They are always ready to sacrifice, but seldom to show mercy. They are they who are represented as professing to love God whom they have not seen, whilst they hate their brother whom they have seen. They love the heathen on the other side of the globe. They can pray for him, pay money to have the Bible put into his hand, and the missionaries to instruct him; while they despise and totally neglect the heathen at their own doors. (156)

Just as damning is what Douglass relates concerning the effect that "getting religion" had on Master Auld:

> In August, 1832, my master attended a Methodist camp-meeting held in the Bay-side, Talbot county, and there experienced religion. I indulged a faint hope that his conversion would lead him to emancipate his slaves, and that, if he did not do this, it would, at any rate, make him more kind and humane. I was disappointed in both these respects. It neither made him to be humane to his slaves, nor to emancipate them. If it had any effect on his character, it made him more cruel and hateful in all his ways; for I believe him to have been a much worse man after his conversion than before. (97)

In Twain's original manuscript for his novel, the king describes to the duke how he makes his living from "most any kind of gospil work: boosting revivals along, or getting 'em up; working camp meetings; 'occupying' for a preacher that wants to take a week's rest; and missionarying."[27] He explains that "folks will plank out cash for the heathen mighty free, if you only locate your heathen fur enough off. I've took in as much as seventeen dollars at one grist for the pore benighted Goojoos—invented 'em myself—located 'em away up jest back of the North Pole. Seeing that that worked so good, I kind of strained myself, next time, and located some in a comet."[28] Although the section in which this statement appears was eliminated from the published version of *Huckleberry Finn*, we are nonetheless treated to the "Pokeville camp-meeting," where the faithful are far more interested in the heathen in the Indian Ocean than those closer to home. The king, in the role of a pirate who has seen the light, collects a tidy sum at the meeting for the purpose of converting his fellow pirates, and the participants at the camp meeting are, as Douglass could have predicted, far more interested in "the heathen on the other side of the globe" than in their "brother whom they have seen." One would be optimistic indeed to nurture even Douglass's "faint hope" that anyone's conversion at such a meeting would lead to "more kind and humane" treatment of those "brothers," much less to their emancipation.

At exactly the same moment as the king is pulling off his pirate swindle, his partner the duke—illegally, as might be expected—is printing up a handbill describing Jim as a "runaway nigger." The purpose of the handbill is to provide the two reprobates with a cover story to justify having Jim "in custody" and thus make it possible to "run" the raft during the daytime. Since the handbill is to be widely circulated, the threat of exposure for the king and duke will seriously diminish while Jim's will correspondingly increase. The duke's handbill-printing activity and the dreary daily reality of threats to Jim's life, even as a partially free man, in the hands of people like the duke and the king, are thus consonant with the glaring absence of any reference at the camp meeting to the plight of American slaves. The king's and the duke's simultaneous undertakings support each other seamlessly. And whether or not the inspiration for this parallel came straight from Douglass, Twain lays distinct stress on precisely the same idea: it would be difficult to imagine "revivals of religion and revivals of the slave-trade" going more closely "hand in hand together."

There is a good chance that Twain was also familiar with "What to the Slave Is the Fourth of July?" an address that has been termed "the most

famous antislavery speech Frederick Douglass ever gave" and that is included in the appendix to *My Bondage and My Freedom*.[29] In this speech,
delivered on 5 July 1852, only seven years following the publication of
his *Narrative,* the outspoken abolitionist explained to his audience that
"the rich inheritance of justice, liberty, prosperity and independence, be-
queathed by your fathers, is shared by you, not by me. The sunlight that
brought life and healing to you, has brought stripes and death to me. This
Fourth [of] July is *yours,* not *mine. You* may rejoice, *I* must mourn."[30] Douglass then went on to make certain there could be no doubt as to the tenor
of his message: "What, to the American slave, is your 4th of July? I answer;
a day that reveals to him, more than all other days in the year, the gross
injustice and cruelty to which he is the constant victim."[31] In *Huckleberry
Finn,* Joanna Wilks's question as to whether servants in England are not
"like our niggers" given holidays "the way we do, Christmas, and New
Year's week and fourth of July?" is answered by Huck with the explanation
that English servants "never see a holiday from year's end to year's end;
never go to the circus, nor theatre, nor nigger shows, nor nowheres" (223).
No major stretch of the imagination is required to see Mark Twain as retroactively taking up in this exchange the challenge that Douglass had issued
so many years before in his lecture: "At a time like this, scorching irony,
not convincing argument, is needed."[32]

From Douglass's *Narrative,* we learn that it is possible that Twain was
not innocently mentioning Christmas and New Year's week either. Conscious of Douglass's description of those holidays, he would doubtless be
agreeing with the erstwhile bondman, without alluding more directly to the
fact in his novel than he does, that

> from what I know of the effect of these holidays upon the slave, I believe
> them to be among the most effective means in the hands of the slaveholder
> in keeping down the spirit of insurrection. Were the slaveholders at once to
> abandon this practice, I have not the slightest doubt it would lead to an
> immediate insurrection among the slaves. . . . The holidays are part and
> parcel of the gross fraud, wrong, and inhumanity of slavery. . . . This will be
> seen by the fact, that the slaveholders like to have their slaves spend those
> days just in such a manner as to make them as glad of their ending as of their
> beginning. (115)

Douglass explains that by luring slaves to drink to excess,

> the result was just what might be supposed: many of us were led to think
> that there was little to choose between liberty and slavery. We felt, and very
> properly too, that we had almost as well be slaves to man as to rum. So,
> when the holidays ended, we staggered up from the filth of our wallowing,
> took a long breath, and marched to the field, feeling, upon the whole, rather
> glad to go, from what our master had deceived us into a belief was freedom,
> back to the arms of slavery. (116)

After hearing Frederick Douglass's strong opinion on this topic, can we, as
readers of *Huckleberry Finn*, allow ourselves to safely assume that Mark
Twain was mentioning any of these "holidays" without an ironical glint in
his eye or a wink of complicity at Douglass?

Holidays, however, did not represent the only area of their lives where
slaves found themselves defrauded of something they had earned through
hard physical labor. Douglass describes at one stage in his *Narrative* how
his master rewarded him for the toil he carried out for another man and for
which he was paid a salary. "When I carried to him my weekly wages, he
would, after counting the money, look me in the face with a robber-like
fierceness, and ask, 'Is this all?' He was satisfied with nothing less than the
last cent. He would, however, when I made him six dollars, sometimes give
me six cents, to encourage me" (139).

It is not inconceivable that Mark Twain recalled this scene at the moment when he was bringing his novel to a close and having Tom reward
Jim with forty dollars while Tom and Huck have over six thousand dollars
apiece. Such an egregious example of injustice closely parallels and could
easily have been inspired by Douglass's story. As Huck tells it, Jim "was
pleased most to death" and exclaimed, "I *tole* you I ben rich wunst, en gwi-
neter be rich *agin;* en it's come true" (361). While Huck does not notice
anything untoward, it would be hard to believe that Jim does not perceive
the enormous difference in amounts when it is revealed a few moments
after he receives his money that Huck has six thousand dollars coming to
him. Twain dramatically contrasts the two figures and underlines the in-
equity by having Jim himself break the news that Huck's father has not
gotten hold of the money and drunk it up. It is also Jim who says to Huck,

"Well, den, you k'n git yo' money when you wants it" (362). Twain thus leaves us little leeway to take for granted that the Jim we have come to know as a particularly savvy individual is insensitive to the divergence between the two sums. After all, the recently freed man has full knowledge of two things that make such an assumption doubtful: he is fully cognizant of the fact that Huck and Tom *each* have a six-thousand-dollar nest egg, and he knows from his own experience the going price for a slave. Since he must somehow come up with what he is fully aware will be a large sum of money in order to be able to free his wife and two children, either through legal or illegal channels, as he himself indicates earlier in the book, it is obvious that he must be painfully conscious of the fact that forty dollars will not go far in aiding him to carry out his plan.[33] The depth of the newly liberated man's joy at Tom's modest reward would, then, at the very least appear to be open to question.

Whatever might have been Jim's deeper response at that moment, Frederick Douglass's reaction to his own treatment was anything but one of gratitude. He tells us that his feelings were just the opposite of what his white master probably intended: "I regarded it as a sort of admission of my right to the whole. The fact that he gave me any part of my wages was proof, to my mind, that he believed me entitled to the whole of them. I always felt worse for having received any thing; for I feared that the giving me a few cents would ease his conscience, and make him feel himself to be a pretty honorable sort of robber" (139). In *Huckleberry Finn*, Tom Sawyer clearly feels that he is behaving honorably. He blindly believes he has deprived Jim only of his "time," and that forty dollars is handsome compensation for what the ex-slave has lost. Given the gross insensitivity embodied in that fact, we should not simply assume that Jim is as genuinely and naively pleased as he appears at the end of the book. It would seem far more likely that his joyful expression conceals precisely the kind of acute discontent that Douglass felt, and that somewhere underneath it all Jim feels that forty dollars plus emancipation does not completely write off the debt.

Mark Twain would also appear to owe a rather substantial debt to Frederick Douglass. Although the former Missourian knew first-hand the world Douglass described and could have acquired all of the above information from other sources, the fact that he knew, respected, and supported the

African American leader increases the probability of his having absorbed ideas and aspects of that man's thinking and writing. Douglass's work crystallizes the world of the American slave in a way that could have provided a handy springboard for Twain's creativity.[34] Just how much of that creativity was stimulated by Frederick Douglass may never be known, but the close parallels that exist between the *Narrative of the Life of Frederick Douglass, Written by Himself* and *Adventures of Huckleberry Finn* strongly indicate that, whether or not either man ever came to fully realize it, that influence was stronger and more profound than has hitherto been understood.

CHAPTER THREE

"Right" in *Huckleberry Finn*

W HEN THE UNITARIAN minister Theodore Parker delivered
"A Sermon on the Dangers which Threaten the Rights of
Man in America" on Sunday, 2 July 1854, only two days before
that year's Independence Day celebrations, he spoke as one of the most
important preachers of his era to the largest congregation in the city of
Boston, Massachusetts.[1] At the core of his sermon were the ideals that Thomas Jefferson had enumerated in the Declaration of Independence concerning the equality of "all men" and the "inalienable" right to "life, liberty
and the pursuit of happiness," which Jefferson believed governments were
"instituted" to safeguard. Parker added a religious note to Jefferson's original words in telling his congregation that "government derives all its *divine*
right from its conformity with these ideas, all its human sanction from the
consent of the governed" (363, emphasis added). He went on to explain his
own understanding of where this "idea of freedom" originated and what it
led to in practice:

> It is derived from human nature; it rests on the immutable laws of God; it is
> part of the natural religion of mankind. It demands a government after
> natural justice, which is the point common between the conscience of God
> and the conscience of mankind, the point common also between the inter-
> ests of one man and of all men.
>
> Now this government, just in its substance, in its form must be demo-
> cratic: that is to say, the government of all, by all, and for all. You see what
> consequences must follow from such an idea, and the attempt to re-enact
> the law of God into political institutions. There will follow the freedom of
> the people, respect for every natural right of all men, the rights of their
> body, and of their spirit—the rights of mind and conscience, heart and soul.
> There must be some restraint—as of children by their parents, as of bad
> men by good men; but it will be restraint for the joint good of all parties

concerned; not restraint for the exclusive benefit of the restrainer. The ultimate consequence of this will be the material and spiritual welfare of all—riches, comfort, noble manhood, all desirable things. That is the idea of freedom. . . . [It] is a religious idea; and when men pray for the "reign of justice" and the "kingdom of heaven," to come on earth politically, I suppose they mean that there may be a commonwealth where every man has his natural rights of mind, body, and estate. (363–64)

In contrast, "the idea of slavery . . . must lead to a corresponding government; that will be unjust in its substance—for it will depend not on natural right, but on personal force; not on the constitution of the universe, but on the compact of men. It is the abnegation of God in the universe and of conscience in man. Its form will be despotism—the government of all by a part, for the sake of a part" (365).

In these words we can hear the haunting "of the people, by the people and for the people" that later became famous in Abraham Lincoln's slightly altered use of Parker's rhythm and concept in the Gettysburg Address. We can, in addition, see what kinds of ideas were circulating in the North with respect to the theory of equal civil rights for all people, whether slave or free. The perception of natural right was not a new one, of course, but Parker and others of his day were founding much of their case upon it. An appeal to a higher "constitution of the universe" rather than to a "compact of man" permitted interpretations of "rights" to be founded on *instinctive* understanding of what was equitable rather than on more limited legal perceptions and therefore left considerably more freedom of action. With God as the ultimate arbiter, the abolitionist position could find support in religion rather than in principles of law, thus allowing for even greater flexibility in justifying the cause of human rights. Parker, as a spokesman for the Jeffersonian position, explained to his congregation on that July Sunday: "The idea which allows slavery in South Carolina will establish it also in New England. The bondage of a black man in Alexandria imperils every white woman's daughter in Boston. You cannot escape the consequences of a first principle more than you can 'take the leap of Niagara and stop when half-way down'" (367–68). Parker felt that no one living in a slave society could ever be truly free and that all members were soiled when even a single individual or group within the society was victimized. He strongly believed that denying equal rights to a slave would, in the long run, lead to disintegration of the fabric of society, since, from the very start, both the idea of natural and unalienable rights as well as the Christian concept of the brotherhood of all human beings would be compromised. As these qualities, in his view, were the principal foundation stones upon which the United States of America had been built, denial of equal rights to anyone—even a slave—ultimately threatened to lead to a collapse of the ideal of democracy as government "of all, by all and for all."

The ideas that Parker espoused were in the air at the time, and he was only one of those giving them voice. His potential for influencing leaders of his day was considerable, however, since he spoke regularly to an audience of between three and five thousand each Sunday;[2] was an extremely active abolitionist who helped runaway slaves; and even belonged to Boston's "Secret Six," a group that contributed money and support to John Brown prior to his raid at Harper's Ferry.[3] Many political leaders, including Lincoln, could not openly recognize Parker's efforts without the risk of losing votes,[4] but this in no way diminished the minister's central role in the civil rights debate going on in the United States prior to the Civil War. The questions being raised concerning those rights touched not only on the enslavement of those of African heritage but also, for example, on how women, children, and other less-favored members of society were treated, as Parker, who covertly helped to found homes for "street" children and "friendless girls," was fully aware.[5]

The debate regarding civil rights was not aided by the fact that a certain blurring of the question was discernible in the U.S. Constitution itself. That document spoke of slaves only as "certain persons" when defining the possible future limitation of the slave trade or as "persons held to service or labor" when stipulating that "no person held to service or labor in one State, under the laws thereof, escaping into another, shall, in consequence of any law or regulation therein, be discharged from such service or labor, but shall be delivered up on claim of the party to whom such service or labor may be due" (article 4, section 2). Nor was the concept of rights simplified when articles 9 and 10 of the Bill of Rights opened the door to a rather liberal interpretation: "The enumeration in the Constitution of certain rights, shall not be construed to deny or disparage others retained by the people" (article 9); "The powers not delegated to the United States by the Constitution nor prohibited by it to the States, are reserved to the States, respectively, or to the people" (article 10).

Consequently, in the early years of the American republic, questions relating to individual rights were looked at from widely different angles. Nevertheless, a certain culmination was reached during the Civil War, when Lincoln finally felt constrained to adopt Jefferson's liberal view that all men were "created equal." This position diverged sharply from the Constitution's more constricted assumption that slaves could not only be legally "held to service or labor" but could also be required to be returned to their "rightful" masters, even if they managed to somehow escape their bondage. By describing Jefferson's idea of equal and unalienable rights for *all* men as a "proposition" to which the nation was "dedicated," Lincoln's Gettysburg Address simplified the constitutional arguments (some would claim beyond recognition) and placed the nation on the path Parker had recommended. That path would lead ineluctably toward a democracy where government "of the people, by the people and for the people" could permit every person in the country to have the "inalienable rights" sacred to Jefferson and the other founding fathers referred to by Lincoln.

As the son of a Missouri slave owner, as well as the brother of a man who had once received an appointment from President Lincoln, Mark Twain was not immune to the potential consequences of the outcome of the debate over rights, and one may presume that his exposure to this discussion was not lessened when he married Olivia Langdon in 1870. Not only had her father harbored abolitionist sympathies,[6] but Olivia herself recorded sayings attributed to Theodore Parker in her commonplace book around the time of her marriage.[7] Hence, it is more than likely that Twain was not unacquainted with the thinking and ideas of Parker and others of similar persuasion. And it is understandable that when writing *Adventures of Huckleberry Finn*, a novel placed in the pre–Civil War period, the author would not neglect to address a number of questions that were uppermost in the minds of those involved in the debate concerning civil rights, a debate to which the cessation of the Civil War had by no means put an end.

But Twain was also sensitive to a much broader range of questions bearing on individual rights than only those directly linked to slavery and the Civil War. This essay undertakes to demonstrate that questions concerning rights are accorded major importance in the novel and that Twain's comprehension and approach to the rights of other human beings was anything but categorical or simplistic.[8] In fact, it would seem that for the author it was often the interaction of the rights of different individuals that could create the most riveting situations; and he seems to have felt that in such situations, as with Huck's attitude toward food, "the juice kind of swaps around, and the things go better" (2).

Huckleberry Finn is the son of a ne'er-do-well father and has no mother, and some of the rights that surface at an early stage in Twain's novel are those with which parents are invested in regard to their children. An example of what such rights can mean in practice to a child like Huck is seen when a new judge, possessing solely theoretical knowledge, arrives in town with the attitude that "courts mustn't interfere and separate families if they could help it" and that "he'd druther not take a child away from its father" (26). Only after a failed attempt at reforming pap does the new judge come to understand that, if given the chance, pap will continue to abuse his rights over his son. Thoroughly shaken by the experience, the judge abandons for the time being his idealistic attitudes, forced into facing the stark reality that "a body could reform the ole man with a shot-gun, maybe, but he didn't know no other way" (28).

For pap, Huck represents merely a form of property that has value only insofar as it can be exploited. Pap returns from his wanderings not to find Huck for Huck's sake but solely because he believes that his "rights" as a parent will allow him to get his hands on the money the boy has come into. He reveals this in telling Huck, "I've been in town two days, and I hain't heard nothing but about you bein' rich. I heard about it away down the river, too. That's why I come" (25). Pap's unhappiness at not being able to fully capitalize on his "rights" as a father is also partly at the root of his complaint about the "govment":

> "Call this a govment! why, just look at it and see what it's like. Here's the law a-standing ready to take a man's son away from him—a man's own son, which he has had all the trouble and all the anxiety and all the expense of raising. Yes, just as that man has got that son raised at last, and ready to go to work and begin to do suthin' for *him* and give him a rest, the law up and goes for him. And they call *that* govment! That ain't all, nuther. The law backs that old Judge Thatcher up and helps him to keep me out o' my property. Here's what the law does. The law takes a man worth six thousand dollars and upards, and jams him into an old trap of a cabin like this, and

lets him go round in clothes that ain't fitten for a hog. They call that govment! A man can't get his rights in a govment like this." (33)

It is clear to all but pap that if he gets what he interprets as *his* "rights," *Huck's* will be trampled on. Pap obviously wants everything but responsibility, and his holier-than-thou declaration about the "trouble and anxiety and all the expense of raising" his son rings as hollow in this context as his subsequent threat "to just leave the country for good and all" (33).

Pap is also highly conscious of the priority he feels his rights should take over those of even a free, light-skinned black. In complaining about "a free nigger there, from Ohio; a mulatter, most as white as a white man" (33), pap can be seen as speaking, prior to the Civil War, for the postwar bitterness produced in many whites by the internal upheaval precipitated through the freeing of the slaves. Pap is forced to learn, however, that even in his day freedmen have some limited rights. In this particular instance pap is informed that the man "couldn't be sold till he'd been in the State six months, and he hadn't been there that long yet" (34). At the root of pap's complaints, however, are not *his* rights so much as the rights that were slowly opening up to blacks, and the ones that were important are easily discerned from pap's comments on the "free nigger":

> "He had the whitest shirt on you ever see, too, and the shiniest hat; and there ain't a man in that town that's got as fine clothes as what he had; and he had a gold watch and chain, and a silver-headed cane—the awfulest old gray-headed nabob in the State. And what do you think? they said he was a p'fessor in a college, and could talk all kinds of languages, and knowed everything. And that ain't the wust. They said he could *vote*, when he was at home." (33–34)

Twain makes it obvious that for pap, wealth, education, and power are areas that should be accessible only to the elect, chosen by the serendipity of birth. There is also little doubt that pap's drunken harangue revealed the inmost thoughts of more than one of Twain's contemporaries. During another of pap's alcohol-aided frenzies Huck's own life is threatened, and he manages to escape only by slipping out of his jacket at the last minute and then outlasting his fatigued father. It is this incident that leads Huck to understand that in order to protect his own right to life he must, in the final analysis, be prepared for patricide or flight. To avoid being forced into the former he swiftly organizes the latter.

Under such circumstances one would assume that Huck would be sensitive to similar situations affecting other human beings, but we may see how ingrained and distorted is his concept of the rights due to slaves when Jim, in anticipation of arrival at Cairo and freedom, explains to Huck that "the first thing he would do when he got to a free State he would go to saving up money and never spend a single cent, and when he got enough he would buy his wife, which was owned on a farm close to where Miss Watson lived; and then they would both work to buy the two children, and if their master wouldn't sell them, they'd get an Ab'litionist to go and steal them" (124). Far from being sympathetic to Jim's plan, Huck responds with pap's, and the South's, ideas on the rights of the children of slaves, not from the point of view of his perception of his own rights. In Huck's words:

> It most froze me to hear such talk. He wouldn't ever dared to talk such talk in his life before. Just see what a difference it made in him the minute he judged he was about free. . . . Thinks I, this is what comes of my not thinking. Here was this nigger which I had as good as helped to run away, coming right out flat-footed and saying he would steal his children—children that belonged to a man I didn't even know; a man that hadn't ever done me no harm. (124)

Huck finds it easier here to condemn this proposed action by his friend, through reducing Jim, as in the earlier "Sollermun" discussion, to "nigger" status once again. That Jim has no right to his own children is self-evident to this teenage white boy in pre–Civil War America and at this stage of his development. Huck sees no logical inconsistency in the fact that Jim, even when free, and in his own as well as society's view, would be doing wrong to feel that he has any right to the children that he has sired but that, according to existing laws, are not his "property." Twain also slips in the significant and ironic fact that Jim's wish is to first try to *buy* his wife and children out of slavery and thus respect the prevailing, if unjust, laws governing property rights in human beings. This critical detail is completely overlooked by Huck in his overwrought, pap-like reaction. Huck misses as well the irony in the fact that, as Fritz Oehlschlaeger observes, "Jim's children do belong, in the natural and not simply the legal sense, to a man Huck does not really know in any deep way at this point in the novel, a man who also has never done Huck any harm, only good—Jim himself." [9]

It takes Huck many more joint experiences with Jim before finally coming to realize that "I do believe he cared just as much for his people as white folks does for their'n. It don't seem natural but I reckon it's so" (201). The key word here is "natural," and we would do well to recall that what Jefferson, Lincoln, Parker, and other Americans considered to be "rights" were often preceded by the word "natural," which pointed to the right of an individual to appeal to God-given instinct rather than man-made law books in deciding a moral issue. What is *un*natural for Huck in this instance is for Jim to have the same reactions as "white folk." At issue is hence the entire question of Jim's essential right to the status of human being. As Huck gradually struggles with this dilemma, it becomes apparent that the argumentation he employs is generally based on an instinctive grasp of "natural right" rather than on the prevailing laws of the day. In another context, Huck reveals that such is, indeed, his personal approach to solving problems when he states: "I go a good deal on instinct" (279).

Jim's freedom is understandably in jeopardy from the moment he escapes from Miss Watson, and the runaway slave undergoes many terrifying moments as he drifts toward New Orleans. It is in connection with the king and the duke, however, that the question of Jim's *right* to his freedom is brought into exceptionally sharp focus. From the moment the two hustlers land on the raft, it takes only the wink of an eye before they transform themselves into royalty, and it is highly revealing that the duke calls himself the "*rightful* Duke of Bridgewater" while the king makes claim to being the "*rightful* King of France" (163, emphases added). Huck and Jim, of course, are swiftly relegated to the role of servants, with Jim, because he is black, drawing the short straw and being treated worse. Both are seen by the king and duke simply as objects to be exploited rather than as human beings with rights, and the two impostors tend to assume this same attitude of superiority toward all with whom they deal: all are taken advantage of and treated as fools. Twain thus utilizes the notion of false royalty to illustrate just how few rights those neither born nor fraudulently *re*born to the purple possess. This "rank" injustice is further dramatized by the fact that it can occur in a world where titles of nobility are formally prohibited by a legal constitution and even in the "new" world, represented by a free-floating raft whose occupants have no formal ties to the "old" shore-world, save those that they choose to bring with them. That Jim and Huck are swiftly stripped of any "natural rights" and quickly made subservient to "divine right" can easily be seen as Twain's satirical comment on just how rapidly the old imposes itself on and corrupts the new. And that the first thing the king asks of Huck and Jim is to be treated "according to his rights" (164), to which, it is clear, he has no legal or justifiable claim, only serves to underscore the intensity of Twain's attack on royal, or other, presumed prerogatives.

The cold-blooded and self-centered attitude of the aristocracy with regard to the rights of others warrants Twain's attention not only in connection with the king and the duke but also in the Grangerford and Shepherdson section, in which both families are said to be of the "aristocracy" and deemed free to go about killing one another "honorably." In addition, we find a similarly ridiculous portrayal of "aristocracy" in the Sherburn-Boggs encounter, when the "injury" to Colonel Sherburn's honor supposedly justifies his "injuring" Boggs to the extreme extent of depriving him of his right to exist.

In *Huckleberry Finn*, Twain also shines a harsh light on the "rights" that mobs arrogate to themselves. Unless stopped in their illegal actions (and Colonel Sherburn shows that even a single individual with sufficient backbone is capable of doing this), they are quite capable not only of inflicting the pain and suffering of being tarred and feathered but also of murder, of which lynching is the physical and legal equivalent. In the Boggs episode, shortly after Boggs has died in a "little drugstore," our attention is drawn to a ridiculous, not to say sick, conception of the "rights" assumed to be possessed by members of a crowd. Huck describes the struggle to see the dead victim in the following way:

> Well, pretty soon the whole town was there, squirming, and scrouging and pushing and shoving to get at the window and have a look, but people that had the places wouldn't give them up, and folks behind them was saying all the time, "Say, now, you've looked enough, you fellows; 'taint right and 'taint fair, for you to stay thar all the time, and never give nobody a chance; other folks has their rights as well as you." (187)

This kind of twisted perception of the rights supposedly belonging to the general public has paid the wages of more than one member of the scandal media over the years, and Twain portrays the kind of morbid curiosity displayed by the masses as anything but admirable.

The question of rights seems ubiquitous in the novel and even intrudes itself into the discussion between Bill, Jake Packard, and Jim Turner, the thieves on the sinking steamboat *Walter Scott*. In the past, Turner has evidently managed to browbeat his two partners-in-crime into always allowing him a disproportionately large share of the "truck" through the threat of turning "State's evidence" against them. Now that they have Turner at their mercy, and because he killed "old Hatfield jist the same way" (83), the two scoundrels feel that they possess a clear and justifiable "right" to kill *him*. Bound and helpless, he pleads for his life, claiming he "hain't ever goin' to tell" (81). The response of his partners, however, shows that even among such reprobates the reaction to what is considered a violation of rights can be just as powerful as at any other level of society: "Hear him beg! and yit if we hadn't got the best of him and tied him, he'd a killed us both. And what *for?* Jist for noth'n'. Jist because we stood on our *rights*— that's what for" (82, emphasis Twain's).

"Good morals" is the excuse given by Bill and Jake for not doing away with Turner immediately and for leaving him bound and gagged to undergo the "natural" fate of drowning when the *Walter Scott* sinks. But intricate final irony is woven into the fact that the two partners ultimately share Turner's fate when, at the last second, they climb out of the skiff that would have carried them to safety in order to unjustly deprive Turner of his "rightful" share of cash not rightfully acquired. This enables Jim and Huck to take advantage of the moment and save themselves by stealing the skiff that "rightfully" was to be used by the thieves. By not clarifying how the thieves came to be in possession of the skiff, Twain nevertheless leaves open the possibility that Jim and Huck are "borrowing" a previously "borrowed" possession and are thus in some way less guilty of doing wrong, although depriving the thieves of their "rightful" property and ultimately of their right to life. It is assuredly not by a mere quirk of fate that the preceding scene of this same chapter shows Huck and Jim joining wits to work out a pragmatic solution to dealing with pap's moral philosophy regarding the "borrowing" of other people's chickens.

In stealing the boat, Huck leaves the men to die what many would probably see as a "rightful" death. But even in this seemingly simple case Twain indicates that there may be more to a question of rights than is always immediately apparent. Huck's original intention is simply to deprive the men of their boat so that the "sheriff 'll get 'em," but fate decrees that Huck and Jim need the boat for themselves since their raft has broken loose and drifted away. Their own right to live thus takes precedence, under duress to be sure, over that of the thieves. Nonetheless, Huck feels sufficiently guilty and remorseful to try to get the "murderers" out of their scrape. When the scheme fails, and it turns out that the thieves probably died as a result of his theft, Huck reacts with a remark that writes off rather flippantly the rights of the dead men in favor of his own "natural right" to life: "I felt a little bit heavy-hearted about the gang, but not much, for I reckoned if they could stand it, I could" (91). Huck would not seem here to have distanced himself all that much from pap's position on the circumscribed rights due to the owners of chickens. "Borrowing" must ostensibly fit within pragmatic parameters; "rights" in the final analysis are to be considered, and if necessary qualified, in the light of personal priorities.[10]

In the closing, Evasion section of Twain's book, the discrepancy between the rights possessed by Tom and those possessed by Jim is assigned particular emphasis. Tom, for example, feels he has the right to act unconscionably in using Jim's imprisonment as the basis for an "adventure" that provides fun and diversion for himself but mainly misery for Jim. And while Jim seemingly respects the white, stylish boy at this point just as much as he did before running away from Miss Watson in the early pages of the novel, Tom, who knows that Miss Watson's will has now granted Jim his freedom and with it the right not to have to take part in the troublesome "adventure," purposely keeps silent about what he knows. After almost letting the information slip out, he carefully refrains from revealing to either Jim or Huck the fact that Jim now has the right to live his own life in his own way. He therefore treats Jim no differently now from the way he has treated him in the past. Since Jim, because of his color, belongs to an inferior group within Tom's white world, the boy evidently feels no pangs of conscience in failing to respect Jim's right to know about the altered circumstances concerning his sacred right to live as a free man. Had Jim become aware that he had acquired this basic right, he almost certainly would not have participated in Tom's "game." It is not only conceivable but probable that he would have left immediately in order to put into effect his earlier plan of freeing his wife and children, rather than playing the fool for a childish lark.

   As it turns out, the only "right" with which Tom is careful to provide

Jim is, tellingly, not one that is essential to a free man but, rather, one that Tom believes should belong to a prisoner or, more significantly, to a friend or associate of a prisoner, one that permits the stealing of anything that can be considered necessary to escaping from an unjust imprisonment. This right must, in general, be regarded as a "natural" one, possessing only possible moral suasion, since in practice the controlling physical power, whether wielded legally or otherwise, is in the hands of the imprisoner. Tom can justify to himself this break with the prevailing legal order on the basis of the fact that the thefts represent only minor infringements of the system. He obviously feels these can easily be excused since he does not yet belong to the adult world and because he knows that "freeing" an already free man can only be seen by adults as a prank, not an implied threat— however childish—to the status quo. Tom's prank would take on an entirely different coloring, however, and be sharply condemned were Jim really a "runaway nigger." And since the "right" that Tom arrogates to himself and Huck allows the boys to pilfer in good conscience whatever they wish, as long as it can be seen to serve the Evasion, it is evident that this "right" is one that is more important to Tom than to its actual possessor, the compliant Jim.

Tom's rights with regard to Jim are not, of course, based on merit or ability, though Jim appears to admire Tom greatly throughout the novel, but on a social position conferred by the thin difference of skin color: the same thin difference to which pap appealed. In this circumstance, as in that earlier one, the person on the "wrong" side of the dividing line paradoxically at once possesses and is deprived of the full rights open in many states to a free former slave:[11] Jim because he is being wrongfully detained due to Tom's silent lie, and pap's "p'fessor" because he is not back home in Ohio and consequently is in the wrong state at the time he meets up with pap. Theodore Parker would no doubt have appreciated the involved irony connected with a dilemma of this nature; Tom Sawyer, on the other hand, and by extension all those like him, can be considered incapable of discerning even the possibility of such irony.

Mark Twain, however, did not need to limit himself only to irony in treating a subject on which he had trained his sights, and it would appear that as a writer he was well aware of the wealth of possibilities available to him in connection with the word "write," a homophone of "right." Instances of word play based on this parallel are numerous in the novel and are often directly linked to literacy.[12] We find, for example, that Jim, who possesses the fewest rights among the main characters in the novel, is severely limited by his inability to write; and Huck, who learns to "read and write a little," is restricted at times in his freedom of action by the talents of the more literate Tom. Again, in the Wilks section of the novel, Twain appears to derive enjoyment from verbally maximizing the linkage of rights with writing. When an attempt is made to decide which set of "brothers" has a *right* to the deceased Peter Wilks's property, the claimants are required to produce samples of their handwriting in order to prove which, if either, is the "right" pair. After this effort fails to produce the desired result, the lawyer, Levi Bell, expresses the general frustration of the citizens in words that include an unintentional pun appropriate to the subject: "Well, well, well! I thought we was right on the track of a slution, but it's gone to grass, partly" (254).

A similar instance of word play occurs when Huck decides to betray Jim and do, as he expresses it, "the right and the clean thing, and go and write to that nigger's owner and tell where he was" (269). If Huck were actually to carry out this plan, it would surely result in Jim being effectively deprived of his human rights. But, after producing the required lines, Huck has his well-known change of heart about Jim when he can't find in his memory any justification, as he puts it, "to harden me against him" (270). Huck then does what he believes is the right thing by Jim, if not by society, in tearing up his letter to Miss Watson. (His first plan is to write to Tom in order to have *him* transmit the information to Miss Watson and thus bear the onus of doing the "right" thing.) But it happens that at the precise moment when the letter is being eliminated the word "right" surfaces once again, as if inadvertently, when Huck exclaims, "All right then, I'll go to hell" (271). The seeming innocence of the statement is belied by Twain's quietly dazzling wit in showing that the rights of a man who cannot write are preserved by a sense of higher right on the part of a boy who in destroying what he writes goes counter to what society says is right. Whether or not Huck will truly be able to silence his conscience with this simple commitment to burn in the future rather than betray in the present, the fact remains that for the moment a relative sort of peace has been attained, with things seeming somehow to be "all right" once Jim's present rights have been safeguarded.

In connection with the subject of homophones, it is important to realize that the word "rite" is also pronounced in the same way as "right." And although the term would hardly have been in young Huck's vocabulary, it was most certainly in that of the widely read and traveled Mark Twain. For the author had been required to consciously go through his own often involved and stressful rites of passage on the way to becoming a printer, steamboat captain, newspaper correspondent, book author, high-society husband, and traveling lecturer by the time he began *Adventures of Huckleberry Finn*.

Of this novel, in which rites of various kinds and forms play a significant role, Betty H. Jones observes that Twain "uses the ancient archetypal symbolic patterns of the initiation rites to comment on the problems that beset his own times. As with all of the archetypal mentors who have preceded him, Jim's primary duty as mentor to the young initiate is to instruct, to guide him in his search for knowledge. Huck like all initiates, seeks knowledge of self, others, and his God." [13] Yet while it may be suggested that Huck must undergo rites of passage in order to become a morally conscious young adult, it should not be overlooked that Jim, too, experiences extended testing before the dominant society will consent, at least formally, to fully recognize him as a human being who truly "owns" himself.

Huck's personal ordeal begins early in the book when he returns to society and suffers spoon-fed religion lessons in order to be able to join Tom Sawyer's gang. Before he can attain full rights as a member, he is required to undergo additional rites determined by Tom such as taking an oath, signing in blood, or offering up someone to be killed should the oath be broken. Soon after finally freeing himself from this childish bind, Huck finds himself subjected to yet another, more adult rite of passage when he is kidnapped by his father. Jones in this instance argues that "in an ironic use of the ancient mythic pattern of initiation, in which the young hero is spirited away by older male relatives from the protective but ultimately constricting presence of the mother and other females, Pap kidnaps Huck, stealing him from the 'sivilizing' influence of the widow Douglas and her sister." [14]

Submission to a further rite of passage is required of Huck not long after this when he is driven to break with the last remnant of his family, fittingly, his father. He is forced to go through the symbolic rite of sacrificing an animal and using its blood in order to be able to "die" to his old life and be reborn into a "new" one. Thereafter, the rest of the novel finds Huck frequently involved at one level or another with formal or informal rites as he drifts slowly down the Mississippi and passes through regular ritual deaths and rebirths on his way toward young manhood and the concomitant rights of a full-fledged adult.[15] James L. Johnson suggests that in the Grangerford section of the book,

> what Buck wants most of all is not to be himself, but to be another Col. Grangerford, and the murder of a Shepherdson would be for him a baptismal rite confirming him in that identity and in a long-sought adulthood. Ironically but appropriately, it is his own death that performs that function. . . . As a surrogate Huck, Buck in his death signifies Huck's own death *out* of this family, and Huck uses it as a second counterfeit suicide.[16]

Since Buck's death occurs in the waters of the Mississippi, Huck realizes that it will be assumed that he too has been killed there and that his body has drifted on down the river. In Huck's case, therefore, this reverse "baptism," exemplifying another "death" by water, serves to free him from the world of the feud and provide him—once again through the shedding of blood not his own—with another "new" life.

Jim's own initial experience with a rebirth by immersion also occurs in connection with the river when he flees his owner and takes to the river to avoid making any traceable track. The difficulty he subsequently encounters in finding suitable food on Jackson's Island represents just the beginning of a series of often painful moments of "initiation" to be undergone and overcome before he can attain the freedom he so earnestly desires.

Before Huck and Jim can finally complete their rites and thus acquire the freedoms—or rights—connected with entry into "new" lives, not only are they forced to undergo a variety of trials, but those trials often consist of being deprived of what each conceives of as basic (or natural) human rights. Jim is generally expected to be respectfully subservient, despite being subjected to a variety of unpleasant experiences connected with unjust imprisonments, while Huck, too, is little better than a slave to the king and duke.

Many of the rites with which Huck and Jim come in contact or conflict—particularly in association with religious and social hypocrisy—also interfere with their enjoyment of their rights by troubling their consciences while simultaneously infringing on their physical freedom.

Thus, although the word "rites" itself never appears in Huck's novel, the emphasis Twain placed on the words "rights" and "writes" in a work where "rites" are so prominent disposes the reader to at least a subconscious awareness of the unmentioned, though ever-present, third member of this homophonic troika.

The intricate matrix produced by the interplay of "right," "write," and "rite" thus supplied the author with just the sort of opportunity for multiple inferences and echoes he so often favored. One can easily imagine that, for a man as attuned as was Twain to the rhythms and effects to be procured from the written as well as the spoken word, such a pyrotechnic display of the intermingling of meaning with repetitive chiming offered undeniable delight. And by considering questions concerning rights from viewpoints to be found in the Declaration of Independence, the Constitution, the Gettysburg Address, and Theodore Parker's sermon on the "Rights of Man in America," Twain also participates—often as a devil's advocate—in the ongoing attempt to discover viable responses to the need of all members of society for practical ways of coexisting.[17] He understands that though the struggle is to be ever renewed, it is never to be completely resolved, and he does not appear to wish to offer facile answers. Nor would he apparently want us to forget that things may already be going "to grass" even at the very moment when we clever mortals are thoroughly convinced that we are "right on the track of a slution."

CHAPTER FOUR

Finishing *Huckleberry Finn*

T HE YEAR IN WHICH Mark Twain began writing *Adventures of Huckleberry Finn* was the centennial year of 1876, during which the United States of America celebrated the adoption of Thomas Jefferson's Declaration of Independence as the official beginning of the country. It was also, however, the year in which the death knell of Reconstruction was being sounded and along with it any serious chance of implementing Jefferson's ideal of equality for all Americans. Not until seven years after this did Twain finally finish his book,[1] and this occurred within only a few months of the Supreme Court's decision to declare unconstitutional the Civil Rights Act of 1875—an act that Massachusetts senator Charles Sumner, who during his lifetime often urged passage of such a bill, had hoped would bring about true desegregation.[2] According to Eric Foner, "as a broad statement of principle, the [senator's] bill challenged the nation to live up to what Sumner called the principle of 'equal rights promised by a just citizenship.' He explicitly, moreover, repudiated the legitimacy of separate but equal facilities; 'equivalent' was not the same as 'equality.'"[3] More specifically, the bill "made it illegal for places of public accommodation and entertainment to make any distinction between black and white patrons, and outlawed racial discrimination in public schools, jury selection, churches, cemeteries, and transportation."[4] By the time the measure was voted into law in March 1875, both the church and public school features had been carefully struck out by opponents of the integration of schools and places of worship. That the bill was passed at all was primarily due to the tireless efforts of Sumner, who, beginning in 1870, introduced the measure in every session of Congress until 1874.[5] It was not until shortly after the senator's death, however, that the bill managed to garner enough support from his congressional colleagues to make its pas-

56

sage possible.[6] While the final version did not represent a complete victory
for Sumner supporters, even in its truncated form the new law was seen as
a serious contribution to the struggle to secure equality of opportunity and
rights to former slaves, wherever in the United States they might happen
to reside. In the opinion of Kenneth M. Stampp: "The Civil Rights Act of
1875 was significant . . . because it was the first federal attempt to deal
directly with social segregation and discrimination by the states or by private enterprises established to serve the public. 'It is the completion of the
promise of equal civil rights,' said *Harper's Weekly.*"[7]

   Although the Civil Rights Act of 1875 was never to fulfill the high hopes
placed in it at the time of its passage, *Harper's Weekly* was not alone in wel-
coming a measure that seemed to promise to add a large number of social
rights to the legal guarantees included in the Thirteenth, Fourteenth, and
Fifteenth Amendments. Mark Twain may have been among the many citizens who looked with favor and optimism on the prospects of former slaves
following the passage of the bill, since it is known that the author greatly
admired President Ulysses S. Grant and made a special effort to meet the
president in 1870 (the year in which Sumner first introduced his proposal).[8]
It is also a matter of record that in 1873, in his second inaugural address,
Grant openly endorsed the idea of a Sumner-type bill—though not without a major reservation on the question of equal social rights.[9] Another two
years would be required before the initiative was finally approved by Congress, but, less than one month following the final vote, Twain expressed
in a letter to his brother Orion the highest praise for Sumner.[10] This would
scarcely have occurred had the author had major reservations at the time
about the act that many saw as the final jewel in Sumner's crown and the
senator's last, if posthumous, service to the nation.

Only a little more than three months following his letter to Orion, Mark
Twain announced to his close friend William Dean Howells that he had
finished *The Adventures of Tom Sawyer*, stating in passing: "By & by I shall
take a boy of twelve & run him on through life (in the first person) but not
Tom Sawyer—he would not be a good character for it."[11] What may be
the first mention of the idea that would come to fruition as the novel *Adventures of Huckleberry Finn* thus occurred within a short time of the passage
of the Civil Rights Act and on the day following the Fourth of July, 1875.

Around the next Fourth of July, in 1876, Twain launched on the actual writing of what was to become, in the eyes of many, his masterpiece. The precise date when the writer began his novel is still a matter of conjecture, but by 1 August 1876 Twain could confidently tell Moncure Conway that "I am booming along with my new book—have written 1/3 of it and shall finish it in 6 working weeks." [12] A little over a week after this, on 9 August 1876, Twain also informed Howells:

> The double-barreled novel lies torpid. I found I could not go on with it. The chapters I had written were still too new & familiar to me. I may take it up next winter, but cannot tell yet. I waited & waited, to see if my interest in it would not revive, but gave it up a month ago & began another boys' book—more to be at work than anything else. I have written 400 pages on it—therefore it is very nearly half done. It is Huck Finn's Autobiography. I like it only tolerably well, as far as I have got, & may possibly pigeonhole or burn the MS when it is done. [13]

It is Twain himself, then, who provides the most precise evidence we have that *Adventures of Huckleberry Finn* was begun in early July 1876. We do not know, however, whether the author consciously considered the Fourth of July dates at either the moment when he conceived the idea for his novel or when he commenced writing it almost exactly one year following his initial inspiration. It would nevertheless appear fitting and understandable for a novel dealing to a large extent with the struggle for independence of a young white boy and a black slave to be conceived and later begun on or near anniversaries of the birth of independence of the nation in which those characters were given life. That the Philadelphia Centennial celebration of 1876 also held a definite importance for Twain may be deduced from the fact that he not only attended sometime in July but also penned a tribute to Francis Lightfoot Lee for the Congress of Authors, which took place on 1 July. [14] If we accept as accurate Twain's account in the 9 August letter to Howells concerning the date when the writing of *Huckleberry Finn* was first commenced, it would seem that the new novel was begun approximately one month before sending that letter, on or around 4 July, and quite possibly in a certain centennial-inspired euphoria.

When Twain first mentioned the rough idea for his new novel to Howells on 5 July 1875 there was no reference to Jim, and we can only speculate as to what role, if any, a former slave was to play in the work (in *Tom Sawyer*, Jim's role is a minor one). The confluence of political events in the nation at that moment, however, could have suggested to Twain's sensitive antennae that a trip down the Mississippi, undertaken by representatives of the two major races in the United States at the time, would be a suitable subject. In post–Civil War and Reconstruction America both characters could easily be imagined questing after a form of freedom inspired by the myriad implications of the Fourth of July date. To what extent Twain's ideas had developed and taken form or what role Jim was destined to play in the book at the moment when the author actually began writing his novel in July 1876 is an open question, however. But at that initial stage, it is conceivable that the celebrations of the centennial year may have brought home to Twain the germane nature of the subject matter and encouraged him to develop it, especially as immediately prior to undertaking the book he seems to have been hitting his head against an unyielding wall in connection with his "double-barreled novel."

When one takes into account that *Huckleberry Finn* was begun only a little over a year subsequent to the adoption of the Civil Rights Act of 1875 and completed only shortly prior to Supreme Court decisions of October 1883 that struck down all aspects of the 1875 act except for the right of African Americans to serve on juries, it is possible to see the writing of Twain's novel as fitting approximately within the time-frame of these legal actions. As a keen observer of the political scene, Twain could not have been unaware of the developments going on in the intervening years with respect to the treatment of former slaves and their progeny, nor is it inconceivable that those developments could have influenced the author's thinking during the creation of his novel.[15] This possibility is enhanced when we consider that one of the central characters in that novel is a slave who is granted freedom during the course of the story but until the final pages of the book is generally presumed—by himself included—to have been *illegally* free for the entire time and therefore deserving of shackles when they are reimposed on him.

In considering the ideas mentioned above, two other major developments of the period should be kept in mind. The first concerns two Supreme Court decisions taken in the spring of 1876—shortly preceding the Centennial celebration—that seriously damaged the Civil Rights Act of 1875 and effectively made of it a toothless tiger incapable of defending those for whom it was created. According to James M. McPherson, "The effect of the *Reese* and *Cruikshank* decisions, combined with the Northern loss of will to carry out reconstruction, was to inhibit further enforcement efforts."[16] Within a year of these decisions, another development with far-reaching consequences also took place: Rutherford B. Hayes was elected president of the United States on the basis of the infamous, back-room Compromise of 1877. This corrupt political arrangement, which gained Hayes the presidency, was concluded not only at the expense of Hayes's opponent, Samuel Tilden, but also at the expense of many of the civil rights of blacks in the South.

The Supreme Court decisions of 1876 as well as the Compromise of 1877, the first occurring shortly prior to and the second shortly following Mark Twain's completion of "half" of *Huckleberry Finn*, could easily have inclined the author to question the wisdom of writing, or continuing, a novel incorporating the friendship of a black and a white (if such a friendship was indeed part of the author's plans for his book in early July 1875 and/or during the summer of 1876). It may be of significance, therefore, that following the Compromise of February 1877, at a time when the tide of political events in the United States clearly began running against the rights of blacks, Mark Twain's creative well also dried up with regard to his novel. It would not be until the summer of 1883 that the author would again find the water in the well high and ready to be drawn.

Between the passage of the 1875 Civil Rights Act and the Compromise of 1877—and in spite of *Reese* and *Cruikshank*—Twain did, nevertheless, conceive and begin the writing of *Adventures of Huckleberry Finn*. By the time he wrote Howells on 9 August 1876 to explain that he was "very nearly half done," many of the political developments that would eventuate in the 1877 Compromise were thus already under way, with Twain certainly aware of a number of them, although, understandably, not of the full range of their potential ramifications.

One reason why Twain may have discounted *Reese* and *Cruikshank* and launched on the writing of his novel in July 1876 may be linked with the letter Rutherford B. Hayes wrote by way of accepting the Republican nomination to run for president of the United States. Appearing at almost exactly the moment when, according to Twain's letter to Howells, the writing of *Huck* had begun, Hayes's letter of 8 July expressed support for the spirit of Reconstruction and promised to counter the effects of the two Supreme Court decisions. Hayes wished to "assure my countrymen of the Southern States that if I shall be charged with the duty of organizing an administration, it will be one which will regard and cherish their truest interests—the interests of the white and of the colored people both, and equally; and which will put forth its best efforts in behalf of a civil policy which will wipe out forever the distinction between North and South." [17] On 5 August Howells informed Twain that "now I'm about to begin a campaign life of Hayes, which Mr. Houghton wants to publish. (You know I wrote the Life of Lincoln which elected him.) I expect that it will sell; at any rate I like the *man*, and shall like doing it. Gen. Hayes is Mrs. Howells's cousin, and *she* thinks that any one who votes for Tilden will go to the Bad Place." [18] In replying to Howells on 9 August (in the same letter in which he apprised his friend of the *Huckleberry Finn* novel), Twain revealed how optimistically he viewed the Hayes candidacy by promising that "I shall read that biography, though the letter of acceptance was amply sufficient to corral my vote without any further knowledge of the man." He urged Howells to "get your book out quick, for this is a momentous time. If Tilden is elected I think the entire country will go pretty straight to Mrs. Howells's bad place." [19]

Mark Twain, along with many others in the land, unfortunately had no way of realizing at this point what Hayes's election would ultimately mean to the country and its black citizens. Since the nominee had committed himself to the "enforcement of the recent amendments to the Constitution," clearly referring to those that guaranteed the rights of former slaves, there was presumably little reason to expect the worst. Yet, despite his pledge, Hayes would disappoint many supporters during his administration through failing to defend the menaced rights of the Southern freedmen and by allowing the Civil Rights Act of 1875 to remain a "dead letter." [20]

One may therefore wonder if Mark Twain would ever have undertaken the writing of *Huckleberry Finn* had he had the slightest suspicion that the words he so much admired in Hayes's letter were "writ in water." Can it truly be the irony of fate—irony Twain would no doubt have appreciated—that it may have been Rutherford B. Hayes's deceptive letter we

somehow have to thank for the fact that the man from Missouri was inspired with the courage to begin his novel in the first place? The question,
in Huck's language, seems "interesting, but tough." No matter what answer may be given to that question, however, the book that the author had
begun in such a white heat in 1876 would fail to be completed (except for
revisions) until August 1883.[21] Although Twain would inform Howells on
20 July of that year that he had "half-finished [*Huckleberry Finn*] two or
three years ago,"[22] a letter he sent to the curator of the Buffalo Young
Men's Association Library on 12 November 1885 seems to contradict that
statement. Twain reported that "between the writing of the first & last
halves of Huck Finn, five or seven years elapsed."[23] And Walter Blair has
carefully cataloged a number of pieces of evidence concerning possible efforts by Twain to come to grips with his book on other occasions between
1876 and 1883.[24] But whatever may have been the specific stages in Twain's
struggle, the simple fact remains that the author somehow found it impossible to bring the novel to a conclusion for seven full years.

When considering that period of seven years, it is important to remember
that between the dates when Twain began and finished *Huckleberry Finn* he
had many other irons in the fire, including *The Prince and the Pauper, A
Tramp Abroad,* and *Life on the Mississippi,* as well as a collection of short
pieces entitled *The Stolen White Elephant.* These efforts alone could easily
explain the hiatus in completing the novel that he had begun in 1876. Yet
another reason for Twain's problem might also have existed. Taking into
account that the Compromise of 1877, which signaled the formal end to
Reconstruction, was agreed to not many months subsequent to the author's
initial burst of writing on his novel and that he found it impossible to complete his work until 1883, it would not seem out of the question for the
nation's confused situation concerning former slaves during the years that
intervened to be reflected in Twain's inability to create a conclusion that
satisfied him.[25]

In 1882 several challenges to the Civil Rights Act of 1875 were filed with
the United States Supreme Court, and decisions were reached on these
cases in October 1883. The result of the Court's decisions was to legally
nullify almost every feature of the act that Charles Sumner had so long
struggled to see adopted.[26] Although the measure had been ineffective al-

most from its inception, it was, at least, on record and thus in a position to trouble consciences. But when for all practical purposes it was stricken from the record by the highest court in the land, consciences could once again rest easy with regard to the proper place of ex-slaves and their children within the social fabric of the nation. By 1883 the attitude of the country itself had also stabilized, with a much smaller number of real rights being granted African Americans than Sumner had envisioned many years before.[27] It is not unfair, therefore, to suggest that the mood of the country in 1882 and 1883 portending the end of the Civil Rights Act of 1875, a development that from one standpoint could be seen ironically as freeing free whites from the final shackles of Reconstruction, might also have contributed to freeing Mark Twain's creative genius and simplifying his task with regard to finding a way out of the cul-de-sac in which he had been languishing with his novel.

Huckleberry Finn has often been faulted for possessing an ending—the so-called Evasion section—that seems at odds with its beginning, and an explanation for this contrast might be discovered in the influences, subconscious or otherwise, exerted on its author by the political world in which he was living. If Twain found it easier to write in 1883 than during the six preceding years, one of the reasons might be that the Civil Rights Act of 1875 was going through its final agony in that year, and whites, especially in the South, were developing viable ways to detour around many of the pressures and problems that the freeing of the nation's slaves had engendered. The mood then prevailing in the country that would allow the Supreme Court to nullify most provisions of the Civil Rights Act without serious outcry meant that, in practice, whites were once again being liberated from problems of conscience with regard to their darker fellow citizens. It would not seem inconceivable, then, that this calmer, less troubled atmosphere aided Twain to clarify and resolve the difficulty he had been having with finishing a novel in which the interrelated humanity and rights of a black man and a white boy were of central importance. In considering this possibility, a brief look at the final, much-maligned Evasion section of Twain's book may prove helpful.

In the United States of 1883, it was free whites who were being released from the bonds of Reconstruction, whereas a more involved process was

going on in Mark Twain's novel. One feature of that process entailed the
fact that Jim, the runaway slave, was, after being imprisoned, learning that
he had already become free long before but had been exploited by the
young Tom Sawyer for "fun." This "freeing of the free Negro"—paralleling in many ways and with possible reverse irony the freeing of free
whites—occurs in the final section and would seem, in view of the critical attention it has received, difficult any longer *not* to see in a post-
Reconstruction light. As Louis J. Budd has said of the novel, "In 1885 it
unmistakably read as a commentary on the Southern question; to believe
this was accidental is to be naive." [28] Jim's frustrating experience with pre–
Civil War imprisonment all the while he should have been benefiting from
the rights of a liberated man clearly corresponds to the situation of former
slaves after 1877 and up to late 1883 who were hindered, primarily in the
Southern states, in almost every way possible from enjoying what they had
been guaranteed by amendments to the Constitution as well as by the Civil
Rights Act of 1875. Though "free," Jim is subjected, in his ignorance of
the full extent of the truth concerning his actual condition and rights, to a
variety of minor tortures in the name of finally gaining genuine and complete freedom. As it so happens, it is a white boy with the Everyman name
of Tom who, through the dishonest maneuver of not revealing what he
knows, is at the source both of Jim's ignorance of his actual condition as
well as of his suffering. By interpreting the final portion of *Huckleberry Finn*
partly as a commentary on the state of ex-slaves in the period following
Reconstruction, it becomes possible to see the Evasion section as showing
whites depriving blacks, through silence and subterfuge, of rights that are
at long last theirs in order to exploit these innocently trusting human beings for selfish and even frivolous purposes. But Mark Twain was too subtle
a writer to have limited himself simply to Jim's problem.

It cannot be ignored that when Huck in the closing chapter finds himself
finally free of pap, with over six thousand dollars available to him "for to
buy the outfit" with which to strike out for the Territory and no longer
morally and socially entangled in a struggle for Jim's liberty, he suddenly
becomes a man, albeit a young one, in full possession of the means, the
birthright, and the skin color to guarantee him a particular kind of freedom. Hence, it is not surprising that he does not care to step backward in
time—"I been there before"—in the manner Twain has done in placing

his novel in pre–Civil War America. The direction in which Huck's freedom lies, at least as long as he can stay "ahead of the rest," is westward and toward the future.[29] With all that he has going for him, and despite the fact that he is now an orphan, it would be hard to see Huck's future as one devoid of hope.

Jim's future, on the other hand, can also only be surmised, but it would certainly not seem as bright as Huck's. With the paltry sum of forty dollars in his pocket, a wife and children whose freedom cannot be purchased for even thirty times that amount, and a dark skin that cannot be hidden during the journey he must undertake in order to find and attempt to free his family, Jim's possible fate is not too difficult to imagine.[30] What is striking, however, is that his fate no longer seems to involve the young, white, financially independent Huck in an assumption of responsibility or a problem of conscience. Jim, it appears, has at his disposal all the money and rights either Tom or Huck evidently feel he has any justifiable need of or claim to. Meanwhile, as with many whites in the post-Reconstruction period around 1882–83, during which the Civil Rights Act of 1875 was an ineffective, soon-to-be-abolished instrument, Huck seems shamefully "comfortable" with a socially unequal status quo that promises to leave him free of the former weight of his black friend.[31]

At this point it may prove worthwhile to go beyond what appear to be rather blinkered attitudes on the part of the boys concerning Jim's future prospects and examine whether in the closing portion of his book Twain gives clear indications as to what he considers to be the general direction the country is to take in the foreseeable future. What in his view is to be the ultimate fate of former slaves, now once again deprived of many of the fundamental civil rights which post–Civil War freedom had seemingly guaranteed them? And can he actually be considered to have revealed much of his thinking on this issue in his novel?

Throughout the final portion of the book, Huck continually betrays Jim's trust through a lack of resistance either to Tom's often cruel initiatives or to Jim's brutal treatment by his adult captors. One instance of this takes place early in the Evasion section when Huck informs us of a fact he obviously never shared with Jim. In answer to Jim's understandable reservations about being imprisoned, Tom has told the worried man "not to be the least afraid, because we could see he got away, *sure*" (309). Tom's true opinion, however, was revealed to Huck immediately after they left Jim's cramped prison:

> He said it was the best fun he ever had in his life, and the most intellectural; and said if he only could see his way to it we would keep it up all the rest of our lives and leave Jim to our children to get out; for he believed Jim would come to like it better and better the more he got used to it. He said that in that way it could be strung out to as much as eighty year, and would be the best time on record. And he said it would make us all celebrated that had a hand in it. (310)

Tom's wish that Jim might be left "to our children to get out" can easily be seen as foreshadowing attitudes of Tom-like whites, following the effective demise of Reconstruction, toward the physically liberated, though in most other ways still unfree, former slaves. And that Tom-like opinions would be of interest in that day to the Jims of America cannot be doubted. What is more, the time-span of eighty years, even if calculated from the period in which the novel is set, would offer whites the promise of postponing ultimate emancipation until well into the following century. But why would the author specify exactly eighty years?

Reflecting on this question, Spencer Brown suggests that "eighty year after Emancipation would be 1943, which deliberate speed would thus seem to be the limit of Mark Twain's pessimism."[32] On the other hand, L. Moffitt Cecil, taking up where Brown leaves off, also sees the Emancipation year of 1863 as the crucial date but turns to the past in order to discover Twain's reason for choosing to limit the number of years to that "unexpectedly precise" figure mentioned by Tom.[33] Cecil surmises that "Mark Twain, writing in the 1880's, knew all too well that eighty years elapsed between our nation's peace treaty with England (1783) and the issuing of the Emancipation Proclamation (1863). Reckoning by those two significant dates, it took our nation eighty years to set Nigger Jim free."[34] There would seem little doubt but that Cecil and Brown correctly perceive the importance to the book of both the Emancipation Proclamation as well as Twain's choice of the exact figure of eighty years. There is reason to believe, however, that in addition to, or in place of, the dates they propose, the author had yet another year in mind.

If we examine the passage in question once again, it would seem difficult not to conclude from such lines as "we would keep it up all the rest of our lives and leave Jim to our children to get out" and "it could be strung out to as much as eighty year, and would be the best time on record" that it is, as Brown suggests, toward the future rather than the past that Twain seeks to direct our attention. Recalling that the book, according to the author, is set in the period around the year 1835, adding eighty years to that date, or even to 1863, would not seem to point to a specific year in the future whose unique historical importance would significantly undergird either Cecil's or Brown's assumptions. If, on the other hand, we remember that the Evasion portion of the book was apparently written in 1883,[35] when the author was finally bringing *Adventures of Huckleberry Finn* to a close, simple mathematics shows that by adding Tom's eighty years to *that* date we arrive at the year 1963.

Twain, who first mentioned the idea for *Huck* on the day following 4 July 1875 and began writing his novel one year later—on or very near the date of the American Centennial—was a man whose fascination with history motivated him to create a memory game that could facilitate the learning of important dates. Since the first mention of this game occurred in the early pages of a notebook that he began in the spring of 1883,[36] it can be assumed that he could easily have been aware in the summer of that same year, while completing his novel, describing Jim's present situation, and mapping out the ex-slave's prospects, that eighty years into the future America would be able to celebrate a notable *double* centenary. Not only would Abraham Lincoln's Emancipation Proclamation be one hundred years old in 1963 but, equally important and appropriate, so would the former president's Gettysburg Address, in which he had promised the country "a new birth of freedom," committing its citizens "to the proposition that all men are created equal." For Mark Twain, who had begun his novel during the centennial of Thomas Jefferson's Declaration of Independence, a future centennial celebration—held on a meaningful anniversary of the completion of the novel and directly connected with Lincoln's use of the Declaration's most famous phrase, together with that phrase's significant influence on freedom for America's slave population—could well have been considered a stylish form of closure.[37]

Evidence that Twain was in the habit of musing on what the distant future might hold may be seen in a January 1885 notebook entry: "America in 1985. (Negro supremacy—the whites under foot.)"[38] This idea for a prospective sketch or story, set one hundred years off,[39] demonstrates the pleasure Twain frequently found in reversing given situations, while allowing for Huck-like ambivalence, if not worries, about what coming years could bring. As this was written at the moment when *Huckleberry Finn* was finally reaching the public, it indicates that the author was consciously contemplating a time-span that would exceed even Tom's "eighty year" and shows Twain to have been fully cognizant of the potentially far-reaching effects of historical changes then under way. And despite what may have been ambiguous private concerns about what the future might bring, this passage, when compared with *Huck*, illustrates that Twain firmly wished his published words to champion human dignity and freedom.

The idea of celebrating Jim's liberation only in 1963 can thus be viewed as allowing Twain to underscore the overlong wait for freedom that— given the conditions prevailing in 1883—seemed likely to be forced on ex-slaves (and their offspring), who would have erroneously believed they had already become fully free exactly twenty years earlier. In addition, the author's playful attitude in the novel toward dates and numbers—which included a special emphasis on the figures two and forty,[40] along with repetitive stress on pairs and duality of various sorts—would suggest that he took pleasure in creating a dramatic flourish whose historical significance might dawn on readers only twice forty years later, around the date of a double centenary celebration. By the time that eighty-year-distant date rolled around, many an earlier, ineffectual, Tom-like effort at procuring complete liberation for the freedmen might well be "celebrated" rather than understood and condemned for what it was: a cosmetic solution or half-serious distraction, with "style," not substance, as the primary objective.

In reflecting on Twain's vision of what the future holds for the freedmen, it should also be remembered that Jim, as the main representative of his race in the novel, apparently rejoices at receiving the forty dollars Tom bestows on him at the end of the book, deeming himself rich, while Tom and Huck, in contrast, are in possession of over six thousand dollars each. This glaring disparity would suggest that, while legally free, Jim cannot, and will not any time soon, be allowed to even pretend to be on an equal economic footing with whites.[41] Nor would it appear at the end of the book that anywhere in the foreseeable future will Jim be fully liberated from the belief that it is somehow the justifiable "right" of whites to be exorbitantly rich while blacks remain pitifully poor.

If the attitudes of Jim, Tom, and Huck are given careful consideration, the ending of the novel would thus seem to incline toward the assumption that the promise of 1863 might well have to wait at least a century before being fulfilled and that "separate and unequal" would continue to be the order of the day for a long time to come.[42] In the interim, the only options seemingly open to sympathetic whites would appear to be limited, as with Huck, to ineffectual, muted opposition—approximating, if not exactly equivalent to, quiet complicity[43]—or else flight to an area of the country as yet little affected by the evils of the slave system.

The closing section of *Huckleberry Finn* may, therefore, still be regarded as being at odds with the earlier portion of the book; but an awareness of the historical contexts during which the major parts of the work were apparently created can contribute to making that fact more comprehensible.[44] For when Mark Twain finally managed to overcome the problems he had experienced for so many years with bringing his novel to a close, it was in a manner that harmonized well with the general political mood prevailing in the United States in 1882 and 1883.[45] That mood strongly reflected the feeling of relief that came with the liberation of whites from the legal constraints of Reconstruction, and that feeling, to which Twain was apparently sensitive, would also seem to have significantly aided in liberating his pen. The closing section of the book reverberates with a sense of release and the lightened mood the author obviously felt in at last being able to finish his novel. Since he had commenced writing that novel during the high season of euphoria connected with the centennial celebration of the founding of the United States, it seems appropriate, if not inevitable, that the book had to await a similar season of renewed hope before being completed. The sad truth, however, is that the mood of the country at that moment represented a distinct contrast with the one that had reigned in the land when work on the book was begun, and that the sense of inebriation so welcome to so many came at the expense of the desires and dreams of many others.

CHAPTER FIVE

Huck and Jim on the Mississippi: Going with the Flow?

T HE MAJESTIC MISSISSIPPI RIVER is of central importance to Mark Twain's *Adventures of Huckleberry Finn* and, over the years since the novel first appeared, an impressive amount of scholarly effort has been expended in evaluating its role. While many perceptive observations and theories have been put forward to explain various aspects of the qualities that the river displays and embodies, relatively little consideration has been given to the fact that neither Huck nor Jim wish, or originally intend, to board a raft and float down the river with the current; for neither character is life on a southward-drifting raft a first choice. Nor is it certain that Twain himself had this in mind for his characters. According to Franklin R. Rogers, "[Bernard] DeVoto assumes that Twain planned from the beginning to take Huck and Jim on a journey downstream to the Phelps's farm, but if such had been Twain's original intent, he would not have destroyed the raft in the first place. . . . The resurrection of the raft is understandable only if one assumes that Twain had made changes in his plans for the novel."[1] Rogers further posits that

in its early stages *Huckleberry Finn* was to be a burlesque detective story. Apparently its denouement was to feature Jim's trial for Huck's murder, a crime never committed; Pap's murder as well as the mock murder were to be connected with the Grangerford-Shepherdson feud in a plot-complex similar to that of *Simon Wheeler* . . .

However, as Note A-10, urging the resurrection of the raft, indicates, Twain found the structural plan of his second work period insufficient for some reason, possibly because it was not readily expandable. Faced with the necessity of carrying on with a story he apparently had thought was almost finished he sought a means of adding to what he had already written. The device he adopted, as the resurrection of the raft suggests, is . . . to drop the culmination which would coincide with the feud and to continue Huck's journey downstream in the company of two tramp printers.[2]

A realization of the fact that neither Jim and Huck nor their creator initially envisioned a raft journey down the Mississippi can thus contribute to our understanding of unplumbed depths in Twain's novel.

After Huck narrowly escapes being killed by his father during one of the old man's drunken binges, he decides to flee in a canoe he has found, informing us that "I judged I'd hide her good, and then, stead of taking to the woods when I run off, I'd go down the river about fifty mile and camp in one place for good, and not have such a rough time tramping on foot" (38). The words "for good" point to Huck's stopping more than temporarily, not to a continual push to put increasingly many miles between himself and his father. A little later, shortly after Huck escapes from the confinement imposed upon him by pap, we also learn that the boy's first act is to hide in his canoe, have a snack, and then "smoke a pipe and lay out a plan." His line of reasoning is clear:

> I says to myself, they'll follow the track of that sackful of rocks to the shore and then drag the river for me. And they'll follow that meal track to the lake and go browsing down the creek that leads out of it to find the robbers that killed me and took the things. They won't ever hunt the river for anything but my dead carcass. They'll soon get tired of that, and won't bother no more about me. All right; I can stop anywhere I want to. Jackson's Island is good enough for me; I know that island pretty well, and nobody ever comes there. And then I can paddle over to town, nights, and slink around and pick up things I want. Jackson's Island's the place. (41)

It is evident that Jackson's Island is to serve as a base and that Huck will depend on the town for necessary supplies. He has absolutely no intention of setting off on a river journey.

Jim is another who does not foresee risking his future on the river. His plan calls for him to travel by land rather than water. For Jim, the river is simply an impediment that must be dealt with in a manner that will not betray him. As he explains to Huck: "I'd made up my mine 'bout what I's agwyne to do. You see ef I kep' on tryin' to git away afoot, de dogs 'ud track

me; ef I stole a skift to cross over, dey'd miss dat skift, you see, en dey'd
know 'bout whah I'd lan' on de yuther side en whah to pick up my track.
So I says, a raff is what I's arter; it doan' *make* no track" (53). Jim at this
point decides to swim out to the middle of the river in order to hitch a
surreptitious ride on a passing raft; and when he finally manages to catch
hold of one and clamber aboard, he "reck'n'd 'at by fo' in de mawnin' I'd
be twenty-five mile down de river, en den I'd slip in, jis' b'fo' daylight, en
swim asho' en take to de woods on de Illinoi side" (54).[3] When one of the
raftsmen approaches with a lantern, however, Jim's plan to completely
abandon the river goes awry. He is forced to slide overboard, swim to Jackson's Island, and survive as best he can for the moment, encircled by the
waters of the Mississippi.

It is by this circuitous course that Jim and Huck happen to be thrown
together on an island refuge in a manner that owes much to Daniel Defoe's
Robinson Crusoe.[4] The island itself, however, is depicted as much more than
a refuge from the storms of life or from the natural storm from which Jim's
knowledge of the actions of birds saves Huck. From Huck's description of
the island during the spring rise of the river, we are led to see it as a combination of Paradise and Noah's Ark:

> Daytimes we paddled all over the island in the canoe. It was mighty cool
> and shady in the deep woods even if the sun was blazing outside. We went
> winding in and out amongst the trees; and sometimes the vines hung so
> thick we had to back away and go some other way. Well, on every old
> broken-down tree, you could see rabbits, and snakes, and such things; and
> when the island had been overflowed a day or two, they got so tame, on
> account of being hungry, that you could paddle right up and put your hand
> on them if you wanted to; but not the snakes and turtles—they would slide
> off in the water. The ridge our cavern was in, was full of them. We could a
> had pets enough if we'd wanted them. (60)

Even the catfish Jim and Huck catch while living on the island is a fisher-
man's dream of almost miraculous proportions. As Huck describes it, the
catfish "was as big as a man, being six foot two inches long, and weighed
over two hundred pounds. . . . It was as big a fish as was ever catched in the
Mississippi, I reckon. Jim said he hadn't ever seen a bigger one" (65–66).

But Huck has also informed us that there are untamed serpents in this

"Paradise," and the boy's joke with the dead snake, whose mate bites Jim and endangers his life, harbingers the finish to the two friends' idyll. It is, in the end, Huck's desire for knowledge that leads to departure from "Paradise." Huck, disguised as a girl, decides to "slip over the river and find out what . . . [is] going on" (66). And the fact that a woman, in this case Mrs. Judith Loftus, is at the source of the information about the impending threat to Jim's freedom, posed by her husband, is not surprising when we consider the many biblical features of Twain's story. Understandably, it is the knowledge obtained from Mrs. Loftus that requires Huck and Jim to flee "Paradise."

At this stage in the novel Huck and Jim are forced to begin continually using the flow of the river to avoid capture, and only after this is the plan of abandoning the raft and the Mississippi at Cairo, with the intention of boarding a steamboat in order to go counter to the flow of the Ohio and *toward* freedom, adopted as a new strategy. The critical decision to leave Jackson's Island and drift down the Mississippi is taken unwillingly, is seen at best as a temporary state of affairs, and can by no means be construed as a propitious choice.

The mode of escape opted for by the two runaways must also be considered as less than ideal, since the piece of raft they utilize in making their departure has the major disadvantage of being distressingly sluggish as a means of travel. Huck tells us that "it must a been close onto one o'clock when we got below the island at last, and the raft did seem to go mighty slow" (77). At a later stage of the narrative, it is just this torpid movement that allows the king and the duke in a skiff to catch up with Jim and Huck only shortly after the raft has cast off. The lack of speed at that moment proves crucial as well as frustrating, since Huck believes he and Jim are at last rid of the two frauds and is already rejoicing in the fact that "it *did* seem so good to be free again and all by ourselves on the big river and nobody to bother us" (259). When the king and the duke manage to reach the raft, however, Huck feels crushed: "So I wilted right down onto the planks, then, and give up; and it was all I could do to keep from crying" (260).

Although we witness several idyllic scenes in the novel in connection with life on a raft, we gradually come to realize that the raft is a dangerously slow, unwieldy object. Even worse, it is subject to being torn from its moor-

ings at critical moments, such as during the risky "adventure" on the sinking *Walter Scott* or in the frightening fog episode. And, as if the disadvan-
tages already mentioned were not enough, Huck and Jim are also fully
aware, in particular after having "watched the rafts and steamboats spin
down the Missouri shore, and up-bound steamboats fight the big river in
the middle" (77), and after unintentionally missing Cairo in the fog, that it
is well nigh impossible to "take the raft up the stream of course" (129). A
raft, despite certain agreeable qualities, represents a powerless conveyance
always at the mercy of the weather and the current, and, what is more,
continually in danger of being destroyed by a steamboat. Despite Huck's
claim that there "warn't no home like a raft, after all" (155), existence on
the drifting and uncertain collection of logs never quite measures up to the
stable, calm contentment that Jim and Huck shared in their lost "Paradise."
For want of an energy source that would enable it to oppose the movement
of the current, a raft is only capable of going with the flow.

Nor is the river itself always the most hospitable of places. Beginning
with the decomposed body mistakenly identified as pap, Twain populates
the river at frequent intervals with hapless victims. There is, of course,
pap's own body, found in the floating house, as well as that of Huck's proxy
pig. And Buck Grangerford along with his cousin Joe also quickly become
lifeless corpses when they seek refuge in the nonpartisan river. Instead of
providing them protection, the Mississippi helps make them easy targets
for their pursuers by slowing rather than speeding their escape: once in the
water they immediately become "sitting ducks" for the men on shore. The
three criminals aboard the *Walter Scott* represent additional sacrifices to the
river's relentless flow, while Mary Jane Wilks points to another potential
source of victims when she indicates that the usual fate of scoundrels in her
town is what she thinks ought to be done to the king and the duke: "we'll
have them tarred and feathered, and flung in the river" (240).[5]

At times it might seem that Twain overemphasizes the connection the
river has with death, unless we take into consideration the importance of
the assorted myths to which he refers, myths that serve as a commentary
on the ways in which human beings attempt to relate to the river and its
bodies. Huck, for example, "knows" the body found in the river and taken
to be pap's has been falsely identified since it was discovered floating face
upward. According to the myth, in which Huck firmly believes, women's

bodies always float face upward while men's float face downward.[6] Then, too, there is the belief that bread containing some quicksilver will, in Huck's words, "always go right to the drownded carcass and stop there" (46).[7] Firing a cannon in the general area where a corpse is suspected to be located is also shown to be a method presumed effective for causing a body to come to the surface (45). All of these beliefs are scientifically unfounded, but the fact that they existed and are mentioned by Twain points to the need that people had for them, a need that must have been based on a sufficiently regular occurrence of death by, or in some way coupled with, the river.

Rivers are not, however, seen from only one point of view in the book. As Mark Twain well understood, rivers represented major thoroughfares in the years preceding the advent of railroads and paved highways. Dirt roads could become impassable during certain seasons or in certain kinds of weather, while rivers, because of their movement, usually remained navigable even in winter, hence the frequency with which towns were built along rivers and, consequently, the importance of the river as a means of linking places and experiences during the period covered in Twain's novel. Lionel Trilling points to that importance in suggesting that

> The form of the book is based on the simplest of all novel-forms, the so-called picaresque novel, or novel of the road, which strings its incidents on the line of the hero's travels. But, as Pascal says, "rivers are roads that move," and the movement of the road in its own mysterious life transmutes the primitive simplicity of the form: the road itself is the greatest character in this novel of the road, and the hero's departures from the river and his returns to it compose a subtle and significant pattern.[8]

Whether or not one accepts Trilling's view concerning the comparative significance of the river as a "character," his conception of the complexity that Twain's use of the river contributed to the form merits noting.

Careful examination of *Huckleberry Finn* reveals that Twain's attitude toward the river is certainly not simplistic or one-dimensional. This irresistible flow carries objects and people with it indiscriminately, shows no favoritism, and has parameters that seem much broader than any perception of the river as the embodiment of a single god might offer. It displays, among its myriad qualities, beauty, mystery, power, gentleness, generosity, constant threats, and an often deceptively benign surface, covering an interior that is not easy to fathom. Nor are its islands presented simplistically. Generally they are seen in the novel as safe havens, but Twain does not hesitate to represent them either as a sort of earthly paradise that can serve to bring humans and other creatures together in peaceful harmony, as noted earlier, or as a formidable hindrance to a fervently wished for reunion, as in the fog episode when Jim and Huck drift along opposite sides of an island.

Even crossing the river can be viewed as problematic. Jim, for example, is thwarted in his attempt to escape across the river and leave the threat of enslavement completely behind; this inexorably leads to a multiplicity of difficulties and a "loss of time" for him as he lives on the river in a sort of limbo, neither completely slave nor completely free. Harney Shepherdson and Sophia Grangerford, on the other hand, succeed in crossing the river and thereby escape becoming slaves to an ancient feud mentality.

The river also takes Jim and Huck past Cairo and safety and ever deeper into slave country, but for this it is in no way to blame, unless it is seen in an anthropomorphic light. Huck never sees the river in such a light, however, and his uncomplicated attitude toward this powerful entity seems apparent in a brief comment he makes shortly after the dissipating of the fog, along with its fears. Displaying awe and his habitual lack of prejudice, Huck remarks, "It was a monstrous big river here" (102). For anyone who has ever experienced a feeling of insecurity at being alone in a small craft far from shore, these words are probably not devoid of meaning.[9]

As Huck and Jim drift down the Mississippi toward adventures that would make Tom Sawyer's mouth water, were he only aware of them, we may therefore wonder if our heroes are really going to "go with the flow" of that mighty river. Is their fate to move through life and, like a raft, "make no track"? Or will they, like a steamboat or a canoe, be able to go counter to the flow when and where necessary?

The contention of this essay is that the primary thrust of Twain's novel is against "going with the flow" and that Huck's character is defined, and Jim's revealed, step by step as these two chance comrades find themselves in successive situations that require them to act or make a decision in some way running counter to major pressures being brought to bear on one or both of them.

Huck, for example, gradually finds the ways of the widow and Miss Watson, as well as Tom's imaginary "adventures," wearing on him and feels pressure building in himself to break away, when pap suddenly steps in and momentarily resolves the dilemma by removing him from the claustrophobic environment of the town. Prior to being kidnapped by his own father, however, Huck already gives a hint of what is to come when he realizes, immediately after pap's return to town, that "I warn't scared of him worth bothering about" (23). When pap challenges him with the comment "You think you're a good deal of a big-bug, *don't* you?" we see the spirit of teenage revolt rise to the surface in the reply, "Maybe I am, maybe I ain't" (23–24). A few pages later Huck expresses similar defiance in explaining that "I didn't want to go to school much, before, but I reckoned I'd go now to spite pap" (29). It therefore comes as no surprise that when pap becomes an actual danger to Huck's existence, the boy is willing to go against both pap and the flow of events by taking his pretended "suicide" into his own hands.

At almost exactly the same moment, back at the widow's, Jim, too, feels compelled to go against a flow of events; in his case it is one that could take him to New Orleans and a worse form of slavery than he has ever before experienced. Huck and Jim thus fortuitously break away from the grasp of a powerful current of circumstances almost simultaneously, and they continue to have this spirit of opposition in common throughout the book.

Huck again evinces his willingness to go against the flow when he makes an attempt at humor in the Raftsmen episode by claiming to be Charles William Allbright, the long-dead subject of one of the tall tales being told. In mocking his own identity, Huck not only challenges the essence of the tale but also makes a wry comment on what he thinks of all the blustery balderdash he has just heard. It is a risky maneuver for a young boy amidst men, but he dares to take the risk, just as he dared to flout pap's authority. He chooses to test his strength at this juncture and does not completely accommodate himself to the flow, unless we see his decision as one that he is certain will produce mirth in the tall-tale tellers by fitting in with the spirit of the moment. Given the situation, however, it would not seem to be a foregone conclusion that the reaction of the men will necessarily be what Huck could conceivably hope for. What does appear evident is that the fourteen-year-old Huck is constitutionally unable to accommodate himself easily to a situation that requires him to submit to an adult authority for which he obviously feels little respect.

Huck's father is also incapable of accommodating himself easily to society for more than brief moments, and his pattern of not doing things according to "reasonable" ground rules, such as not collecting and selling more driftwood at one time than is necessary to enable him to purchase enough liquor for a binge, can be seen as setting a pattern for his son. Huck has difficulty in understanding what he deems to be pap's shortsighted attitude toward the driftwood, but he comes much closer to making peace with society than pap ever does. Huck is, however, pap's son in not hesitating to go counter to the flow whenever his craw gets too full. Just as pap allows the new judge in town to go only to a certain limit in "converting" him before reverting to form, Huck also possesses definite limits as to what he is willing to tolerate.

Evidence of this may be seen in the Wilks episode when Huck sees the misery that the Wilks girls experience after a family of three of their "niggers" is split up and sold by the king and the duke. Huck is able to look on in silence only because he possesses secret knowledge:

> The girls said they hadn't ever dreamed of seeing the family separated or sold away from the town. I can't ever get it out of my memory, the sight of them poor miserable girls and niggers hanging around each other's necks and crying; and I reckon I couldn't a stood it all but would a had to bust out and tell on our gang if I hadn't knowed the sale warn't no account and the niggers would be back home in a week or two. (234)

The kindness that the girls had shown the boy at an earlier moment in the novel stirred him at that point to steal the six-thousand-dollar bag of gold coins from the king and the duke; and this latest display of greed infuriates him enough to cause him to take things into his own hands once again and initiate a plan to once more counter the flow of the situation. Huck's clear revolt against the members of what he calls "our gang" comes about in spite of pap, who has shown by bad example that "the best way to get along with his kind of people is to let them have their own way" (165). In this instance, Huck decides not to let the king and duke "have their own way" and manages to stand firm against the twin flow of forces represented by their direct acts and by pap's indirect teaching.

In what are often considered some of the most dramatic episodes in the novel, Huck goes against the flow of society in trying to save Jim from slavery, and his decisions in this connection all run counter to the practice of the period. In taking his stand, Huck is, as we know, required to oppose received religious beliefs that could find justification in the Bible for holding slaves. He must also go counter to received political practice, which, according to the stipulations of the Constitution, required slaves to be returned to their masters. Huck's opposition to this dual flow exposes him, he believes, to being condemned at death to hell and condemned in life to being regarded as a "low-down Ablitionist" (52), but he cannot find it within himself to accept either the religious or the political precepts that might allow him to avoid such a fate.

With Huck, it is clearly his humane nature that gets in the way when it conflicts with the inhumanity he encounters. He feels that he should oppose the seemingly just hand of nemesis in order to try to save the criminals on the drifting and doomed *Walter Scott* "so they can be hung when their time comes" (87), and he goes to a good bit of trouble for them. It is against the flow of common sense, perhaps, but Huck cannot completely abandon either the men or his natural instinct to save life. Significantly, he goes with his *own* flow in an attempt to counteract what the flow of the river threatens to produce. He realizes only too well that he too could be hung one day and thus identifies with the murderers. Such an unexpected reaction reflects a tolerant ability to identify with all levels of imperfect humanity, contradicts the norm, and contributes in a major way to making Huck the universal symbol he has become. He can even find it within himself to try to counter the flow of lynch mob justice and attempt to warn the king and the duke of their impending tarring and feathering, despite the fact that they have sold his friend Jim into slavery for a paltry "forty dirty dollars." In both of the above cases Huck applies his own sense of a more humane level of fair play to situations that apparently have already been decided by some power greater than himself. In each set of circumstances he displays the individual strength to resist the flow of what is seemingly preordained.

Twain also indicates that Jim, no less than Huck, ceaselessly strives to counter the flow. This begins early in the book when Jim seeks to carry out his escape by hitching a ride on a raft and must first swim to the middle of the river where, in a symbolic indication of his need and willingness to go against the flow, he significantly tells Huck that he "kinder swum agin de current tell de raff come along" (54). But Jim's opposition to the flow is not displayed solely in physical resistance to the river itself. He firmly opposes the movement of the current in spirit through never abandoning his goal of becoming free all the while he and Huck are drifting south. Jim's overtly rebellious acts, such as challenging Huck's "white" authority in the "Sollermun" and "Frenchman" arguments or daring to indicate that Huck is "trash" in the follow-up events to the fog scene, also add supporting evidence of Jim's strength of character.[10] Jim has the courage to oppose the flow of events as long as will be necessary for him to reach his goal of freeing not only himself but also his wife and children. At no point does he alter his stance or display the least inclination to waver on this issue, despite the mistreatment he undergoes at the hands of almost all of the whites with whom he comes in contact. In this manner, Jim is portrayed as just as stubborn as Huck in steadfastly, if quietly, going against what he feels to be the frustrating flow of events.

There are several other characters besides Huck and Jim who also display a willingness to resist the flow of events. Colonel Sherburn, for instance, coolly faces down a lynch mob that has flowed in a seemingly unstoppable mass toward his home. The doctor in the Wilks section dares to go counter to the crowd, the king and the duke, and even the Wilks girls themselves in his attempt to expose fraud. And, whether or not the gesture is seen as a deus ex machina, Miss Watson, who was originally planning to sell Jim, decides instead to oppose the practice of the day and liberate her slave, despite the fact that he ran away and thereby failed to honor the code of obedience that could have been expected to earn him his freedom. In each of these cases, individual courage claims the ultimate prize.

The final break with the flow occurs on the last page of the novel when Huck, after once again trying to find an acceptable existence in living according to Tom Sawyer's "style" and rules, realizes that Tom, with his "bullet around his neck on a watch-guard for a watch," will, for too long to come, always be "seeing what time it is" (362). That Huck notes and mentions Tom's vanity allows us to understand that at some level he is disturbed by the dreary implication of the new habit.[11] The ramifications of that fact and the possibility of having Aunt Sally as a surrogate for the widow Douglas and Miss Watson provide the motivation for Huck to once again oppose the flow. Huck valiantly attempts to diplomatically say no to further "adventures" with Tom over in the Territory by claiming not to have the "money for to buy the outfit" (361). But when Tom counters with the fact that Huck actually has more than six thousand dollars at his disposal, the scene is set for Huck to react once more in the only way he can conceive of to the kinds of pressures he experienced once before in the early pages of the novel.

In the end, the Mississippi must finally be left behind by both Huck and Jim. Neither character wished at the outset to be on the river, and neither now expresses regret at abandoning it. During a trip that has largely been defined by the current of this "road that moves," they more often than not have found themselves in conflict with the deceptively "comfortable" but unrelenting motion of its flow. Huck's final decision is a resolute rejection of life on and along the river in favor of the obvious risk involved in heading west onto dry land and into an un-"sivilized" world where, contrary to the flow of accepted logic, the unknown appears less threatening than the known. It seems plain that neither the raft nor the river can offer Huck or Jim an acceptable future, and this should come as no revelation after watching the two friends struggle, each in his own way, so long against the downstream flow.

It is therefore back on terra firma, but in terra incognita, that Huck's struggle promises to continue; Jim's plans for the future, which have long been apparent, also exclude both raft and river. Neither character would appear at this juncture to harbor any illusions, romantic or otherwise, about the Mississippi, but it would not seem beyond imagining that memories of their recent experiences together might not be forgotten in the years to come. For Mark Twain could never forget the Mississippi he came to understand so well as a young man, despite the fact that the flow of his life ultimately separated him physically—although never spiritually—from the movement of that restless river. As a former steamboat captain he never forgot the difficulties involved in traveling upstream against the current, all the while clearly realizing that the responsibility for facing and overcoming those difficulties belonged in the end to only one person on the boat. When *Adventures of Huckleberry Finn* is regarded from this vantage point, the novel would appear to bear permanent witness to its author's understanding of the continual and complex challenge involved in not going only with the flow.

CHAPTER SIX

Reflections on *Huckleberry Finn*'s Floating House

IN MARK TWAIN'S *Adventures of Huckleberry Finn*, the "Floating House," often dramatically dubbed the "House of Death," has primarily received attention in connection with Jim's covering of pap's face to keep Huck from discovering the identity of the corpse.[1] Although Jim's action is commonly seen as one of simple kindness, several scholars have interpreted it as possibly one of clever self-interest.[2] In the view of Thomas Weaver and Merline A. Williams, "Jim withholds the knowledge of pap's death because to do so best serves his plan to escape to Cairo"; and for Forrest G. Robinson, "Jim's seeming generosity, by veiling the truth about Pap's death, artificially preserves Huck's principal motive for flight. So long as Jim controls this information, he maintains the balance of power, and thus retains a substantial measure of control over Huck."[3] Such interpretations, in tandem with a tendency to accord Jim similar credit on other occasions and see him as possessing more subtlety than the ingenuous Huck, serve to raise his status as a character through revealing qualities of mind and sensitivity that might otherwise be overlooked. These perceptions are important to understanding the complex richness of Twain's achievement, for whether Jim's action in the floating house is seen as selfless or self-serving, our opinion of him rises, since in the first case he can be considered kind and in the second clever or even, in a third possible scenario, a combination of the two.

Once pap has been carefully covered and Jim's action duly noted, however, the floating house is usually allowed to drift quietly on down the river. The concern of scholars generally extends to little beyond the fact that the upstairs room where pap's body is found has all the signs of a bordello and that Huck's use of "ignorantest" in describing the words scrawled on the walls of the house points either to growth in his level of literacy or to his perception that he "can recognize degrees of knowledge; he understands that he is at least not as ignorant as the inhabitants of this ghastly house."[4] There are, nonetheless, a number of other aspects worthy of notice that have received at best only fleeting attention.

The river, as Huck has told us a few lines before the scene begins, had been "raising and raising for ten or twelve days, till at last it was over the banks. The water was three or four foot deep on the island in the low places and on the Illinois bottom. On that side it was a good many miles wide; but on the Missouri side it was the same old distance across—half a mile— because the Missouri shore was just a wall of high bluffs" (60). This would suggest that the house that will shortly come drifting past the island has been washed off the low-lying Illinois bottomland and not the high bluffs of the Missouri side. But Twain quickly casts doubt on this assumption by specifying that the house comes down the river "on the west side," thus indicating that, while there are bluffs located across from the island, the house could conceivably have been washed off the Missouri side from a lower site farther up the river.

Once the house appears, Huck informs us that he and Jim "paddled out and got aboard—clumb in at an up-stairs window. But it was too dark to see yet, so we made the canoe fast and set in her to wait for daylight" (60). Twain also decided to wait for daylight, since at this point in the tale he chose to omit from his original manuscript "a smell in there that warn't agreeable."[5*] Although at a later stage in the book Huck mentions the smell of rotting fish, it may well be that the smell of rotting human flesh (mixed, as we shall soon discover, with whisky) struck Twain as overly explicit for young or more innocent readers.

With the arrival of the new day, Jim enters the house first and before covering pap with "some old rags" informs Huck that the man has been shot in the back, estimating the length of time pap has been a corpse at "two to three days." Jim does not reveal his reasons for making this precise judgment any more than he exposes pap's identity to Huck, but his action can be interpreted as a selfless attempt to spare Huck serious shock and discomfort. In support of the "clever self-interest" thesis, however, it should be recognized that Jim is aware after the hairball experience and after Huck's flight from pap's captivity—presumably discussed at length by the two refugees—that the passing of Huck's father would be more likely to bring his son relief rather than regret.[6] Spencer Brown argues that Jim's withholding of that information maintains Huck in a state of slavery to the fear of having pap again catch up with him.[7] Jim's two-to-three-day assumption concerning pap's corpse also points to the maximum length of time the house, whether moving or not, has been at the mercy of the river and confirms that this cannot have been long. One conclusion to be drawn, therefore, is that pap was not very far up the river when he met his death. It is possible to surmise that Twain's decision to make the time span so short may thus have been linked in a direct way to editing out the smell that "warn't agreeable." The author also diminishes the brutality of the moment and distracts the reader at the point where Jim urges Huck to look away from the body. Jim's mispronunciation of "ghastly" as "gashly" beguiles us into chuckling at a linguistic slip, while Twain profits from that split second of relaxed inattention to slip in a possible hint as to a grisly detail linked with the victim's demise.

Having climbed into the house through a second-story window—made possible by the fact that the house, necessarily floating partly submerged, is also "tilted over considerable"—the two companions discover an unmistakable but humble "house of pleasure" scene. Huck, failing to comprehend the full picture painted by the details, records that, in addition to the body,

> There was heaps of old greasy cards scattered around over the floor, and old whisky bottles, and a couple of masks made out of black cloth; and all over the walls was the ignorantest kind of words and pictures, made with charcoal. There was two old dirty calico dresses, and a sun-bonnet, and some women's under-clothes, hanging against the wall, and some men's clothing, too. We put the lot into the canoe; it might come good. There was a boy's old speckled straw hat on the floor; I took that too. And there was a bottle that had had milk in it; and it had a rag stopper for a baby to suck. We could a took the bottle, but it was broke. There was a seedy old chest, and an old hair trunk with the hinges broke. They stood open, but there warn't nothing left in them that was any account. The way things was scattered about, we reckoned the people left in a hurry and warn't fixed so as to carry off most of their stuff. (62)

From Twain's original manuscript we know that he eventually substituted "ignorantest" for "vulgarest" and dropped "that they called a 'sugar teat'" from the final printed version.[8] "Perhaps," as Victor Doyno suggests, "Twain deleted 'sugar teat' because that word choice was too racy for his initial audience."[9] And even from the few indications thus far noted, it would seem that the author was continually conscious of the delicate line he was treading by inserting this kind of house into the story at all. Yet he chose to do so. Why?

One plausible reason for Twain's decision may have been that the house, while reflecting pap's tastes and values, also provided the author with another opportunity for humor. If for a moment we allow our imagination freer play than Huck's, it is not difficult to conceive of a situation in which the occupants of the room where pap died were engaged in riotous activities connected with cards, whisky, and bareness of body. From the pointed mention of two black masks and two calico dresses, it is quite possible that in addition to at least one baby and perhaps a boy old enough to wear the straw hat Huck finds on the floor, the house held more than one woman and almost certainly the "couple of mighty hard-looking strangers" Judith Loftus will shortly describe to Huck as the last companions to have been seen with pap. Given the number and nature of the articles of clothing left hanging "against the wall of the room," it is also highly probable that pap was not the only person naked, or close to it, around the time of his death. Huck will learn from Judith Loftus that pap had received money from Judge Thatcher to hunt for Jim, Huck's presumed killer, "all over Illinois with" but may never have gotten that far since he and the strangers did some serious drinking together before leaving town. Judith Loftus's information would suggest that the two deadbeats brought Huck's father back to the house in order to strip him of the rest of the funds he had received from Judge Thatcher, hence the empty whisky bottles, the playing cards, and the women's dresses and underclothes. From this knowledge it can also be inferred that the riotous activities going on within the room where the clothing is found had continued for some time, and the cocktail becomes complete if we add to this steamy potion a rising river.

The fact that Huck finds a boy's hat but no boys clothing could indicate that a boy, wearing all the clothes he owned and possibly acting as a lookout on behalf of the adults, was the first to notice the threat that the river posed to the house and its occupants. If we imagine him excitedly rushing up the stairs to warn the rioters, the fate of the hat in the ensuing flurry is easy to deduce. In such a situation it is also understandable that those in the room, under the influence of whisky and possibly, in the most literal sense, caught with their pants down, would quickly become panicky and scramble wildly toward doors and windows. If pap had not already been done away with by this time, it is also probable that his companions, rather than waiting any longer to extract his money slowly, dispatched him under the pressure of the moment and took whatever cash he still possessed that they had not already obtained by other means. Huck informs us that all signs indicate a hurried departure by the scalawags, which would point to the rising river rather than to pap's death as the cause of their rapid exit. Without the threat of the river it seems only logical that the departure—if such a move were even under consideration—would have been carried out in a more leisurely and organized fashion, with the disposal of pap's body one of the first priorities.

Twain's well-known enjoyment of ribaldry would suggest, moreover, that it was the Walpurgis Night wildness of a scene similar in its broad outlines to the one described above that appealed to him enough to justify its inclusion in this "boy's" book; and that it should be seen as at least partly humorous is further indicated by Huck's laconic "the way things was scattered about, we reckoned the people left in a hurry and warn't fixed so as to carry off most of their stuff." The available evidence thus points to the people in the house being intoxicated and less than fully clothed when they suddenly found themselves inside a house beginning to tremble in the grip of the swirling waters of the rising Mississippi. Under such circumstances, it should come as no surprise if items and objects that might otherwise have been swiftly stuffed into the pockets of pants, shirts, coats, or dresses—such as the "bran-new Barlow knife worth two bits in any store" listed by Huck as part of the "truck" he and Jim fall heir to by default—would have to be abandoned in the frenzy of the moment and in the absence of those handy pockets.[10]

The terror that being trapped on an unstable and undulating floating platform can inspire is later experienced directly by Huck and Jim when they realize aboard the sinking *Walter Scott* that their raft has broken loose and that they are cornered on the doomed steamboat along with men planning murder. For them there is nothing funny at that moment. But if the Floating House scene was envisioned by Twain in something like the manner just suggested, one can easily picture a mild but roguish smile playing over the writer's countenance as he was creating the subtle minimum of detail indispensable to bringing it alive. The screaming and scurrying of pap's "friends," in their inebriated and barely clothed state, seem only too audible, while the sloshing, spluttering, and swearing as they try to reach dry land ahead of a speedily encroaching river takes little effort to imagine. Rats leaving a distressed ship would appear elegant in comparison. What is more, "warn't fixed so as to carry" is just the kind of underplayed, dramatic "snapper" Twain delighted in delivering.

The Barlow knife that Huck pockets is also the kind of linking element Twain took pleasure in creating. We know from an earlier scene in the book, where Huck is carrying out his plan to escape from pap and needs to cut open a "bag of meal," that he has no knife. He explains how he must resort to using an old saw with which he had managed to cut his way out of the cabin where he was imprisoned, because "there warn't no knives or forks about the place—pap done everything with his clasp-knife, about the cooking" (41). The Barlow knife, therefore, fulfills Huck's need for a knife of his own. And since it was the best-known brand of pocketknife available in its day, it also gently directs our attention once again to those pockets that were not available to receive this small but valuable item when they were most needed.

But Mark Twain was not one to waste ammunition or even a folding blade. The knife now belongs to Huck, and it is this particular knife that he will take out of *his* pocket on the *Walter Scott* to cut the rope connecting the sinking steamship to the skiff he and Jim are in the act of stealing from the intended killers. It thus turns out that this Barlow knife, which could conceivably have been purchased by pap and which is found in the place where Huck technically becomes finally free of his father, will serve—with the rich irony Twain so loved and manipulated so well—to save the lives of Huck and Jim, thereby sparing them from undergoing an experience eerily similar to the one that befell pap in the floating house. This "inherited" object will allow the son to literally cut himself loose from his father's fate and, for good measure, permit the rescue of a member of the race pap so thoroughly detested.

Twain had not, however, exhausted the house's repercussive ammunition with his use of the Barlow knife. Articles in the sinking house that will serve a similar if slightly less direct purpose to that of the knife happen to be one of the calico dresses and the sunbonnet. Huck dons these for the exploratory trip where he encounters Judith Loftus, and he manages to glean information from her that will enable him to keep her husband from catching up with Jim and himself. The clothing that Huck wears on that occasion is thus clearly linked with the function of the Barlow. The son's "inheritance" from his father's antisocial way of life is to fulfill a positive purpose for which it was never intended, and again it will contribute to a result pap could not have abided: the rescue of Jim.

Once Mark Twain has driven the original reprobates from their troubled dwelling and brought the two intrepid adventurers inside, he has Huck list all the other items left behind, articles that tell their own grim story about the kind of life led by those who only recently abandoned them. The candlestick and cup are of tin and not silver or even pewter or crockery, while a humble gourd bears witness to the modest circumstances of those who used it. The quilt, which will later serve to cover Jim during daytime travel, and a fiddle-bow, which no doubt contributed its share to the recent merriment but which without the player and the fiddle now lies useless, are both described as "ratty" and "old," whereas there is reason to be suspicious of "some vials of medicine that didn't have no label on them," as well as of another unusual object: a wooden leg.

Huck remarks: "The straps was broke off of it, but barring that, it was a good enough leg, though it was too long for me and not long enough for Jim, and we couldn't find the other one, though we hunted all around" (62). Twain's original manuscript read "as good as new,"[11]* but his subsequent alteration to "good enough" lowers it a notch to the level of the other objects and effectively prevents the reader from being distracted from its more important message into musing on less essential questions. That the straps were "broke off," not simply unbuckled or detached, betokens a violent separation of the leg from its original owner, and here again Twain softens the tone of the passage through describing how Huck and Jim first measure the leg and then, after confirming that it suits neither of them perfectly, look high and low for the "other one."

The wooden leg and the unsuccessful search for its matching counterpart during Huck's inventory of the objects encountered in the house also attract T. S. Eliot's attention. As Eliot sees it:

> This is the sort of list that a boy reader should pore over with delight; but the paragraph performs other functions of which the boy reader would be unaware. It provides the right counterpoise to the horror of the wrecked house and the corpse; it has a grim precision which tells the reader all he needs to know about the way of life of the human derelicts who had used the house; and (especially the wooden leg, and the fruitless search for its mate) reminds us at the right moment of the kinship of mind and the sympathy between the boy outcast from society and the negro fugitive from the injustice of society.[12]

Eliot offers a sensitive reading but seems oblivious to the humor connected with the search for the "absent" leg. In commenting on the same passage, Louis J. Budd clearly perceives the possible shortcoming in Eliot's remarks, pointing out that "comedy, to be sure, is more idiosyncratic than tragedy and entails a cruel paradox: the harder we try to explain or just insist on humor, the sillier we look. So I am embarrassed to confess uncertainty whether T. S. Eliot, in his elderly reverence toward *Huckleberry Finn*, misses a joke or else disposes others to do so."[13] The difficulty here pertains to the fact that what seems to go without saying for Huck and Jim does not actually hold true in practice. The supposition made in all seriousness by the two companions—that since human beings normally have two legs, even a wooden leg must always have a mate—is obviously a mistaken one. But Mark Twain is clearly not the man to ask about that, nor, seemingly, are Huck and Jim. The reader, however, would be justified in assuming that our two heroes should be aware of the fact. For as recently as the preceding chapter, they were heard discussing Jim's unwise investment in the bank set up by "dat one-laigged nigger dat b'longs to old Misto Bradish," and, as we can observe from E. W. Kemble's illustration, that "banker" seems to get along quite well with merely *one* wooden leg. But as Huck and Jim seem totally unaware of such a possibility, one may ask whether the requirements of humor demanded that Twain authorize his characters to momentarily forget at this point the knowledge they must be assumed to possess concerning the physical limitation of the one-legged man who fleeced Jim of five dollars.[14] Whatever the reason for this apparent memory lapse, the humor that springs from the dislocated logic that causes Huck and Jim to try to find a second leg certainly merits a moment of amnesia on their part—and on ours.

Following their return to Jackson's Island from the visit to the floating house and after having breakfasted, Huck relates how he and Jim "rummaged the clothes we'd got, and found eight dollars in silver sewed up in the lining of an old blanket overcoat. Jim said he reckoned the people in that house stole the coat, because if they'd a knowed the money was there they wouldn't a left it" (63). Jim's assumption represents another example of the practical logic for which Huck so often expresses private admiration, and the conclusion Jim draws is clearly a viable one unless the coat belonged to pap, the unknown amputee, or another victim of pap's murderers. In that case it would have been simply a leftover, the contents of which were unknown to the killers. The case for the coat belonging to pap would seem to be a strong one, however, because we know that the coat he was furnished by the new judge in town was sold for money with which to buy "forty-rod" liquor, and, needing a coat, pap could subsequently have acquired this cheap one. We also know that Judge Thatcher had given pap money *before* his drinking bout with the "hard-looking strangers" and that the wily pap could well have hidden some of the cash in the lining of the coat (though his penchant for immediate gratification would speak against such a supposition). It can, in addition, be assumed that the fleeing occupants of the house would have been more likely to have snatched up their own coats rather than "an old blanket overcoat"; that the coat, if pap's, would have belonged to a recently murdered man, thus bearing an unspoken yet unforgettable curse; and, finally, that the coat could have potentially served as evidence against the perpetrators of the crime, and for that reason alone it would have been imperative to abandon it.

The novel's only other plausible candidate for ownership of the coat would appear to be "dat one-laigged nigger," although no further information is ever conveyed to the reader as to any of the man's actions or whereabouts following his successful bank scam in chapter 8. Nonetheless, the poor quality of the coat, as well as the money sewn into its lining and the abandoned wooden leg, could also point to this one-legged hustler, who, after fraudulently collecting a goodly sum from his fellow slaves, declared bankruptcy and failed to return the funds entrusted to him. We know that he had Jim's five dollars in addition to money from all the other investors he had duped, so hiding some of the cash in a coat that would be unlikely to betray its presence would certainly not conflict with the character traits he had so far exhibited. The signs pointing to violent removal of the wooden leg could also mean that he, like pap, had been lured to the house before the dark deed was carried out, while ignorance of the content of the coat's lining on the part of the house's occupants indicates, as Jim correctly notes, the probability that the coat did not belong to any of them.

It would thus appear that by never again referring to the "banker" in the novel, Twain succeeds in providing the reader with at least two different *possible* owners for the coat, both of whom had recently benefited from an influx of funds about which they may not have kept sufficiently silent. But even that dual offering does not completely exhaust all the options. There is the possibility that the coat belonged to neither of the candidates mentioned so far but to another victim of the murderous crew—conceivably one possessing a wooden leg. In that case Twain will have laughingly allowed us to "bank" on pap or the Bradish slave and, by "specalat'n," lose—like Jim—our investment. Yet another possibility that, despite Jim's assumption, cannot be completely written off is the chance that the coat *did* belong to one of the murderers, or possibly to another member of their gang, but was overlooked or forgotten in the heat of the moment.

In all of these cases it is the economical precision of Twain's elliptical information that obliges the reader to remain forever in the realm of uncertainty with regard to the complete picture. In a related manner, as well as in connection with the money hidden in the coat, it is of interest that in the original manuscript of the novel Twain struck out the words "We was rich."* that in the published book would have followed "and so, take it all around, we made a good haul" (62).[15] This deletion seemed to have been owing to the fact that the words might appear repetitious, since the preceding chapter had closed on a similar note, with Jim saying, "Yes—en I's rich now, come to look at it. I owns mysef, en I's wuth eight hund'd dollars. I wisht I had de money, I wouldn' want no mo'" (57). Twain was no doubt aware when making his revision that the irony inherent in Jim's statement about himself bore far more significance than Huck's three words concerning "truck" ever could and therefore deserved not only to take precedence but should in no manner be watered down. The eight dollars that would be found in the coat a few lines subsequent to the deletion could have seemed to echo Jim's "eight hund'd dollars" sufficiently to have satisfied the writer's meticulous ear and to have convinced him that even without Huck's words he had already created an adequate number of understated links between events, scenes, and chapters. Since it is apparent that the "haul" had provided riches beyond what Huck—or even Jim, who was aware of so much more at that moment—could divine, it is conceivable that Mark Twain decided as he was striking out "We was rich."* that he had created a trove whose value it would be better to downplay at that point in order to more fully exploit its ironical import at later stages of his book. Again, less promised more.

CHAPTER SEVEN

The Figure Forty in *Huckleberry Finn*

Scholars have often noted the possible importance of the fact that the sum of forty dollars is linked with Jim several times in Mark Twain's *Adventures of Huckleberry Finn*.[1] Meaningful aspects of Twain's use of the number forty have nevertheless been overlooked, with the reason seeming to stem from the fact that authors on the subject have limited their observations to dollars.[2] While dollars are of consequence in the novel, and particularly in connection with the figure forty, their glitter, together with the fact that the forty-dollar sum appears three times at critical moments, has apparently concealed the possibility that the figure may have a yet wider significance.

Before turning away from dollars, however, we should recall, as has often been noted, that in each instance where the forty-dollar figure surfaces in the book the dollars are soiled. The forty dollars from the slave catchers are clearly blood money earned by doing their job too well; the money the king receives for Jim is, in Huck's eyes, "dirty" and quickly wasted on gambling and liquor; while the forty dollars Tom gives Jim serve as a reward to Jim for having been misused and willfully kept in ignorance of his true freedom. In each of these situations at least one of the parties to the exchange is shown to be a kind of Judas willing to sell or take advantage of a fellow human being for some manner of profit: the adults for money, the child for "adventure."[3] That Twain was conversant with the story of Judas is clearly demonstrated both in the published novel, when Huck praises Mary Jane Wilks for having "the grit to pray for Judus [*sic*] if she took the notion" (244), as well as in the author's original manuscript, where he carefully spelled Judas's first name correctly but created a pun on the last name in having Huck misspell it as "Iscarott."[4] The pun was eliminated prior to publication, but it was Twain's thorough familiarity with the biblical story that allowed him, through three references to forty dollars in connection with some form of betrayal of Jim, to call up in the minds of his readers the echo of "thirty pieces of silver." The use of different situations, each of which could be seen to reflect in some way the Judas story, evidently served in his eyes to obviate the need to specify either the number thirty or silver currency. Nevertheless, during the first of the forty-dollar exchanges and thus possibly the most propitious moment for setting a pattern, Twain is more explicit in drawing his parallel than in the subsequent two situations. While at no point in the scene does the word "forty" actually appear, Huck is told that he can "make some money" by turning in "any runaway niggers," and Twain employs the term "piece" and indicates rare-metal coinage when he has the slave catchers make the boy a gift of two twenty-dollar gold pieces (126–28).

It is necessary to realize, however, that in *Huckleberry Finn* Mark Twain does not confine himself to mentioning the number forty solely on those occasions where money changes hands. A close examination of the text reveals that rather than being "obsessed with the sum of forty dollars," as Arthur Pettit maintains,[5] Twain actually used the figure forty more frequently without a direct reference to dollars than with one and in an even wider structural pattern than has hitherto been perceived. The number first appears on the title page, where the time of the novel, "Forty to Fifty Years Ago," was originally limited to "Forty,"[6] and by the third chapter we already find Tom mentioning the figure in connection with the work of genies who can "build a palace forty miles long" (16). Other uses of the number may be found in the name of pap's favorite beverage, "forty-rod" (27), in Huck's description of the ridge on Jackson's Island as "about forty foot high" (58), and in his appraisal of Judith Loftus as being "about forty year old" (169). It is again encountered in his portrayal of the king, impersonating Harvey Wilks, as having "showed in forty ways that he *was* Harvey" (218), as well as in the duke's subconsciously guilty use of the number—after he has just revealed that the king received forty dollars for Jim—in lying to Huck that the man who bought Jim "lives forty mile back here in the country" (274). The duke is also at the source of another fraudulent measure of distance, since it is he who produces the fake circular describing Jim as having "run away from St. Jacques' plantation, forty mile below New Orleans" (174). In reciting to Jim the names of a number of kings, Huck concludes his inventory with "and forty more" (199) and later in the book depicts the rope-ladder pie prepared for Jim's "escape" as containing "rope enough for forty pies" (319). Jim himself employs the number in declaring that he will not abandon the wounded Tom "'dout a *doctor;* not ef it's forty year!" (341), while Brer Hightower, in the "gossip" scene, uses the figure when offering an estimate of the number of people he supposes have been active in freeing Jim from his Phelps plantation prison: "A *dozen,* says you!—*forty* couldn't a done everything that's been done" (346).[7]

Twain's original manuscript for his novel furnishes even more evidence indicating that repetition of the number forty was not inadvertent. In the rope-ladder pie section of chapter 37, for instance, the words "a lot of," describing the pies, are crossed out in favor of the word "forty";[8] and although in the scene in chapter 32 where Huck first meets Aunt Sally, Twain's first impulse was to use exactly the same words and age as for Judith Loftus, "about forty year old," the "forty" was later revised upward to "forty-five or fifty."[9] We also learn of a table "'bout forty foot long" and a "fat nigger woman about forty."[10]

Of yet wider significance, as Victor Doyno notes,[11] is the fact that in the final chapter of Twain's work, where the manuscript reads simply "And we had him [Jim] up to the sick room; and had a high talk; and Tom says, le's all three slide out of here,"[12] the book as published in both England and America incorporates the following segment, inserted between "Tom" and "says":

> give Jim forty dollars for being prisoner for us so patient, and doing it up so good, and Jim was pleased most to death, and busted out, and says:
> "*Dah,* now, Huck, what I tell you?—what I tell you up dah on Jackson islan'? I *tole* you I got a hairy breas', en what's de sign un it; en I *tole* you I ben rich wunst, en gwineter be rich *agin;* en it's come true; en heah she *is!* *Dah,* now! doan' talk to *me*—signs is *signs,* mine I tell you; en I knowed jis' 's well 'at I 'uz gwineter be rich agin as I's a stannin' heah dis minute!"
> And then Tom he talked along, and talked along, and (360–61)[13]

Judging from the content of the above portion of the novel, it would appear that it was added with the purpose of creating linkages with earlier scenes, such as those where "signs" and superstitions play a role.[14] Twain's choice of the figure forty would therefore point not only to conscious

awareness of its suitability to such an aim but to the clear intention to make
the most of that suitability. That this section was not simply inserted on a
whim we also know from the author's working notes for his novel, which
include the notation "$40 for Jim—who says '*told* you I'd be rich agin.'"[15]

Through frequent repetition, therefore, Twain lays particular stress on this
number, which he first employs at the opening of his novel and later inserts
near its close.[16] One explanation for this emphasis may be that he began the
writing of *Huckleberry Finn* during his fortieth year. Consciousness of that
fact may have contributed to his decision to place the novel's events precisely forty years back in time and to incline him to reiterate the number in
the book, even at the later stages of its creation. As Walter Blair has pointed
out:

> November 30, 1875, Clemens' fortieth birthday, doubtless had even more
> of an impact upon this sensitive man than the completion of the fourth
> decade of life has on most people. . . . Clemens in his forty-first year was
> feeling decrepit . . . perhaps recalling [John] Hay's dismal prophecy ["A
> man reaches his zenith at forty, the top of the hill. If you have any great
> undertaking ahead, begin it now. You will never be so capable again"], he
> predicted the end of his literary career . . . This was Clemens' mood about
> a month before he started to write *Huckleberry Finn* in his peaceful study
> high above the distant city of Elmira.[17]

In that same month, the author also completed "The Facts Concerning the
Recent Carnival of Crime in Connecticut," in which the protagonist's hos-
tile and soon-to-be-strangled conscience is described as seeming "to be
about forty years old" and bearing "a sort of remote and ill-defined resemblance to me!"[18]

Another link between Twain's age and the frequent recurrence of the
figure forty may be seen in the fact that it was during the summer of his
fortieth year that *1601*, originally titled *Fireside Conversation in the Time of
Queen Elizabeth*, was written.[19] This pastiche, dealing largely with flatu-
lence, was, as Twain later recalled, "a letter which I wrote to [Joseph]
Twichell, about 1876, from my study at Quarry Farm one summer day
when I ought to have been better employed,"[20] and was subsequently circulated privately for the enjoyment of a limited group of friends.[21] Looking

back at that period of his life from a distance of thirty years, Twain permitted himself to wonder "if it would be as funny to me now as it was in those comparatively youthful days when I wrote it."[22] But in that earlier season the forty-year-old writer's evident appreciation of off-color humor would suggest that the fun he had experienced in creating this ribald account of an imagined social occasion—perhaps best, if broadly, described by replacing *o* with *a* in the word "forty"—might well spill over into the novel begun that same summer, yet manifest itself for public consumption in a less pronounced manner. The use of such word play as a means of drawing a laugh was, after all, far from foreign to this master wit. And, as Justin Kaplan observes, *Huckleberry Finn* and *1601* "were related in important respects. Both were implicit rejections of the taboos and codes of polite society, and both were experiments in using the vernacular as a literary medium."[23]

It was, moreover, during Twain's fortieth year that the United States of America celebrated the first centennial of its own birth. And it would not be inconceivable that realization of the fact that both he and his country had reached significant milestones within several months of each other could have suggested itself to the man who had chosen the pen name Mark Twain and who was ever conscious of parallel structures, duality, and the pairing of unlikely twins.

Twain's familiarity with the Bible and his direct and indirect references to the story of Moses would also indicate that by originally placing his story forty years back in time he may have been inviting readers, even at the outset of the book, to compare the wandering of Huck and Jim with the forty years of wandering in the wilderness that were required for the children of Israel to reach their goal.[24] The pleasure Mark Twain took in playing and singing spirituals would, moreover, point to his clear realization of the fact that such songs often contained thinly veiled references to the connection between the stories concerning the suffering of the Israelites and the plight of black slaves in the South. The repeated use of the number forty could thus have served in Twain's eyes to remind readers periodically of the length and the kind of misery experienced by an earlier group of slaves whose history would have been only too familiar to a large portion of those readers.

The effectiveness of the repetition of the number forty could have been suggested as well by the chantlike beat of such a line as "And the rain was upon the earth forty days and forty nights,"[25] which appears in the story of Noah and the flood, recounted in Genesis, the First Book of Moses (7:12),[26] a story that is clearly alluded to in Twain's novel.[27] But not only in the tale of Noah is the number forty given special emphasis in the Bible. In Exodus, the Second Book of Moses (34:28), we are told that Moses "was there with the LORD forty days and nights," and in Matthew 4:2 it is after having "fasted forty days and forty nights" that Jesus is tempted by the devil. For an ear as attuned to both music and language as that of Twain, the increased power and rhythm obtained from repeating such a number would have been more than apparent; and the fact that the author chose precisely the figure forty for a novel in which Moses, the flood story, and a frustrating and meandering quest for freedom figure prominently cannot easily be ignored. Nor should we ignore Mary Kemp Davis's germane observation that "on the religious level, Jim's temporary recovery of his freedom in the fortieth chapter of the novel is certainly suggestive, given the earlier allusions to Moses and the Exodus story."[28]

All of the reasons thus far proposed to explain Mark Twain's repeated use of the figure forty are rather straightforward, and each possesses its own merit. I would submit, however, that a more arresting and subtle explanation may be connected with the phrase "forty acres and a mule."

James F. Light informs us that at the close of *Huckleberry Finn* Tom Sawyer feels that "he should pay Jim something for being such a good prisoner even when actually free. He gives Jim forty dollars (reminiscent of forty acres and a mule) and Jim is grateful. In his new 'freedom' Jim feels himself to be wealthy, just as once before, when he had fourteen dollars, he had felt himself a rich man. That Jim had earlier been defrauded of his riches is suggestive of the future fate of the forty dollars."[29] Light does not touch on the forty-dollar pattern pointed to by earlier writers on the subject, but his parenthetical remark concerning "forty acres and a mule" warrants exploring further.[30]

Twain realized in 1876, when beginning his novel, that a book set in a period preceding the Civil War could not make use of knowledge that would have been unavailable to the characters of that period. The author apparently slipped up in the use of twenty-dollar gold pieces, which were not minted until 1849,[31] but this was an exception. By the time he began writing *Huckleberry Finn*, the phrase "forty acres and a mule" had taken on a particular onus. Twain was no doubt sensitive to that fact and, as a professional writer and practiced public speaker, realized that repetition of the number forty could ring a bell in the minds of his readers and call the subconsciously available "acres" phrase to the surface, in particular when associated with money and a black man. Given the time span during which the events in the novel were taking place, however, Twain would certainly have felt precluded from incorporating a *direct* reference to "forty acres and a mule," even though the exploitation of a naive ex-slave was a concept that could be considered highly appropriate to his portrayal of Jim. The potential that the "forty acres" theme offered for underscoring the deceptions practiced on ignorant and vulnerable former slaves during Reconstruction was, therefore, great but had the serious drawback of being anachronistic. The problem facing the author could thus be seen as one of simultaneously using and yet not using that theme. This conundrum was solved, I believe, by the frequent repetition of the first word of the phrase: "forty." In this manner the weight of the full expression was made available, allowing the complete idea to be insinuated without warping the time frame to which Twain had limited himself.

"Forty" is therefore the key number and is repeated often, while the substitution of "acres" for "dollars" follows easily since both terms define a quantity of property. It is also conceivable that the three uses of the forty-dollar figure in a Judas-story context can be viewed as simply one of Twain's variations on a more broadly and subtly developed theme of deception and betrayal. Jim himself describes how he once became the victim of both self-deception as well as deception by others at a time when, in his own view, he was a "rich" man in possession of fourteen dollars. That the money was soon lost through misplaced credulity can be seen as pointing not only, as Light indicates, to "the future fate of the forty dollars" but also to the future fate of all those who place their faith in the concept of "forty acres and a mule." And since "fourteen" can act as an approximate homophone for "forty," this allows it—as with the repeated "fo' dollars" in the same passage—to sound again the opening notes of the leitmotif. But what about that infamous mule always yoked to the forty acres?

Light catches a reverberation of what Twain may have been suggesting in seeing the forty dollars Jim receives as "reminiscent of 'forty acres and a mule,'" but he concentrates his attention on the probable financial disillusionment in store for Jim. Doyno, too, hearkens to the faint tinkle of Twain's bell but might also have listened longer. His conclusion is that "in offering Jim 'forty dollars,' Tom gives not 'forty acres and a mule,' but a simple cash nexus. Tom denies Jim's humanity and takes an action that puts him in structural resemblance to the two slave hunters and the king." [32] In Twain's working notes, however, there is a clue as to how the number forty was perhaps being used in a much broader structural context.

The first entry on the first page of Twain's working notes is "De Mule" with a line drawn through it, underlined three times, and followed by a period. [33] Since Twain's novel contains no mention of any mules other than the "thousand 'sumter' mules, all loaded down with di'monds" that exist only in Tom Sawyer's imagination (15), [34] the riddle as to what Twain was referring, or what he might have had in mind, is left open to conjecture. Nevertheless, the fact that the mule in question is preceded by "De" clearly points to "Missouri negro dialect," according to the linguistic parameters Twain had set for himself in *Huckleberry Finn*. It is thus connected directly to the black world, whose most prominent representative in the book is Jim. In this manner we are led to see "De Mule" as situated in the mind and mouth of a black person, and from this it seems only a short jump to the "forty acres" image, since it was ex-slaves who were victimized by their trust in the concept embodied in the words "forty acres and a mule." The triple underlining of "De Mule," added to the line crossing out the words, also allows for the possibility that "De Mule" was in some way considered of primary importance by Twain but could not, in his judgment, be openly referred to in the novel.

There is also another possibility. According to Appendix A of the Blair and Fischer edition of *Adventures of Huckleberry Finn*, "Mark Twain's deletions sometimes indicate not that he rejected an idea, but that he had completed his use of it in the story" (712). The fact that "De Mule" is crossed out thus suggests that, as no mule is to be found in the novel, the idea had indeed been incorporated, but without mention of the specific term. The regular reappearance of the number forty may have been seen by Twain as effectively making the heavy-handed addition of an actual mule as unnecessary to the text as an exact mention of "thirty pieces of silver." Assuming these suppositions are correct, "De Mule" can be seen as linked to the number forty in the manner discussed above and, if so, would fully deserve the triple underlining, capitalization, and period with which it is embellished. This could also help to explain its place of honor as the first item in the working notes and even, perhaps, why Twain decided to add Jim's forty dollars to the end of the novel.

As the working notes also mention "$40 from men,"[35] the likelihood of a connection between the concept and the act cannot be ruled out. For if the working notes were written in 1879 or possibly before chapters 17 and 18—as is suggested in Appendix A (711–12)—this could contribute to explaining the increasingly frequent use of the figure forty in the portion of the book subsequent to the mention of "De Mule" and the "$40 from men." It might also aid in clarifying why Twain would wish to insert the number one last time before bringing his book to a close. Since Jim's childishly innocent assumption that with forty dollars, just as with fourteen dollars, he had become a rich man is flagrantly mocked by the fact that Huck and Tom have over six thousand dollars apiece at *their* disposal, this points once again to the kind of self- as well as societal deception connected with the concept of "forty acres and a mule."

All these arguments suggest that what originally may have begun in the author's mind as rather uncomplicated reasons for incorporating the number forty into the texture of *Huckleberry Finn* developed, during the changing times and the sporadic creation of the novel, into a deeper and richer web of significance the further the writing progressed.[36] Can it therefore be mere happenstance that when Twain was deciding on the precise number of orders to be obtained before allowing the book to be published, he settled on the figure 40,000?[37]

CHAPTER EIGHT

The End, Yours Truly Mark Twain

URING SEPTEMBER 1884, shortly before *Adventures of Huckle-berry Finn* was to be published, Mark Twain was in steady correspondence with his nephew, Charles L. Webster, concerning whether to include a portrait of a bust of himself at the beginning of the book.[1] On 8 September he sent "a photograph from the bust," asking:

> How would it do to heliotype it (reducing it to half the present size), & make
> a frontispiece of it for Huck Finn, with
>
> MARK TWAIN
> ———
> *from the bust by Karl Gerhardt*
>
> printed under it.
> ———
> Would the whole thing (binding into the book included), cost more than
> 2 cents? Otherwise we couldn't afford it. And could we delay the canvassing
> copies & put it in them? I suppose it would help sell the book.[2]

The following day Twain forwarded a further advisory: "The bust was made in Elmira & is just finished. The photos were taken here & I have the negatives myself. But do nothing in the matter unless you find *advantage* for us in it.———I thought maybe it would advantage the book."[3] And on 20 September we find him worrying that "that heliotype Co hasn't sent me that bottle of ink yet for the autographs."[4]

Although the picture of the bust is presumably the subject under discussion, it would appear that for Twain the signature to be supplied below the picture represented an essential part of the package and even justified reducing the size of the picture by half in order to accommodate it. The author obviously realized that the pen name he had been making famous on the lecture circuit and with his previous books could be a strong plus in selling his newest work and does not even raise the question of its importance with his nephew, who, since the publishing company actually belonged to Twain, occupied his position at Twain's pleasure.

As Webster offered no objection, the American edition was eventually provided with the picture of Gerhardt's work, beneath which was to be found the impressive flourish of an autograph by Mark Twain. Since that name also appeared on the cover and the title page,[5] there could, despite the modest mention of the name Samuel L. Clemens in small print underneath the copyright date, be no doubt that Twain had a serious connection with the tale ostensibly recounted by a certain fourteen-year-old youth who went by the curious and somehow catchy name of Huckleberry Finn.[6]

On the opening page of the novel, Twain also made certain to underscore his association with the work by incorporating the name Mark Twain in the first paragraph, which begins with Huck telling the reader, "You don't know about me, without you have read a book by the name of 'The Adventures of Tom Sawyer,' but that ain't no matter. That book was made by Mr. Mark Twain, and he told the truth, mainly" (1). In these lines Twain manages not only to advertise *Tom Sawyer* but also to link, through Huck's knowledge, the name of the author of the quite successful earlier book to the one the reader has just taken in hand; in this fashion he achieves a double use of the sales value of his name.[7] It is thus apparent that Samuel Clemens felt strongly conscious of the name he had created for himself and was not at all averse to drawing attention to it whenever he felt that could be of "advantage." This becomes all the more evident if we consider, as Louis Budd points out, that "both for better and worse, Twain thought of himself as publishing under a brand name, tied first to the Jumping Frog story and then to *The Innocents Abroad*, which, he bragged, kept selling right along like the Bible. As early as 1873 he fought literary pirates by contending in court that Mark Twain was a trademark, not a pseudonym, and he pushed another such case in 1883."[8] These dates would indicate that at the time he was beginning his novel in 1876, as well as when writing to Webster in 1884 concerning the heliotype frontispiece for the completed work, the author was not insensitive to the value of displaying prominently the name Mark Twain.

As a former riverboat pilot, Twain was also cognizant of the multifaceted quality possessed by his adopted name, and it is of interest that in *Adventures of Huckleberry Finn* the number two is mentioned in some connection in every chapter but one, beginning, as might reasonably be suspected, with chapter 2. If this level of consistency can be taken to indicate that the use of the number was intentional on Twain's part, it would be logical for the omission of the number two in chapter 1 to be compensated for by the writer's conspicuous use of his own nom de plume to "mark twain" within the text. There is, moreover, another significant statistic that merits attention: not only does Twain employ the figure two at least once in forty-two out of forty-three chapters of his novel, he further underlines its importance by resorting to its use no less than 140 times during the course of the book. (In addition, it may be noted that the words "couple" and "twice," often written as "twyste," also appear frequently.) Through regular repetition, therefore, Twain places distinct stress on this number in a manner that harmonizes well with the emphasis on ambivalence, duality, duplicity, and character pairs that the novel also displays. Might not one conceivable reason for this be that Twain is drawing the reader's subconscious attention to a fact he himself was keenly aware of: that with *The Adventures of Tom Sawyer* successfully in print, this was to be the *second* of his "boy books" for adults? Or should we perhaps look beyond this obvious possibility for his dependence on the ubiquitous number, mentioned so often directly or manifested in such a rich variety of alternate guises?

In recent years much has been made of the fact that in several respects Twain brings his book full circle, for instance through having many of the characters from the opening chapters reappear either in person or in name during the closing chapters. More than one critic has referred to or quoted from the following key paragraph in the final chapter:

> And then Tom he talked along, and talked along, and says, le's all three slide out of here, one of these nights, and get an outfit, and go for howling adventures amongst the Injuns, over in the Territory, for a couple of weeks or two; and I says, all right, that suits me, but I ain't got no money for to buy the outfit, and I reckon I couldn't get none from home, because it's likely pap's been back before now, and got it all away from Judge Thatcher and drunk it up. (361)

Words often cited from this passage are "for a couple of weeks or two," with the inference usually being that Twain is chuckling ironically once again, either at the fact that Tom, despite heady pretensions, is seriously

lacking in both precision and polish, or at the boy's narrowly limited conception of the length of time needed to carry out an "adventure."[9] It is
possible, however, that Twain may have been doing rather more than
simply drawing attention in a humorously unsubtle fashion to a failing on
the part of Tom. If we take into account the somewhat extraordinary attention that the writer appears to pay to the number two elsewhere in his
novel, it would seem important when examining Tom's "a couple of weeks
or two" to avoid dismissing the "mistake" too quickly and to consider
whether or not the young man is actually capable of perceiving the difference between "a couple" and "two." In chapters 35 and 37 Twain offers
incontrovertible proof that Tom is, indeed, aware of the distinction.

Tom's plan for stealing Jim requires case knives for the task of slowly
digging Jim a hole through which he can escape, and the original conception of the plan, as Tom describes it to Huck, demands "a *couple* of caseknives" (304, emphasis added). Consequently, once Huck is finally convinced that the plan is acceptable, he tells Tom: "I'll mosey along, now, and
smouch a couple of caseknives" (305). At that instant Tom betrays unmistakable knowledge of the meaning of "a couple," and thus of the number
involved, when he counters Huck's plan for carrying out the original proposal to "smouch" only two knives. Revising his own thinking, Tom increases the number of knives needed by one, ordering Huck to "smouch
three . . . we want one to make a saw out of" (305). When Huck responds
with "Tom, if it ain't unregular and irreligious to sejest it . . . there's an old
rusty saw-blade around yonder sticking under the weatherboarding behind
the smokehouse" (305), Tom, Huck informs us, "looked kind of weary and
discouraged-like, and says: 'It ain't no use to try to learn you nothing,
Huck. Run along and smouch the knives—three of them'" (305).

Considering the care taken here to showing Tom not once but twice
exhibit his knowledge of what "a couple" means and recalling that in the
succeeding chapter the case knives again become the object of attention
when they blister the hands of their users and are exchanged for a pickax
and a shovel *imagined* to be "caseknives," it would seem difficult to conceive
of the author forgetting such details in the all-important concluding chapter of his novel. In fact, it would be accusing Twain of a major oversight to
assert that Tom makes his humorous blunder in Chapter the Last without
the author's express approval and full awareness of the knowledge with

which he has so conspicuously provided the boy in chapter 35. The possibility of such a thing occurring cannot be totally ruled out, of course,[10] but the emphasis Twain places on Tom's understanding of the difference between "a couple" and "three" does not allow much room for maneuver. Even the rather foolish Tom Sawyer we are presented with in *Huckleberry Finn* must, at a very minimum, be given credit for knowing the difference between two and three. That this is undeniably the case is made abundantly clear in chapter 37, where Tom counts the spoons for Aunt Sally. It is the boy's fraudulent counting that serves as the basis of the humor in this episode and proves conclusively both that Tom *can* count and that his skills in this area are fully developed.

With the words "a couple of weeks or two" Twain may well have been offering a closing remark concerning the doubleness that informs the novel while at the same time making a humorous comment on Tom's superficiality. But he may also have been doing a good deal more. It is my contention that Mark Twain was bringing his book to a close with a veiled reference to his own name. I would submit that throughout the novel the author was in all probability using the number two (and equivalents to it) in each chapter subsequent to chapter 1 as a distinguishing personal stamp—based on his pen name—in order to "mark twain" in a clear but covert manner in each of these divisions. The uncalled-for doubling of the number in the final chapter by the mathematically proficient Tom could therefore indicate that Mark Twain was signing his book in a saucy and slightly more salient manner than he had been using up until that point in "initialing" each chapter with the word "two."

It would also appear that since chapter 1 of *Huckleberry Finn* opens with a reference to *Tom Sawyer*, together with a mention of Twain's name in the first paragraph, the placing of the phrase "a couple of weeks or two" in the mouth of Tom Sawyer at the end of the novel provides a formal link with the beginning of the book through once again "marking" "twain" in connection with Tom. In this circumstance the two words that possess an equivalent value to "twain" are used in an erroneous manner that draws particular attention to them by pairing unlikely pairs.

Shortly after Tom's words have been uttered, Huck himself signs the book, combining a form employed for ending stories with a phrase used for concluding letters to produce "The end, yours truly Huck Finn." Through having Huck doubly close the novel in this manner, Mark Twain may be seen as laying stress on the fact that this book, which can be regarded not only as an independent entity but also as a sequel to *Tom Sawyer*, has, in a sense, come to a double conclusion, with paired works further "coupled" by this form of closure. In addition, the author succeeds in underscoring one last time the complex duality that plays so frequently in the novel and to which Tom's words have so recently lent emphasis—a duality that is embodied in Samuel Clemens's nom de plume as well as intrinsic to the fact that the author could simultaneously possess and make use of two completely different but equally valid proper names.

Through Tom's mistaken usage, Twain would therefore appear to be drawing attention to much more than ignorance, a humorous error, unpolished enthusiasm, or a limited imagination. Considering the author's repetitive use of his pen name at the beginning of the book, his sensitivity to the seemingly inexhaustible potential inherent in that appellation, and the unfailing reappearance of the figure two in each chapter following the first, it would seem entirely justified to accord Mark Twain credit for having ended his novel with a panache that has too long gone unappreciated and unremarked.

CHAPTER NINE

On Black and White in *Huckleberry Finn*

W HEN LATE IN Mark Twain's *Adventures of Huckleberry Finn* Huck says of Jim, "I knowed he was white inside" (341), it requires no effort to accept this statement as an innocent expression of approval of the Southern way of life by an ignorant fourteen-year-old boy. What is "white" is taken by that boy to be good, proper, and right but is contradicted by Jim's black skin, which, according to the teachings of Huck's society, should enclose completely opposite, "black" qualities. Huck's words, however, can be considered pivotal to attempting a deeper analysis of the position of blacks and whites in Twain's novel, since inversion of roles and values lies at the heart of the author's ironic and subversive approach to his subject. Early in the book, Twain wastes no time in beginning to display whites in a negative light while conversely showing blacks to be possessed of the very qualities that the whites consider to be the prerogative of their color only.

Our first encounter with Jim—a man possessing no last name, as was commonly the case, and who is hence easily seen as a rootless black Everyman—finds Tom Sawyer exploiting him for some cheap "fun." Tom settles for hanging Jim's hat from a tree limb, but only after Huck opposes the more radical measure of tying Jim himself to a tree. Tom sees Jim more as a plaything than as a human being with rights equal to his own, while Huck only backs away from Tom's original scheme for the selfish reason that Jim "might wake and make a disturbance, and then they'd find out I warn't in" (7). At the very least, then, the white boys' treatment of the black man must be seen as insensitive, since Jim would not have been likely to share in the "fun" of such an action. Tom and Huck have *their* fun when Jim turns the experience into a story about having been ridden around the world by witches, but it is Jim who has the last laugh when he uses the tale,

108

together with the "five-center piece" left behind by Tom as payment for candles, to make profit from curious fellow slaves.[1] The talent of the black man in this instance far outshines the actions of the white boys.

A further display of Jim's intelligence may be seen in the soothsaying he practices, using a hairball taken from the stomach of an ox. In making his predictions, he follows the widely accepted white-black, good-bad pattern of the dominant white culture. Questioned by Huck about the feared return of pap, Jim assuages his friend's worry about his father by telling the boy: "Dey's two angels hoverin' roun' 'bout him. One uv 'em is white en shiny, en t'other one is black. De white one gits him to go right, a little while, den de black one sail in en bust it all up. A body can't tell, yit, which one gwyne to fetch him at de las'. But you is all right" (22). Then, adroitly sliding away from Huck's topic of interest onto a more general and possibly more comforting subject, Jim also claims: "Dey's two gals flyin' 'bout you in yo' life. One uv 'em's light en t'other one is dark. One is rich en t'other is po'. You's gwyne to marry de po' one fust en de rich one by en by" (22). Jim finishes by warning Huck to "keep 'way fum de water as much as you kin, en don't run no resk, 'kase it's down in de bills dat you's gwyne to git hung" (22), but he is doubtless conscious of avoiding risk himself through not straying from the predictable good-bad, rich-poor comparisons correspondingly associated with white and black.

Twain again contrasts white with black in describing pap. The fifty year old has no gray in his hair to indicate a mellowing with age but possesses "all black" hair that is "long and tangled and greasy" (23). Pap's "long, mixed up whiskers" are of the same hue, which produces a dramatic contrast with the color of his face. As Huck describes it, "There warn't no color in his face, where his face showed; it was white; not like another man's white, but a white to make a body sick, a white to make a body's flesh crawl—a tree-toad white, a fish-belly white" (23). This depiction leads us to understand the strange fact that there can actually be negative white (or, in this case, the absence of color altogether), and, from what we later learn of pap and his values, there is little question but that symbolic importance is linked to this perception. The description of pap's hair and his "fish-belly white" complexion also creates a picture of the kind of dead body the river might wash up, and when his corpse does drift by in a floating house, it is, significantly, naked, albeit dry. The antiblack stance exhibited by pap in the novel can, moreover, be viewed as placing him unequivocally at the extreme "white" end of any color scale, since no shadings can be distinguished in the opinions he expresses.

Another instance of the white as black and the black as white is to be found in the scene in which we hear pap bitterly complain that "there was a free nigger there, from Ohio; a mulatter, most as white as a white man. He had the whitest shirt on you ever see, too" (33). Part of the ironic force of this scene depends upon noticing that at that moment pap himself is quite dark in color, since he has been drunkenly lying in the gutter all night, and, as Huck observes, "A body would a thought he was Adam, he was just all mud" (33). In contrast, the black man pap attacks is not only almost white in color but clearly possesses "white" qualities: he is financially sound, serves as a professor in a college, and, according to what pap has heard, "could talk all kinds of languages, and knowed everything" (34). That Twain was consciously underscoring analogous whiteness, and thus creating more irritation for pap, is indicated by the fact that the words "a mulatter, most as white as a white man," were a later insertion in the manuscript.[2] It might also be pointed out that the man from Ohio, unlike pap, manifests the dignity of age in being "gray-headed" and, in further contrast to pap, is cleanly, richly, and neatly dressed. This "free nigger" also possesses one civil right crucial to continued freedom: the right to vote. In pap's eyes this is clearly perceived as a looming threat to the present power structure, since the stride taken by a mixed-blood chattel slave to the voting, well-off status of "free nigger" all too clearly allows the man to bypass pap and other poor whites, threatening to leave them with no underclass to look down on and feel superior to.[3]

The shocking reality of the situation is that black can become "white" and white "black"; it is thus possible for pap's world to be completely upended in one swift motion. Small wonder that he is instinctively terrified and responds accordingly with physical violence, giving the man a shove. Through asking "why ain't this nigger put up at auction and sold?" pap also expresses the wish that the man should be forced to return to his former state of servitude (34). And pap's closing description of his object of hate and fear as "a prowling, thieving, infernal, white-shirted free nigger" labels the man with the stereotypical adjectives "prowling" and "thieving," while the term "infernal" points to a direct connection of this barely black man, paradoxically decked out in a white shirt, with the Prince of Darkness himself. The profound fright pap feels at perceiving this "devil" in light, elegant disguise seems only too tangible.

The vexation that pap displays at the thought of a "free nigger" possessing rights and advantages equal or superior to his own would only have been exacerbated had he ever come to know that when rewards were offered for his and Jim's capture, the runaway slave was considered to be worth one hundred dollars more than he. There is no question but that pap would have felt that there had been a gravely confused evaluation with regard to the relative importance of black and white. The ironic stress Twain was bestowing on this comparison would become even more obvious in the second-to-last sentence of his novel *Pudd'nhead Wilson*, where race and economics receive a similar treatment. At that critical closing moment, Twain no longer relies on the discrete approach he employed in *Huck* but allows the narrator to shine a glaring light on an inversion of the value to be placed on black slave and free white, informing the reader that "everybody granted that if 'Tom' were white and free it would be unquestionably right to punish him—it would be no loss to anybody; but to shut up a valuable slave for life—that was quite another matter."[4]

Twain no doubt enjoys his gentle joke at the expense of the virulently prejudiced, white pap. It meshes neatly with an overall strategy designed to regularly tweak the nose of pat prejudice through making black "white." As might be expected, Jim is the most visible beneficiary of this approach, and we repeatedly find him exhibiting positive qualities and emotions. In addition to being intelligent, this runaway slave is seen as generous, humane, clever, perceptive, faithful, and self-sacrificing, to mention but a few of the "white" features assigned to him. More than once we observe him stand Huck's watch on the raft when the boy is tired, and Huck also informs us, with the offensive if not fully realized condescension that Twain knew to be characteristic of even well-meaning Southerners, that "Jim had a wonderful level head, for a nigger: he could most always start a good plan when you wanted one" (107). It is Jim who knows about "signs" and who has the practical abilities that contribute so much to making the raft more livable and effective as a "home." The first time Huck can bring himself to call Jim "white," however, it is only with great hesitation and under outside pressure from two slave catchers. Twain nevertheless allows Huck to slowly distance himself from pap's narrow views and grow close enough to Jim so that by the late stages of the book the boy *"knowed"* Jim "was white inside" (341, emphasis added).[5]

This development progresses by fits and starts, as with any human relationship, and we more than once see Huck frustrated in his discussions with Jim at what he views as "nigger" obtuseness. In every case Twain has Jim win the argument and defeat Huck by using a logic that is highly effective in spite of not corresponding to the usual "white" pattern. Huck is also troubled by his companion's seeming lack of respect for prevailing laws concerning family members of slaves. Blinded by standard Southern biases, Huck overlooks the crucial fact that Jim's plan for freeing his family calls for him to respect existing laws if at all possible and to resort to the sweat of his brow before having recourse to less legal action. Thus, despite the frequent application to Jim of the demeaning term "nigger" by all and sundry, he is never seen by the reader to be anything less than decent, kind, and tolerant. In Huck's deepest soul searching the boy must also finally admit that "somehow I couldn't seem to strike no places to harden me against him, but only the other kind" (270).

Shortly before coming to this awareness, and while wrestling with his conscience as to whether to opt for Hell or reveal Jim's whereabouts to Miss Watson, a clear realization dawns on Huck:

> And at last, when it hit me all of a sudden that here was the plain hand of Providence slapping me in the face and letting me know my wickedness was being watched all the time from up there in heaven, whilst I was stealing a poor old woman's nigger that hadn't ever done me no harm, and now was showing me there's One that's always on the lookout, and ain't agoing to allow no such miserable doings to go only just so fur and no further, I most dropped in my tracks I was so scared. (268–69)

From what we know of Mark Twain's skills as a writer and humorist, it must be presumed that the relative clause "that hadn't ever done me no harm" is purposely designed to "mistakenly" refer to its immediate antecedent, "nigger," and not to Miss Watson, though Huck's clear intention is to have it the other way around.[6] Twain thus shows Huck, even before coming to the conscious decision to go to Hell, already blurring black-white boundaries and sliding unawares out of the clutches of the slaveholder and onto the slippery path of sympathy toward the slave.

As usual, Jim is the slave Huck has in mind, and during the Evasion section of the novel Jim is exploited by Tom for the selfish purposes of Tom's "adventure." While Jim goes along with the game as best he can, Twain allows us to understand that although the town gossips consider the evidence discovered after the Evasion proves that "the nigger's crazy" (346), every one of the details mentioned actually had Tom at its source. The Evasion is thus used in a humorous fashion, but all its features point to a crazed white world where normal logic is discounted, where a black human being who would sacrifice his own freedom in order to save a young white boy who has treated him as a plaything is regarded by the white community as deserving to be lynched. It is clearly not black values that are insane here.

When Jim is recaptured and returned to his cabin prison after nursing the wounded Tom, the ability of the Southern white world to protect even a recognized black hero is seen to be insubstantial at best. The doctor's intervention on Jim's behalf eliminates only the cussing, while Huck's well-meant but all too painfully silent hopes for better treatment for his friend prove useless and, as might be expected, go unfulfilled: Jim, who, as we learn later, is actually legally free at this point, remains, literally and figuratively, heavily chained. Twain's unusually heavy-handed satire at the expense of even well-meaning pre– as well as post–Civil War Southern whites can, it appears, only be ignored by a conscious effort on the part of the reader. The black man shows uncommon bravery, whereas whites at every level prove ineffectual at providing even minimal recognition or recompense for the accomplishment of a "white" ideal. Twain once again gives us a "nigger" who is "white" to compare with "gentlemen" who are "black."

This is not the first time that Jim has been victimized or put at risk by his trust in whites, as we may remember from the dangerous visit with Huck to the wreck of the *Walter Scott* or the practical "joke" Huck played on him with the dead rattlesnake. More than once Huck only barely manages to overcome his societal scruples about helping this man to escape. Trust in whites, even a young white boy, is demonstrated to be precarious at best and highly hazardous more often than not. Throughout these trials, however, Jim shows himself possessed of a sense of humor (Huck tells us that Jim "was the easiest nigger to laugh that ever was" [168]), depth of feeling and emotion about both his own family as well as the "ole true Huck" (Jim even mentions his own crying in the novel), and kindness in not revealing pap's death to the boy (selfish motivation connected with Jim's own personal safety is, of course, plausible but not necessarily exclusive). Although Huck, because of his upbringing by pap and the white Southern world, is astonished to learn that Jim seemed to "care just as much for his people as white folks does for theirn" (201), Jim proves himself at every turn worthy of Huck's view of him as "white inside," while that judgment would fit few of the white characters in the novel.

When we recall pap's description of the "white nigger" as "prowling" and "thieving," it is evident that these terms can more appropriately be applied to himself. But they would also apply to other white reprobates such as the king and the duke, who fittingly suspect the Wilks orphans' "niggers"—whom the two scoundrels have heartlessly sold off in different directions—of filching the bag of money they themselves are intending to steal. In the king's explanation of how he and the duke came to lose the money entrusted to them by the Wilks children, we find one of Twain's most effervescent inversions of "nigger" and "white":

> Well, when my niece give it to me to keep for her, I took and hid it inside o' the straw tick o' my bed, not wishin' to bank it for the few days we'd be here, and considerin' the bed a safe place, we not bein' used to niggers, and suppos'n' 'em honest, like servants in England. The niggers stole it the very next mornin', after I had went down stairs; and when I sold 'em, I hadn't missed the money yit, so they got clean away with it. My servant here k'n tell you 'bout it, gentlemen. (252)

The black-hearted here are obviously the two scoundrels who have not blanched at selling and separating black families. This dishonest duo nevertheless feel outraged and unfairly put upon when apparently done out of their intended booty by those they not only consider to be racially, socially, and intellectually inferior to themselves but whom they also thought they had victimized. Twain intensifies the irony by having the presumably dishonest "niggers" compared to honest, white English servants, with Huck—the American boy who doesn't believe in risking the truth more than he has to, and the actual "thief" of the money—asked to bear solemn witness to the veracity of the story in his shaky guise as one of those forth-right English menials referred to by the king. There is, moreover, cruel irony involved in the fact that although "the niggers" are innocent of the theft of the money, their fate is exactly, and unjustly, the same as if they were guilty, since their sale means additional illicit revenue for the king and duke. White clearly has the right in this case, as in most others in the novel, though white may not do right.

It is also an undeniable but little noticed fact that throughout *Huckleberry Finn* blacks are generally painted in a positive light. Despite Huck's re-sponse to Aunt Sally's query as to whether anyone was hurt when the steamboat blew a cylinder head ("No'm, killed a nigger" [279]—clearly blatant irony directed at simple Southern prejudice), blacks are frequently shown to be helpful and intelligent. For example, Jack, Huck's "nigger" at the Grangerfords, helps hide Jim, who describes him as "pooty smart." When Jack takes Huck to see Jim, he interests the boy in "water moccasins" in order to be able to deny being implicated in concealing a runaway slave. This subtle strategy parallels Huck's own transferal of his money to Judge Thatcher in order to be able to honestly deny possessing any to pap and thus frustrate pap's designs on it. We also hear Jack quietly reveal to Huck what happened to Sophia and Harney. Jack thus judges the recipient of his information and channels only enough of it to be of use without involving himself in difficulties. He is indeed "pooty smart."

It should also be realized that Jack is assigned to serve Huck, which would possibly indicate that he occupies a position at the lower end of the scale for slaves, at least "house" slaves, since it would be logical to assume that the slaves already assigned to all the other members of the family were chosen because of qualifications superior to his. If this humble representa-tive of the slave caste is compared with Colonel Grangerford, the senior and, according to Huck, superior representative of this white family, one would naturally assume that the Colonel with his "white" qualities would easily outshine Jack. For Huck as well as all members of the Grangerford family, such a correlation is nothing short of inconceivable, but the reader is certainly entitled to consider and contrast these two unlikely personages. Such a comparison reveals that although we learn relatively little about Jack, we cannot avoid seeing that whereas he is involved in saving life and in kind acts toward both blacks and whites, Colonel Grangerford is involved not only in slaveholding but also in leading the members of his family toward ultimate destruction and death. In this manner Mark Twain gently juxtaposes the "civilized" insanity of a white "paragon" and his family and the naturally sane actions of a simple slave, whom the Grangerfords would consider, at best, a semisavage.

Two other incidents in the novel, besides Jim's care for the wounded Tom, show Huck being made aware of a black person saving a white one from a potentially dangerous situation. The king, who had been running a profitable temperance meeting, tells the duke that "when somehow or another a little report got around, last night, that I had a way of puttin' in my time with a private jug on the sly," the only thing that saved him was that "a nigger rousted me out this mornin', and told me the people was getherin' on the quiet, with their dogs and horses, and they'd be along pretty soon and give me 'bout half an hour's start, and then run me down, if they could; and if they got me they'd tar and feather me and ride me on a rail sure" (160). The king never explains why the "nigger" warned him, but from the reader's distance the act would seem to have been a generous one since the king was plainly not going to be around later to express his gratitude or hand out a reward. What the king shows no sign of perceiving is that the "nigger," no stranger to suffering himself, comprehends only too well what the old man would go through if caught and recognizes a brotherhood that transcends color, making black and white equal: that of pain.

On another occasion it is Aunt Sally's "nigger woman" who spots Huck surrounded by yelping hounds and rushes in swinging a rolling pin to save the boy from a threatening situation. Huck notices how the woman's poorly dressed black children and Aunt Sally's white children react in the same way when put in a similar situation. The paralleling of black and white in Huck's description is further emphasized by the fact that the "nigger woman come tearing out of the kitchen, with a rolling pin in her hand," while we are told of Aunt Sally, "and here comes the white woman running from the house, about forty-five or fifty year ole, bareheaded, and her spinning-stick in her hand" (277). Twain, in this fashion, twins the women, their speed of movement, their armament, and the actions of their children. We may note, moreover, that "spinning" contains the letters as well as the sound of "pin," while "spinning stick" and "rolling pin" match in other

ways as well. That Huck perceives at least a portion of this carefully integrated and richly developed image of equality is therefore not surprising. It
should also be evident that such a dawning awareness of nondifference represents a subtle step forward in the boy's progress toward learning that Jim
is "white inside" and acquiring the minimal understanding necessary to the
construction of a true bridge across the chasm that separates black from
white in his world.

It is also vital to understand that Huck is neither above nor outside that
world. He is a Southern boy, powerfully influenced by his upbringing and
the surrounding society. To expect him to easily reject Tom Sawyer's authority in the Evasion section, merely because he has earlier dismissed
some of Tom's imagined "adventures" and because he has experienced a
few enlightened moments in regard to Jim as a human victim of an inhu-
man system, is not a fully fair demand to make of a fourteen-year-old orphan, no matter how much some readers might wish him to express moral
dudgeon. Janet Gabler-Hover holds that "ethically, Huck seems to go
about as far as a child can go toward moral awareness, without guiding
examples within his conventional culture."[7] Tom, not marginal like Huck,
is at home within that culture and has sources of information that have been
unavailable to his friend. As a result, Huck has a decided feeling of inferi-
ority that surfaces frequently in the novel. Twain knows all these things
only too well and never tries to force the boy into the mold of a crusader.
For Frederick Crews, "The whole moral irony of *Huckleberry Finn* depends
on Huck's inability to adopt abolitionist 'principles' that could render him
a conscious critic of the antebellum South."[8] Huck nevertheless often wa-
vers, and in this wavering we see his true humanity attempting to break the
enslaving bonds of the worlds he has grown up with and into. To ask, however, that he take up just causes and lay about him with the noble blade of
a Cyrano de Bergerac would be to ask that Twain knuckle under to Sir
Walter Scott's romantic notions; and we should never lose sight of the fact
that in this novel Scott's namesake steamboat ends up on the bottom of
Twain's Mississippi.

Huck is not, then, a simple avenging angel of righteousness, nor was
Mark Twain.[9] And only someone as purblind as pap would fail to realize
the length of the stride Twain took from Southern slave owner's son to
author of one of the most powerful problack novels ever written. That he,

like Abraham Lincoln, driven by a powerful sense of justice, could manage
to undertake and, however imperfectly, carry through such a major personal revolution in his lifetime represents one more proof of his greatness.
That in *Huckleberry Finn* he could, and can, touch his readers so profoundly
stands as silent but permanently renewable witness to this. As a recon-
structed Southerner living in the North, Twain evidently felt that the
South had to be seen from the eyes of a Southerner if the inconsistencies it
embodied were to be most fully exposed. Huck, therefore, is his instrument
for prying open the door of years of ignorance, prejudice, and hypocrisy.
And Huck's protective, chameleon-like cloak of invisibility is created not
only by being one of "them" and employing "their" language, including
the word "nigger," but also by the fact that he is slowly being educated as
he experiences various facets of life in the pre–Civil War South. Twain, in
this manner, initiates Huck and the reader simultaneously into the mysteries of the black-white dilemma and the savagery of uncivilized "sivilized" Southern society.

An extreme example of this savagery, which paralleled the brutality of
the feud, of riding suitable victims on a sharp-edged rail, or of tarring and
feathering women, was the "good ole" Southern custom of lynching. In his
notes for *Huckleberry Finn*, Twain considers "a lynching scene" (A-11, 731),
and in another entry states: "They lynch a ˌfreeˌ nigger" (C-4, 752). But,
somewhat surprisingly, no one ever experiences this fate in Twain's novel.
Why this was we may never know, since the idea of including such violence
in a "boys'" book apparently would not have overly discomfited the man
who more than once considered including such a scene and who did not
shy away from the somewhat diluted descriptions of Buck's and Boggs's
deaths, the king's obscene Royal Nonesuch display, or the tarring, feathering, and rail riding of the king and the duke. The fact remains, however,
that although Jim is threatened with lynching, the only lynching scene in
the novel has as the intended victim a white man.

Mark Twain refuses to follow the usual script where a black slave,
hence a member of the lowest class, is murdered for a real or imagined
insult to a member of any of the white classes or for a claimed infraction of
either a written law or an unwritten code. In *Huckleberry Finn*, we see instead the white, upper-class Colonel Sherburn murder the white, lower-
class Boggs, calmly and in cold blood for the unwritten crime of insulting
him. When a crowd of citizens sets out to lynch Sherburn, he effectively

counterthreatens them, causing them to back off, and it seems probable that this stalemate will become permanent. Unless, as Sherburn puts it, he is lynched "in the dark, southern fashion," he will go scot-free, and Boggs will remain unavenged. The victory will go not to the legal justice system but to the upper-class white citizen who successfully mocks both the system and his fellow citizens. With this scene, Twain underscores the unstated but understood truth that white royalty does in fact exist in the South. Even a vigilante-type system, used most often for holding slaves in check through terror, is shown to be powerless against the unbending sense of superiority at the core of the "manhood" displayed (and for which Twain seems to evince a certain admiration).

The author thus creates a lynching scene where no lynching takes place. But was this because he did not wish a white to be lynched? Would a "free nigger" have been a more appropriate and, in many quarters, a more acceptable victim? Did Twain feel that a black man could not "believably" defend himself and ultimately avoid being lynched in the pre–Civil War South? Or was this, after all, another instance of Twain's inverting of black and white with the color of the person doing the insulting (and being subjected to Sherburn's lynch-mob-style justice) as well as the "lynching" itself inverted? Given the number of role reversals already encountered in the novel, it would not seem unjustified to credit Twain with creating more here. Such an interpretation would aid in understanding the author's seemingly inconsistent and indirect approach to this aspect of Southern violence and injustice and help explain why in this case the border between black and white, between justice and injustice, appears far from crisply defined. It would also contribute to clarifying why the man who would one day write "The United States of Lyncherdom" would choose to avoid lynching a "free nigger" in *Huckleberry Finn* and substitute an unlynched white member of the ruling upper class.[10] For it was Mark Twain who wrote with biting sarcasm back in 1869: "But mistakes will happen, even in the conduct of the best regulated and high-toned mobs, and surely there is no good reason why Southern gentlemen should worry themselves with useless regrets, so long as only an innocent 'nigger' is hanged, or roasted or knouted to death, now and then."[11]

The inversion of black and white is not, therefore, a simple equation or a neatly predictable feature of *Huckleberry Finn*. There are, as well, several instances where a reader might take offense by not stopping to consider that Twain was showing a world as it existed, warts and all, that that world was one where blacks were considered subhuman, and that "nigger" was the most commonly used epithet, especially among the lowest classes, who had the most to fear from the possible rise of that two-legged "property." Hence, it should not strike us as out of place or improper to find the minstrel-show approach exploited for humorous ends in connection with Jim (as is well known, Twain had a predilection for minstrel shows and mourned their passing). However, as Kenny J. Williams points out, "No matter how foolish Jim may appear and despite the number of times he is called 'nigger,' in the final analysis he cannot be burlesqued. But the fact that he is not absolutely part of that happy lot of plantation slaves who people American literature is lost on those who reduce the novel to an exercise in name-calling." [12]

Nat, "the nigger that fed Jim," is also treated as a fool by Tom and Huck, who take advantage of his belief in witches to trick him into believing his senses have deceived him. His description and treatment represent perhaps the strongest case for insensitivity and a one-sided approach to a black person in the novel. Nat is described as "having a good-natured, chuckle-headed face, and his wool was all tied up in little bunches with thread. That was to keep witches off" (295). (We should recall in this context Huck's own acknowledgment in chapter 1 that "I tied up a little lock of my hair with a thread to keep witches away" [4].) But despite the fact that Nat ends up being the butt of the joke, believing that his senses have betrayed him and that he has not heard what he did indeed hear, an important factor to consider is that he is seen in a softened light as "good-natured." Although he fulfills the stereotypical role of happy, witch-fearing, somewhat benighted slave, no attempt is made to otherwise denigrate him. For some readers the characteristics mentioned may seem sufficient grounds on which to condemn the author, but one should never lose sight of the exculpating fact that it is Huck, the narrator, who sees Nat in this way. We may also note, in this connection, that the description of the way Nat smiled is also relatively mild, though clearly "colored." Huck tells us, "The nigger kind of smiled around graduly over his face like when you heave a brickbat in a mud puddle" (295). The word "mud," like "nigger," is Huck's and that of his society, reminding us once again that we are in the American South.

For those who would nonetheless see Twain as having written a racist novel on the grounds that the word "nigger" appears in its pages and that there is laughter at the expense of some of those "niggers," it may perhaps prove instructive to consider the following facts concerning what the author does *not* include in his work. At no point in the novel does he resort to stereotypical physical descriptions of blacks. Although Jim is given "hairy arms and breast," and Nat's face is described as "good-natured and chuckle-headed" with his smile rendered in the manner mentioned above, we never see any black person in the book endowed with thick lips or the kind of mouth frequently overemphasized in minstrel shows. There are no rolling eyes or flared nostrils, and at no point do Negroid features of any kind find a place within the text of Twain's book. Blacks in the novel are never referred to in any of the demeaning ways all too often resorted to, they are never indicated to be mentally deficient, nor do we find flip comparisons to apes, monkeys, or other animals.

While there are many of the original illustrations for the book where Jim and other slaves are portrayed, and though some of these depictions clearly appeal to stereotypes, none are exaggerated to an extent that exceeds the characterizing applied for the purposes of moderate humor to many of the other personages. It might also be suggested that this limited level of humorous stereotyping served the author as a countertext purposely designed to disarm potential racist critics and thus help his book to reach the widest possible audience for the subversive message he had undertaken to promote. As Earl F. Briden observes, Twain apparently did not want his illustrator, E. W. Kemble, "to encourage the reader to take Jim—and Huck's relationship with Jim—seriously. The reality of the black-white alliance and of the black hero was to be suppressed pictorially, with the result that an additional source of 'genteel' uneasiness would be dissolved in pictorial humor."[13]

In one of Twain's working notes for the novel we do find, on the other hand, the following three lines, which were never acted on: "Turn Jim into an Injun"; "Then exhib him for gorilla—then wild man Arab &c., using him for 2 shows same day"; and "Nigger-skin (shamoi) for sale as a pat med." (757).[14] It is important to recognize with regard to these lines that all of the ideas expressed are appropriate to and most probably meant to be employed in connection with two of the most despicable characters in the

novel, the king and the duke. It is also of interest here that Twain elected
to use only the wild Arab idea, conceivably the least offensive of the lot in
having no link to any major population group in the United States at the
time. Also, the author most often chooses to exhibit qualities in Jim and
other slaves that prove a level of humanity equal or superior to that of
whites. This may not always "seem natural" for Huck or other whites, but,
as has been pointed out, Huck is ultimately obliged to conclude, with respect to Jim, that "I do believe he cared just as much for his people as white
folks does for theirn" (201).

It is equally essential to note that other stereotypical labels attached to
blacks are also explicitly inverted in Twain's novel. For example, all those
human beings faulted for a lack of cleanliness are white. Pap is more than
once seen to be filthy and is known to sleep with hogs. His hair is greasy;
he is, as mentioned earlier, described as "just all mud" in one instance; and
on another occasion the new judge in town has to dress "him up clean and
nice" (26) before he is presentable. By comparison, we never meet an un-
clean black person in the book. Nor do we ever meet one who smells bad.
Despite the continuous closeness of Huck and Jim and their nakedness together, no mention of offensive odor ever occurs. Yet Twain was apparently
not unfamiliar with this stereotype, for he clearly turns it on its head in
having Jim, not Huck, make the observation of the king that "dis one do
smell so like de nation, Huck" (200, emphasis Twain's).

Such inversions and omissions point to anything but a racist novel. There
is little doubt but that Mark Twain wished to create a particularly subtle
but powerful case against racism and facile racist epithets such as "nigger."[15] While Jonathan Arac asks on behalf of black readers: "If Huck has
such moral insight that he is willing to go to hell for Jim's sake, why does
he not find new ways of saying his new sense of the world? Why not stop
using a word that is part of the system he is, we suppose, rejecting?"[16] David L. Smith comprehends that

> a reader who objects to the word "nigger" might still insist that Twain could
> have avoided using it. But it is difficult to imagine how Twain could have
> debunked a discourse without using the specific terms of that discourse. . . .
> The specific function of this term in the book, however, is neither to offend

nor merely to provide linguistic authenticity. Much more importantly, it establishes a context against which Jim's specific virtues may emerge as explicit refutations of racist presuppositions.[17]

In connection with this idea we might also consider what Spencer Brown takes to be a critical purpose served by Twain's "Explanatory":

> In the "Explanatory" note at the head of the novel, the only place where he speaks "in propria persona" and not through Huck, he uses the word "Negro." Everywhere else, including the speeches of the Negroes, the word is "nigger." I cannot believe that Mark Twain would make such a to-do in the introductory note merely to call attention to his not infallible skill with dialects. He wishes to show us the word *he* would use if he, rather than the slave society, were speaking.[18]

Further evidence in support of this position is found in Twain's working notes for his novel where he most often uses such terms as "Negros," "Negress," and "Negro" in referring to blacks and employs "nigger," almost without exception, in contexts where it would appear in that form within the texture of the novel.[19]

It would therefore appear that Mark Twain wished to write a novel in support of the free black in the post-Reconstruction South, and, as Brown perceives, "against the continuation of slavery in Jim Crow (where does Jim get his name?), against the legalist who wants to do everything regular and who forgets Lincoln's stroke of the pen, against the white who wants to wait until the black is 'ready' for freedom, against, finally, any distinction whatever between the races."[20] But this pill was a large one to try to force down a Southern throat constricted by traditional prejudice and deep-seated fears. Twain's use of the familiar negative epithet "nigger" and of gently humorous and mildly stereotypical illustrations for his novel would thus seem to have been designed to allow his deeper message to pass these formidable barriers unobstructed—and initially unnoticed. It may be that the author's subtlety was in some ways more impenetrable than he envisioned, however, for he apparently felt obliged to take a more overt approach to the same problem a few years later in *Pudd'nhead Wilson*, in which received ideas on race are also subverted through the inverting of black and white. It is nonetheless apparent from many of the comments made on *Huckleberry Finn* that the inversion of values is often lost on unwary readers.[21] As Richard K. Barksdale observes: "If the ironic statement made by an author in a work of fiction is too subtly wrought, it will not be effectively communicated to the average reader. The continuing controversy about *Adventures of Huckleberry Finn* suggests that the American reading public, in the main, has never fully understood the author's ironic message." [22]

Luckily, however, that message has not always fallen on deaf ears, as is indicated by the fact that William Faulkner, for one, picked up Twain's torch in order to cast light on and expose what lies in the harsh shadows of a warped Southern world where black and white can often be seen as reversed and contrasted. But it would be unfortunate if Twain's basic aim were to be generally misinterpreted and his effort thwarted, either by blindness to the direction he adopted in his novel or by blinkered "presentism" in feeling that his contradictory, Southern-born, Northern-adopted, nineteenth-century, ever-experimenting, dual-named self can be simply and precisely categorized according to the yardstick of a so-called enlightened value system.[23] For one of the most exciting aspects of Mark Twain's ingenious subversion of racism in *Huckleberry Finn* is the possibility that once it becomes plain what the author is up to, the reader may well experience the urge to exclaim along with Huck, "Well, if I ever struck anything like it, I'm a nigger" (210).

CHAPTER TEN

"I Never Seen Anybody but Lied
One Time or Another"

IGUEL DE CERVANTES, Daniel Defoe, Jonathan Swift, Washington Irving, and Nathaniel Hawthorne are among the writers who pioneered and developed many features of the tradition of insinuating with tongue in cheek—in introductory and closing
statements to their works—that fiction recounts only the unadorned truth.
It is also known today that Mark Twain's personal library contained examples of the writings of each of these authors as well as of others who
were instrumental in formulating or furthering this teasing approach to the
reader of imagined stories.[1] But despite clear indications that Twain was
well acquainted with the efforts of such writers, as well as with the tradition,
little attention has been paid to the pattern and development of the author's
approach to the creation of prefaces for his own writings. I shall therefore
examine Twain's evolution in the art of devising prefatory material for his
works in the hope of indicating just what today's readers of fiction might
owe to it. The prefatory material for *Adventures of Huckleberry Finn* will be
seen to occupy a position of central importance in this study, but in order
to better appreciate many aspects of that importance it will prove helpful
to first examine some of Twain's earlier efforts at finding suitable opening
comments for his works.

In the apparently guileless preface to *The Adventures of Tom Sawyer* it would
be difficult to discern more than a perfunctory bow by the author to the
tradition of pretending to truth telling in works of fiction:

> Most of the adventures recorded in this book really occurred; one or two
> were experiences of my own, the rest those of boys who were schoolmates

of mine. Huck Finn is drawn from life; Tom Sawyer also, but not from an individual—he is a combination of the characteristics of three boys whom I knew, and therefore belongs to the composite order of architecture.

The odd superstitions touched upon were all prevalent among children and slaves in the West at the period of this story—that is to say, thirty or forty years ago.

Although my book is intended mainly for the entertainment of boys and girls, I hope it will not be shunned by men and women on that account, for part of my plan has been to try to pleasantly remind adults of what they once were themselves, and of how they felt and thought and talked, and what queer enterprises they sometimes engaged in.

Hartford, 1876   The Author[2]

As is customary with the convention of mock honesty, we have here the word of an "authority" as to the verity of many of the assertions, but the entire effort appears to lack the telltale irony so prevalent in the works of Twain's predecessors. Although we know that the author was thoroughly familiar with the writings of many previous practitioners of the technique, that familiarity finds only faint reflection in a modest claim to truthfulness that shows no evidence of the sham seriousness usually found in those earlier works.

Nor does the conclusion to *Tom Sawyer* appear to attempt to do much more than create a warm, somewhat philosophical mood, indicate that the characters "still live," and point the way to a continuation of the story:

> So endeth this chronicle. It being strictly a history of a *boy*, it must stop here; the story could not go much further without becoming the history of a *man*. When one writes a novel about grown people, he knows exactly where to stop—that is, with a marriage; but when he writes of juveniles, he must stop where he best can.
>
> Most of the characters that perform in this book still live, and are prosperous and happy. Some day it may seem worth while to take up the story of the younger ones again and see what sort of men and women they turned out to be; therefore it will be wisest not to reveal any of that part of their lives at present.[3]

How much truth may be ascribed to the claim that "most of the characters . . . still live" is clearly debatable inasmuch as we have only the author's word and are limited to the author's understanding of the meaning of the word "character." Otherwise, however, Twain once again gives little cause for suspecting deeper irony or more than a perfunctory bow to the old convention. There is little indication in these two brief paragraphs that Twain would seek to expand on the methods of his precursors in the initial pages of *Adventures of Huckleberry Finn*, the novel he began writing during the same year *Tom Sawyer* was published.

Yet evidence exists that at the time of the publication of *Tom Sawyer* Twain was awake to the possibilities that less than candid prefatory and concluding material could offer. A number of years prior to the publication of his novel he had undertaken to send a certain John Henry Riley to South Africa to gather material for a book dealing with the diamond rush going on at the time.[4] Twain himself was to write the book in the first person, using Riley's "voice"; and by way of justifying this authorship, at one remove from personal experience, he conceived the idea of furnishing his work with a deceptive preface in which he would declare with a straight face: "When Daniel de Foe wanted to know what life on a solitary island was like, and doubted whether he was hardy enough to stand it himself, he sent the ingenious Robinson W. Crusoe; and when I wanted to know all about wild life in the diamond fields and its fascinations, and could not go myself, I sent the ingenious Riley."[5] Although the book was never to get written, the concept of using an earnestly presented preface disingenuously was not forgotten.

By the time Mark Twain got around to publishing *Huckleberry Finn*, he had already experimented with a number of possibilities for poking fun at the somber and frequently saccharine opening and closing statements included in much of the moralistic literature of the day. The targets were evidently too tempting for the author to ignore, and he took noticeable pleasure in lancing what he apparently regarded as boils on the face of fiction. At the beginning of Twain's short story "Lucretia Smith's Soldier"—published in 1864, provided with chapter headings, and presented as a parody novel— we find a "Note from the Author" to "Mr. Editor" in which he jokingly offers bogus "thanks" to several sources, including the "accommodating Directors of the Overland Telegraph Company . . . for tendering me the use of their wires at the customary rates," and impishly declares that "the inspiration which enabled me in this production to soar so happily into the realms of sentiment and soft emotion" has as its source "the excellent beer manufactured at the New York Brewery, in Sutter Street, between Montgomery and Kearny." [6] More important, Twain revealed in his note that even at this early date, preceding by several years the Riley experiment as well as the publication of *Tom Sawyer*, he was well aware of the work of his predecessors. Not only does he jeer at "those nice, sickly war stories in *Harper's Weekly*," but he also claims that his story "can be relied upon as true in every particular," and he even goes so far as to "document" the proof of his claim:

> the facts it contains were compiled from the official records in the War Department at Washington. The credit of this part of the labor is due to the Hon. T. G. Phelps, who has so long and ably represented this State in Congress. It is but just, also, that I should make honorable mention of the obliging publishing firms Roman & Co. and Bancroft & Co., of this city, who loaned me *Jomini's Art of War*, the *Message of the President and Accompanying Documents*, and sundry maps and military works, so necessary for reference in building a novel like this. [7]

As it turns out, the story neither refers to nor is in any way directly related to any of this supposed documentation, and the humor of the note is so transparent that there is little chance of the reader being taken in by it. Several elements found in the prefatory material to *Huckleberry Finn* and other Twain novels are nevertheless adumbrated in "Lucretia Smith's Soldier."

In the "Prefatory" to *Roughing It*, Twain also chuckles at the solemnity of various kinds of seriously intended writing when he avers:

> This book is merely a personal narrative, and not a pretentious history or a philosophical dissertation. It is a record of several years of variegated vagabondizing, and its object is rather to help the resting reader while away an idle hour than afflict him with metaphysics, or goad him with science. Still, there is information in the volume . . . I regret this very much; but really it could not be helped: information appears to stew out of me naturally, like the precious ottar of roses out of the otter. [8]

On the heels of this tortured pun on the word "attar," the author closes with thinly disguised off-color phrasing—designed to describe an overflow of something other than "facts" and "wisdom"—as he plays merrily on the word "tighter":

Sometimes it has seemed to me that I would give worlds if I could retain my facts; but it cannot be. The more I calk up the sources, and the tighter I get, the more I leak wisdom. Therefore, I can only claim indulgence at the hands of the reader, not justification.

The Author[9]

Employing the same teasing tone, Twain ends his book with a mock "Moral":

If the reader thinks he is done, now, and that this book has no moral to it, he is in error. The moral of it is this: If you are of any account, stay at home and make your way by faithful diligence; but if you are "no account," go away from home, and then you will *have* to work, whether you want to or not. Thus you become a blessing to your friends by ceasing to be a nuisance to them—if the people you go among suffer by the operation.[10]

In Twain's first attempt at a novel, *The Gilded Age*, written jointly with Charles Dudley Warner, the preface also begins in a light vein, similar to that of *Roughing It*, jokingly informing the reader that "this book was not written for private circulation among friends; it was not written to cheer and instruct a diseased relative of the author's; it was not thrown off during intervals of wearing labor to amuse an idle hour. It was not written for any of these reasons, and therefore it is submitted without the usual apologies."[11] The truth of the matter is that the authors might in fact have felt a bit awkward in offering apologies, since the preface represents not only a general parody of a genre, as with "Lucretia Smith's Soldier," but also a specifically aimed parody of the preface to Nathaniel Hawthorne's *The Marble Faun*.[12] Hawthorne had ironically bemoaned the situation in America where

No author, without a trial, can conceive of the difficulty of writing a romance about a country where there is no shadow, no antiquity, no mystery, no picturesque and gloomy wrong, nor anything but a commonplace prosperity, in broad and simple daylight, as is happily the case with my dear native land. It will be very long, I trust, before romance-writers may find congenial and easily handled themes, either in the annals of our stalwart republic, or in any characteristic and probable events of our individual lives. Romance and poetry, ivy, lichens, and wall-flowers need ruin to make them grow.[13]

Twain and Warner, taking up the challenge, double the ante by indulging in their own spoofing of Hawthorne's approach, claiming:

> It will be seen that it [this novel] deals with an entirely ideal state of society; and the chief embarrassment of the writers in this realm of the imagination has been the want of illustrative examples. In a state where there is no fever of speculation, no inflamed desire for sudden wealth, where the poor are all simple-minded and contented, and the rich are all honest and generous, where society is in a condition of primitive purity, and politics is the occupation of only the capable and the patriotic, there are necessarily no materials for such a history as we have constructed out of an ideal commonwealth.[14]

After distancing themselves both from the tradition of romance writing and from its contemporary practitioners, the authors move on to justify the placement of "attractive scraps of literature at the heads of our chapters" in a plethora of different languages, "for the reason that very few foreign nations among whom the book will circulate can read in any language but their own; whereas we do not write for a particular class or sect or nation, but to take in the whole world."[15] And in that final phrase lies the nub. For not recounting a tale with any pretension to truth but hoodwinking the "whole world" is the name of the game in this frolicsome novel, whose authors go so far as to make the cocky claim that they "do not expect that the critic will read the book before writing a notice of it."[16]

Other approaches to light-hearted introductory and concluding material are to be found elsewhere in Twain's writings. But it was around the period during which he was wrestling with *Huckleberry Finn* that the author began toying in earnest with the convention of facetiously claiming truth for his longer works of fiction. One experiment of that nature is found in a footnote to the title of the short story "The Stolen White Elephant," where we are presented with the complex claim that this story was "left out of *A Tramp Abroad*, because it was feared that some of the particulars had been exaggerated, and that others were not true. Before these suspicions had been proven groundless the book had gone to press.—M.T."[17] Since the book supposedly went to press "before these suspicions had been proven groundless," there is no chance that the suspicions can ever be eliminated for this or any other edition where the footnote appears. The conclusion to be drawn concerning the truth of M.T.'s claim is therefore inescapable. Despite this joke, and as a further gesture of respect for the procedure of pretending to recount only the truest of true stories, Twain opens the tale with an appealing justification for expecting the reader to believe in the truth of the narrative. We are encouraged to feel confident of its veracity not only because M.T. relates it but because the tale was first recounted by an aged, honorable, and honest "gentleman": "The following curious history was related to me by a chance railway acquaintance. He was a gentleman more than seventy years of age, and his thoroughly good and gentle face and earnest and sincere manner imprinted the unmistakable stamp of truth upon every statement which fell from his lips."[18]

"The Stolen White Elephant" was published in 1882, and during that same year (only a few months before bringing *Huckleberry Finn* to a close) Twain was also in the process of finishing *Life on the Mississippi*, in which he offers the following comment on his professed appropriation of the name Mark Twain from the deceased Mississippi riverboat captain Isaiah Sellers:[19] "I was a fresh new journalist, and needed a *nom de guerre*; so I confiscated the ancient mariner's discarded one, and have done my best to make it remain what it was in his hands—a sign and symbol and warrant that whatever is found in its company may be gambled on as being the petrified truth; how I have succeeded, it would not be modest in me to say."[20] At first glance this statement might seem reassuring, but Twain's ambiguously precarious "gambled on" linked with his "modest" refusal to divulge the extent of his success (?) in dealing with inflexibly lifeless "petrified truth" must cast serious doubt on the amount of credence that may be accorded the "authority" of "Mark Twain" or "M.T." as signs, symbols, or warrants that what he recounts may be accepted as unquestionable and vital truth.[21]

Twain would not hesitate to resort to either of the subterfuges used in "The Stolen White Elephant" again, and the "authorizing" footnote trick is employed, for instance, in the short story "Luck," where M.T.'s note affirms: "This is not a fancy sketch. I got it from a clergyman who was an instructor at Woolwich forty years ago, and who vouched for its truth. M.T."[22] And who (we can hear M.T. going on to ask) would be so disrespectful or irreverent as to suggest that the word of a man of the cloth might be questioned?

Pseudo-authenticity is also conferred on *The Prince and the Pauper*, a novel begun well over a year after but published prior to *Huckleberry Finn* and shortly before "The Stolen White Elephant," through an adaptation of the authorizing approach. In a mildly enigmatic preface to the novel, Twain affirms:

> I WILL set down a tale as it was told to me by one who had it of his father, which latter had it of *his* father, this last having in like manner had it of *his* father—and so on, back and still back, three hundred years and more, the fathers transmitting it to the sons and so preserving it. It may be history, it may be only a legend, a tradition. It may have happened, it may not have happened: but it *could* have happened. It may be that the wise and learned believed it in the old days; it may be that only the unlearned and the simple loved it and credited it.[23]

This patently noncommittal statement is preceded on the first two pages of the novel not, as with "The Stolen White Elephant," by a mere "authorizing" footnote but by something far grander: a reproduction of an original letter from Hugh Latimer, bishop of Worcester, to Oliver Cromwell, copied and transcribed "FROM THE NATIONAL MANUSCRIPTS PRESERVED BY THE BRITISH GOVERNMENT," announcing "*the birth of the* PRINCE OF WALES (*afterward* EDWARD VI.)."[24] The document, which serves to confer authenticity on what follows, is itself succeeded by a page on which the Great Seal and autograph of King Henry VIII are pictured,[25] creating an unvoiced illusion that what is to follow bears the imprimatur of the prince's own father. Twain, highly conscious of his position as a distinctly American writer, possibly drew particular enjoyment from choosing for his novel a letter in which Bishop Latimer makes a shamelessly presumptuous case for God being English: "Gode gyffe us alle grace, to yelde dew thankes to our Lorde Gode, Gode of Inglonde, for verely He hathe shoyd Hym selff Gode of Inglonde, or rather an Inglyssh Gode, yf we consydyr and pondyr welle all Hys procedynges with us from tyme to tyme."[26] At the close of the letter, Latimer indicates to Cromwell that if he "wolde excytt thys berere to be moore hartye ayen the abuse of ymagry or mor forwarde to promotte the veryte, ytt myght doo goode."[27] With these words, not only is the honesty of the document's "berere" called into question but also the overdeveloped creative imagination that makes him prone to abuse "ymagery." It would not seem unfounded, therefore, to draw a parallel between the untrustworthy bearer of the document and the consciously deceptive creator of the fictional world about to be laid before the reader. The "authenticating" document can hence be seen as possibly defeating its purpose in the novel since it can be considered to be both authorizing as well as self-destructing. What seems to be serious and visible authenticity is undercut by the content of the letter when considered within the framework of Twain's novel. And despite the fact that the signatures of a bishop as well as a king contribute to stamping an image of truth on Mark Twain's work of fiction, the author's stratagems would appear to sprinkle fairy dust in the eyes of those who would believe in the literal truth of his tale.

Only a little over a year before beginning his work on *The Prince and the Pauper*, Twain had already produced a large portion of *Adventures of Huckleberry Finn* and, at that stage in his writing career, appears to have been attracted by the promising potential for a complicated form of humor that the convention of employing less-than-genuine prefaces embraced. At the same time, he also seems to have decided to take the idea one step further and joyfully mock its mockery. At the beginning of the novel he includes the following:

NOTICE

PERSONS attempting to find a motive in this narrative will be prosecuted; persons attempting to find a moral in it will be banished; persons attempting to find a plot in it will be shot.

BY ORDER OF THE AUTHOR

PER G.G., CHIEF OF ORDNANCE. (lv)

With these unexpectedly threatening words, the reader is quickly brought to realize that this prefatory comment has little in common with the peaceful preface to *Tom Sawyer*. Indeed, for Neil Schmitz, "The 'Notice' posted at the head of *Huckleberry Finn* evokes Civil War/Reconstruction orders, the bills put up in the courthouse squares of occupied Southern cities and towns."[28] And "The Author" not only appears to disclaim any conscious authorial intent in the areas of motive or plot but also seems to disavow the kind of high moral righteousness to which previous writers in the tradition had often laid claim.[29] He now seems to wish to reject completely even the kind of humorous "moral" offered at the close of *Roughing It;* gone, too, are the rather innocuous phrases of the *Tom Sawyer* preface and conclusion. In addition, the extravagantly exaggerated threats swiftly wrench the reader into a realization that there is little likelihood of being able to approach the coming narrative in anything like a totally serious fashion. By adopting this frontal assault and jibing so openly at several of the widely accepted features of the time-honored tradition of appealing to a *gentle* readership to accept a proffered story as genuine, it is just possible that Twain was attempting to outdo all previous practitioners of an approach to fiction writing that had been in use for many years on both sides of the Atlantic.[30]

In the "Explanatory," which immediately follows the "Notice," one finds Twain continuing in a similarly playful vein. But in recent years there has been a tendency to accept unquestioningly David Carkeet's exclusionary assertion that

> the fact that intelligent sense can be made out of the preface falsifies the view that Clemens was joking when he wrote it. This view never had much merit anyway. While the last sentence of the "Explanatory" might raise a smile, there is nothing rib-splitting about a list of dialects. The existence of a separate comical preface (called "Notice" and published on a separate page in the first English and American editions) is irrelevant; it is certainly possible for an author to write two prefaces to a work, one comical and one serious. . . . Clemens's abiding interest in folk speech, his impatience with [Bret] Harte's use of dialect, and his working notes on the dialects in *Huckleberry Finn* all point to earnestness in the representation of dialects in this novel—as does the evidence of extensive revision of dialect spellings. There are hundreds of corrections of dialect in the manuscript (or discrepancies between a dialect form in the manuscript and the final form in the first edition). A *just* might be corrected to *jest* in the manuscript, for example, and then end up as *jist* in the first edition. Such labored revision makes no sense if the "Explanatory" is frivolous.
>
> Thus Clemens was serious when he wrote the "Explanatory."[31]

When one considers that Twain frequently tended in his writing to juggle more than one ball at a time and that the effectiveness of his humor often depended on the fact that it could easily be read as "intelligent sense," it could perhaps prove helpful to examine the text itself to see whether there is room not only for agreement but also disagreement with the notion that "Clemens was serious when he wrote the 'Explanatory.'"

The evidence thus far presented relating to Twain's history of bantering in his prefatory material would suggest that readers should in general be wary of approaching his prefaces too seriously; and specific exception to Carkeet's conclusion may be taken on the basis of Twain's burlesquing of the pseudo-expertise sometimes pretended to by earlier authors in deadpan prefaces and introductions to their novels and stories. A glance at the professional qualifications that supposedly authorize "The Author" to speak knowledgeably on the subject of dialects demonstrates that, however earnestly they *may* have been meant, they are presented in what would seem possible to interpret as less than an entirely serious manner:

> IN this book a number of dialects are used, to wit: the Missouri negro dialect; the extremest form of the backwoods South-Western dialect; the ordinary "Pike-County" dialect; and four modified varieties of this last. The shadings have not been done in a haphazard fashion, or by guess-work; but pains-takingly, and with the trustworthy guidance and support of personal familiarity with these several forms of speech.
>
> I make this explanation for the reason that without it many readers would suppose that all these characters were trying to talk alike and not succeeding.
>
> THE AUTHOR.   (lvii)

A close examination of the second sentence of the "Explanatory" reveals that the expertise, "the trustworthy guidance and support" appealed to in order to avoid "guess-work" or shadings "done in a haphazard fashion," comes from none other than Twain himself. One need only ask the identity of the trustworthy person who has decided on what "trustworthy guidance" the reader can base trust for the intricate cleverness of the gambit to become evident. The only professional qualification submitted for the reader's approval by "The Author" is "personal familiarity with these several forms of speech." That every reader might not be totally satisfied with such bona fides would seem at least possible, and it would appear equally conceivable that not all readers would accept at face value a mastery attested to only by the self-proclaimed master himself.[32]

In the closing sentence of the "Explanatory" it is also possible to see

Twain as underscoring the comic aspect of his trickery and even gleefully drawing attention to it. In flippantly suggesting that without his explanation "*many* readers *would* suppose" (emphasis added), Twain leaves no room for doubt that a broad spectrum of his reading public could certainly *not* avoid a mistaken perception and that he is charitably rendering this slow-witted group an indispensable service. The concluding clause, which defines the problem that it is *assumed* less perceptive readers would face in supposing "that all these characters were trying to talk alike and not succeeding," can be taken not only as an example of Twain's wit but also as a red herring drawn across the reader's path.[33] There is, after all, little reason to assume that "many readers" would suppose any such thing or that varied dialect spellings or shadings would disturb their equanimity one whit.

It would seem at least conceivable, therefore, that Carkeet has too readily dismissed the likelihood that tongue-in-cheek humor might be embedded in Twain's loop reference to his own authority as the final arbiter for his expertise on the subject of dialects.[34] It also bears noting that the closing sentence of the "Explanatory," the only sentence that Carkeet allows "might raise a smile," is not only closely linked to but also dependent on that previous sentence justifying the "expertise" of "The Author."

It may be suggested, moreover, that Carkeet goes astray in wishing to dismiss as "irrelevant" the comic aspect of Twain's "Notice" preceding the "Explanatory," as well as in failing to take into account the fact that the opening lines of the novel immediately following the "Explanatory" are also presented in a playful manner. If we consider that the "Explanatory" is sandwiched between two elements that clearly employ humor and make allowance for the evidence of Twain's pronounced tendency to have recourse to amusing prefaces, there would seem—even in light of the rather tame *Tom Sawyer* preface—to be sufficient grounds for doubting whether the short statement of "The Author" can be viewed simply as a sober approach to a problem with dialects. To fully accept Carkeet's claim that Twain took pains with the dialect details in his book need not categorically exclude the possibility that the "Explanatory" might also have been written with a twinkle in the eye and a nod of smiling acknowledgment to the predecessors of "The Author" in the sporting art of gulling the unwary reader.

Another possibility that merits consideration has to do with the fact that Twain in his day was in the forefront of those writers using dialect. Yet in *Huckleberry Finn*, as Robert J. Lowenherz notes, "He decided, wisely, not to rely chiefly upon dialect spelling for either verisimilitude or comic effect."[35] Twain, according to Lowenherz,

> generally used dialect spelling functionally and, in Huck's speech as narrator, very sparingly. . . . In the entire first chapter, totaling about 1,400 words, one finds only thirteen words whose spellings reflect Huck's pronunciation.[36] This restriction of dialect spelling to less than one percent of Huck's narrative speech is maintained quite consistently throughout the novel.[37] By using dialect spellings economically, Twain does not force the reader through a verbal obstacle course.[38]

Lowenherz also observes that "hardly a decade before Twain began writing *Huckleberry* Finn, a kind of quirky phonetic orthography, often more quirky than phonetic, was the accepted technique for dialect representation."[39] If it is conceded that by clearly limiting the phonetic spellings in *Huckleberry Finn* Twain was rejecting such "quirky" orthography, might it not also be allowed that in the "Explanatory" he could have been resorting to a mildly humorous "stretcher" to "explain" (excuse?) his technique and thus cover his back with regard to the kind of criticism to which his innovative and often minimalist solutions could conceivably give rise in certain quarters?

If, in light of the preceding remarks, it can be granted that Mark Twain may not have been completely serious in any of the three introductory phases of his novel, it would perhaps warrant examining further the idea that, in the manner of his European and American predecessors, he was experimenting with fresh approaches to the convention of mischievously claiming validity and truth for all or part of his novel. With this in mind, let us turn our attention for a moment to the oft-cited first lines of the book, where Huckleberry Finn tells the reader:

> You don't know about me, without you have read a book by the name of "The Adventures of Tom Sawyer," but that ain't no matter. That book was made by Mr. Mark Twain, and he told the truth, mainly. There was things which he stretched, but mainly he told the truth. That is nothing. I never seen anybody but lied, one time or another, without it was aunt Polly, or the widow, or maybe Mary. (1)

In these lines Twain opens to derision the tradition of passing off fiction as legitimated truth. By admitting to "stretchers," or exaggerations, and through the phrase "told the truth, mainly," he joins Washington Irving in shattering any foundation to a claim of unadulterated honesty, since even a small crack in the structure is more than enough to call the stability of the entire edifice into question.[40]

Gregg Camfield speaks of "the liar's paradox that Clemens invokes at the outset of the story. Everything his book says, everything any book says, is a lie, even if this point, though made by a lying book, is true."[41] When considered together with the "Notice" and the "Explanatory," the novel's opening lines thus contribute to fashioning a discrete unit that represents an ingenious approach and a novel addition to the ideas often displayed in the openings to the works of Defoe, Swift, Irving, Hawthorne, and others. Not to treat these three elements as part of a triad would be to amputate one section at the expense of the other two; and failure to give adequate recognition to the humorous aspects of any one of the elements would jeopardize the integrity of the whole.

In support of this position, it will prove helpful to consider briefly the kind of introductory material employed in several of Twain's subsequent works.

In *A Connecticut Yankee* Twain employs an overtly droll approach and in his preface turns the tradition of pretending to historical accuracy in fictional accounts to amusing advantage when, in a style reminiscent of that of *The Prince and the Pauper*, he informs the reader with obvious relish:

> The ungentle laws and customs touched upon in this tale are historical, and the episodes which are used to illustrate them are also historical. It is not pretended that these laws and customs existed in England in the sixth century; no, it is only pretended that inasmuch as they existed in the English and other civilizations of far later times, it is safe to consider that it is no libel upon the sixth century to suppose them to have been in practice in that day also. One is quite justified in inferring that wherever one of these laws and customs was lacking in that remote time, its place was competently filled by a worse one.[42]

A clear case can be made for interpreting the statements made in this preface, as in the *Huckleberry Finn* "Explanatory," both humorously as well as seriously, and Twain continues his light bantering in "A Word of Explanation," in which he avers: "It was in Warwick Castle that I came across the curious stranger whom I am going to talk about. He attracted me by three things: his candid simplicity, his marvellous familiarity with ancient armour, and the restfulness of his company—for he did all the talking. We fell together, as modest people will, in the tail of the herd that was being shown through, and he at once began to say things which interested me." [43] As with the opening pages of *Huckleberry Finn*, it is easy to overlook some of the elusive irony involved here, such as the fact that the stranger's company is restful because "he did all the talking." The word "modest" is also capable of eliciting a smile, not only for its *immodest* use and its possible wry reference to Swift's famous use of the word in "A Modest Proposal" but also for the fact that Twain and William Dean Howells many years prior to the publication of the novel had initiated the idea of forming what they, with an obvious smirk, modestly called "The Modest Club." [44] (As indicated earlier in connection with *Life on the Mississippi* and Twain's nom de plume, "modest" was a word that the author did not hesitate to employ in referring to himself when wishing to draw a laugh.) In addition, the stranger's "candid simplicity" recalls the "earnest and sincere manner" of the "gentleman" in "The Stolen White Elephant," as well as the "honest" strangers in other stories where Twain resorted to this ploy. [45]

There are a number of subsequent instances in the "Word" where irony also makes itself felt. At the end of this introductory section, for instance, Twain again makes sport of the concept of simulated truth telling, this time in the style of Swift and Hawthorne, by having the "author" solemnly inform the reader that the entire "journal" was received from the unknown, "mysterious stranger," and, in a fashion similar to the document approach employed at the beginning of *The Prince and the Pauper*, reveal: "The first part of it—the great bulk of it—was parchment, and yellow with age. I scanned a leaf particularly and saw that it was a palimpsest. Under the old dim writing of the Yankee historian appeared traces of a penmanship which was older and dimmer still—Latin words and sentences: fragments from old monkish legends, evidently." [46] As is the case with *Huckleberry Finn*, the opening lines of the first chapter of the novel are also presented with a smile (and possibly a private joke, since Twain's close friend Joseph Twichell was the minister of Hartford's Asylum Hill Congregational Church):

> "CAMELOT—Camelot," said I to myself. "I don't seem to remember hearing of it before. Name of the asylum, likely."

It was a soft, reposeful, summer landscape, as lovely as a dream, and as lonesome as Sunday.[47]

If the gently humorous opening of *A Connecticut Yankee* and the semiserious approaches of *The Prince and the Pauper* and *Huckleberry Finn* are now compared, a number of resemblances would seem difficult to dismiss.

When we turn our attention to the introductory material for *Pudd'nhead Wilson*, we find Twain once again treating the reader to a sample of the rollicking pleasure he took in playing with the tradition of opening a novel with counterfeit sincerity—and again in the manner of Irving. He begins his book with "A Whisper to the Reader," and he starts with a quote from "Pudd'nhead Wilson's Calendar." This means, of course, that Twain is shamelessly quoting from none other than himself: "There is no character, howsoever good and fine, but it can be destroyed by ridicule, howsoever poor and witless. Observe the ass, for instance: his character is about perfect, he is the choicest spirit among all the humbler animals, yet see what ridicule has brought him to. Instead of feeling complimented when we are called an ass, we are left in doubt."[48] Whether "we" are truly "left in doubt" is far from certain, but the reader is not long left in doubt as to the level of intended seriousness of these prefatory remarks. For Twain quickly follows up with a long-winded and ludicrous explanation for turning to the "authority" of an American lawyer, whom he smilingly defines, using the chiefly British term, as a "barrister":

> A person who is ignorant of legal matters is always liable to make mistakes when he tries to photograph a court scene with his pen; and so I was not willing to let the law chapters in this book go to press without first subjecting them to rigid and exhausting revision and correction by a trained barrister—if that is what they are called. These chapters are right, now, in every detail, for they were rewritten under the immediate eye of William Hicks, who studied law part of a while in southwest Missouri thirty-five years ago and then came over here to Florence for his health and is still helping for exercise and board in Maccaroni and Vermicelli's horse-feed shed which is up the back alley as you turn around the corner out of the Piazza del Duomo just beyond the house where that stone that Dante used to sit on six hundred years ago is let into the wall when he let on to be watching them build Giotto's campanile and yet always got tired looking as

soon as Beatrice passed along on her way to get a chunk of chestnut cake to defend herself with in case of a Ghibelline outbreak before she got to school, at the same old stand where they sell the same old cake to this day and it is just as light and good as it was then, too, and this is not flattery, far from it. He was a little rusty on his law, but he rubbed up for this book, and those two or three legal chapters are right and straight, now. He told me so himself.[49]

Fascinated with the number of possibilities for humor that a seemingly unending sentence offered, Twain does not resist the temptation to conclude this whimsical "Whisper" with a second one:

Given under my hand this second day of January, 1893, at the Villa Viviani, village of Settignano, three miles back of Florence, on the hills—the same certainly affording the most charming view to be found on this planet, and with it the most dream-like and enchanting sunsets to be found in any planet or even in any solar system—and given, too, in the swell room of the house, with the busts of Cerretani senators and other grandees of this line looking approvingly down upon me as they used to look down upon Dante, and mutely asking me to adopt them into my family, which I do with pleasure, for my remotest ancestors are but spring chickens compared with these robed and stately antiques, and it will be a great and satisfying lift for me, that six hundred years will.

Mark Twain [50]

That the author was aware while writing *Pudd'nhead Wilson* of the humorous aspect inherent not only in the names Maccaroni and Vermicelli (particularly when linked with horse feed) but also in the name Hicks may be concluded from the fact that "hick" was one of the words that Howells, a number of years earlier, had considered offensive and deleted from the proofs of *The Prince and the Pauper*.[51] In sharply contrasting the unpretentious qualities of two Americans, the "hick" lawyer William Hicks and the author himself, with numerous features of a rich Italian tradition painted in preposterously garish colors, Twain also displays the wish to avoid worshipping at a European altar, while simultaneously appealing to the unpolished humor of a wide audience possessed of "American" attitudes. By brazenly quoting from himself and subsequently using the comic figure of Hicks, "who studied law part of a while in southwest Missouri thirty-five years ago" and whose own expertise is self-proclaimed ("He told me so himself"), as the supreme authority for the rightness of "the law chapters," Twain does not appear to have come all that far from having "The Author" appeal to his own "trustworthy guidance and support" in *Huckleberry Finn*'s "Explanatory," or from having Huck comment on Mr. Mark Twain's truthfulness in the opening lines of that novel. There is little semblance any longer of doing more than routine obeisance to the tradition of pretending to truth telling in fraudulent introductions to works of fiction.

Twain reverts to feigned gravity and a more classically complex approach to the hoary tradition in the novel *Joan of Arc* where he has the story told by a certain Sieur Louis de Conte, Joan's supposed page and secretary. According to Albert E. Stone, Jr., Sieur Louis de Conte was "an actual historical personage" although a minor figure, described as a "young man of noble birth" whom Twain had discovered in the fifth volume of Michelet's *Histoire de France* and who bore what for Samuel L. Clemens were "the convenient initials." [52] In addition, Twain puts the preface in the hands of a "translator" by the historically redolent name of Jean François Alden. But even supplied with a frilly French middle name, we can recognize plain John Alden, the admirer of Priscilla Mullins who, according to legend, proposed to the young lady on behalf of Myles (or Miles) Standish. In his role as a translator, however, Alden serves as a go-between for the wily Mark Twain and not for the modest Myles (as Clemens no doubt realized, both "Mark Twain" and "Myles" can be read as measurements), informing the reader in his second prefatory message, "A Peculiarity of Joan of Arc's History":

> The Sieur Louis de Conte is faithful to her official history in his Personal Recollections, and thus far his trustworthiness is unimpeachable; but his mass of added particulars must depend for credit upon his own word alone.
>
> The Translator [53]

The translator's reserved admission of the fact that the "trustworthiness" of Sieur Louis de Conte can be deemed "unimpeachable" only insofar as he keeps to the record should by now no longer surprise us, and the intricately layered disclaimer regarding the fact that responsibility for the "mass of added particulars" can be ascribed solely to Sieur Louis de Conte's "own word alone" is fully worthy of the convoluted wit of the game-loving Mark Twain. Further playful parrying with the truth in this passage is possibly displayed in the fact that Conte's name in French can mean not only "story" or "tale" but, as the author cannot be denied credit for knowing, also "fib" or "yarn."

One of the last of Twain's longer works to be published during his lifetime, *What Is Man?* is admittedly not a novel but is nevertheless provided with a preface that does full honor to the creaky convention of making a claim to truth telling. It is just possible that in this apparently unassuming effort, and with assumed trepidation, the aging writer may have been subtly attempting to slam a final door on a time-worn tradition that he felt had outlived its usefulness. With this idea in mind, let us examine Twain's preface:

> FEBRUARY, 1905. The studies for these papers were begun twenty-five or twenty-seven years ago. The papers were written seven years ago. I have examined them once or twice per year since and found them satisfactory. I have just examined them again, and am still satisfied that they speak the truth.
>
> Every thought in them has been thought (and accepted as unassailable truth) by millions upon millions of men—and concealed, kept private. Why did they not speak out? Because they dreaded (*and could not bear*) the disapproval of the people around them. Why have I not published? The same reason has restrained me I think. I can find no other.[54]

Although the approach to telling the truth appears to mimic to a certain degree the *Tom Sawyer* preface in its seemingly candid and innocent appeal to the good will of the reader, there is a major hoax in progress here, if, perhaps, imperceptible to Twain's unwitting public. James M. Cox describes it in the following way:

> Here in succinct terms is a definition of the suppressed artist. He appears at last with a truth which he has kept secret for half of his creative life because he could not face the disapproval of those around him. Yet for all the pretense of confession in the preface, the inescapable fact remains that the book was released anonymously and copyrighted under someone else's name. Thus the preface becomes the ultimate lie and the ultimate evasion.[55]

But is that all there is to it? Isn't there a faintly perceptible twitch at the corners of Twain's mouth? Of what real importance, for example, are all those attempts to put a time frame around this work? And just where in the name of all that is miraculous did the author (allegedly known only to a certain J. W. Bothwell,[56] whose surname—which could be read as "both well"—no doubt appealed to the love of duality of a man who had elected to be known as Mark Twain) manage to dig up those "millions and millions" of mute, frightened, and cowardly witnesses to the veracity of what he claims to be the "truth" of what we are about to read? We may note in this regard that whereas in the *Tom Sawyer* preface only *"most* of the Adventures . . . really occurred" (emphasis added), and for *Joan of Arc* the "mass of added particulars" were still left open to question, in this case "every thought" in the book has been given a seal of approval not only by the author but also by those "millions." In light of such an extravagant assertion one is inclined to recall "Lucretia Smith's Soldier," which was supposedly "true in every particular." And in view of the development toward this point in the prefatory material for Mark Twain's novels, one may wonder after this whether there were any more rivers for the author to cross. Did he consider that his goal had been attained and that only recrossing would henceforth be possible? If some such notion was indeed flitting about in the consciousness of the writer, this preface can be seen not only as "the ultimate lie and the ultimate evasion" but also, perhaps, as a saucy cry of "touché!" to the tradition of pretending to tell "unassailable truth." It can be considered a closing sally or, as Twain would have called it, a "snapper" in his long-running joke on, but not always with, the "trusting" reader.

If the initial pages of *Huckleberry Finn* are now reconsidered in light of the droll solutions resorted to in the openings to *The Prince and the Pauper*, *A Connecticut Yankee*, *Pudd'nhead Wilson*, *Joan of Arc*, and *What Is Man?* it would seem difficult to preclude the possibility that in the earlier novel the author was regarding his subject with a steady smile and as a humorous whole. It would also appear evident that the general approach to claims of truth telling in the prefatory material for all six works can be considered in a similar light and that the distance traveled since the writing of the preface to *Tom Sawyer* would not seem negligible. With *Pudd'nhead Wilson*, *Joan of Arc*, and *What Is Man?* Twain would appear to have put the finishing touches on what he commenced with *Huckleberry Finn* and *The Prince and the Pauper* and continued in *A Connecticut Yankee;* a definite threshold would seem not only to have been reached but also transcended.

Indeed, it is possible to see Mark Twain as having developed a scofflaw approach to the traditional technique of pretending to truth telling in fiction that effectively delivered a life-threatening blow to that convention. It would appear, moreover, that the convention was weakened to such a degree that authors after Twain found little reason to attempt to revive it, although now and again over the years there have been those who have deigned to give it a quick tip of the hat, or at least prod the apparent corpse in order to see if there might yet be life left in it.[57] But that such writers have not, by and large, found much of a heartbeat would probably not have come as much of a surprise to Twain, who, as we have seen in the *Pudd'nhead* "Whisper," realized what destructive results could be occasioned by ridicule.

One might, then, ask whether what Twain had somewhere in his mind as he was busy writing prefaces for *Huckleberry Finn, The Prince and the Pauper, A Connecticut Yankee, Pudd'nhead Wilson, Joan of Arc,* and *What Is Man?* was not merely to deviate from the time-revered tradition but to so thoroughly deride both earlier European as well as more current American approaches that they would wither in importance and influence. When one considers the writer's far-reaching familiarity with the works of many of the authors who had contributed to creating the rules that he delighted in twisting, as well as the boredom with Hawthorne's writing that he expressed to Howells only a few months following the publication of *Huckleberry Finn,*[58] the possibility of this being the case would not seem excluded.

It may also be recalled that while Twain in his "Notice" to *Huckleberry Finn* warned the reader away from even the kind of spurious moral found at the end of *Roughing It,* Huck, in the opening words to his own novel, warns the reader about Twain's lack of total truthfulness and also indirectly implicates himself in telling untruth when he states: "I never seen anybody but lied, one time or another, without it was aunt Polly, or the widow, or maybe Mary."[59] In subsequently having Huck bid farewell to us at the end of his book with the trite and rather empty words "yours truly," Twain can therefore be seen as pointing not only to the hollowness of such formula phrases but also to the final barrenness of a convention that speciously pretends to truth telling in fiction.[60] In view of the evidence examined thus far concerning the subtle ingenuity of Twain's stratagems, it would not seem unreasonable to wonder if even more levels of irony and perhaps foretastes of future directions are not cunningly cloaked in the fact that *Huckleberry Finn*, the novel in which Twain appears to have undertaken a major onslaught on the long-respected custom of pretending to deal frankly and truly with the reader, closes with the words "The end, yours truly Huck Finn."

Knowledge and Knowing in *Huckleberry Finn*

I
N MARK TWAIN'S *Adventures of Huckleberry Finn*, one of the most frequently addressed notions concerns knowledge: of what it might consist, who does or does not possess it, how it is viewed and acquired,
and how, whether complete, partial, fabricated, or imagined, it is then
transmitted. In a book purporting to be written by a fourteen-year-old boy
in the process of learning about the world and his place in it, an emphasis
on such a subject is understandable. What is exceptional in comparison
with other "boy books" is the complexity Twain employs in dealing with
this topic, as well as the depth of his awareness of the subtle forces involved
in becoming an enlightened human being. For example, while Twain elects
to have Huck and Jim, as well as several other characters, displayed as innocent of knowledge in many situations, their seeming naiveté often reveals
wisdom as profound as that of the wise fools or court jesters of earlier
literature.

But while the mention of *Don Quixote* in the novel points to Twain's
distinct consciousness of the idealistic innocent theme, and although many
of the novel's characters are accounted "fools" at one time or another, the
author's use of such concepts is not so simplistic as to merely mimic his
predecessors. Twain frequently complicates the equation with other elements, such as human failings, that draw us closer to the character in question and contribute to the spirit of tolerance that permeates the novel. As
adventures accumulate and the raft wends its way down the river, we also
gradually discover that much more than "coming of age" is being dealt with
and that the knowledge being absorbed by these "innocents" goes far beyond elementary acquisition of skills or attitudes. Though it is true that
Huck is seen to be in the process of experiencing physical and spiritual
liberation from an inhumane father and an oppressive society, there is em-

phasis throughout the book on educational skepticism or reconsideration of values as new or revelatory knowledge becomes available. At first glance it would therefore seem singular that one major source of such knowledge—books and the information to be found in them—is most often treated with disdain in Twain's novel.[1]

Beginning with Huck's unhappy encounters with the Bible and a spelling book in chapter 1 and ending with his realization of "what a trouble it was to make a book" (362), a negative atmosphere seems to envelop most of the printed matter that appears or is referred to in *Huckleberry Finn*. Tom's uninspired, often cruel notions are generally derived from half-digested romantic fiction, and the books Huck runs into on other occasions are usually seen if not as directly pernicious, at least as not to be taken too seriously— as, for instance, in the Wilks episode with the dictionary Huck realizes is not a Bible and on which he is therefore not afraid to swear an oath.[2] When pap kidnaps his son and takes him across the river, Huck also explains that "it was kind of lazy and jolly, laying off comfortable all day, smoking and fishing, and no books nor study" (30). During Huck's stay with pap there is actually one book present, but it is used only for "wadding" for pap's rifle; its reason for being there is simply to serve as a source of paper rather than as a source of information, mental stimulation, or inspiration.

In the Grangerford home we again observe Huck's innocence employed as a foil in satirizing a list of books that define the limits of the level of "sivilization" reached by this family of Southern "aristocracy." Huck meticulously and in all seriousness describes what he encounters:

> One was a big family Bible, full of pictures. One was "Pilgrim's Progress," about a man that left his family it didn't say why. I read considerable in it now and then. The statements was interesting, but tough. Another was "Friendship's Offering," full of beautiful stuff and poetry; but I didn't read the poetry. Another was Henry Clay's Speeches, and another was Dr. Gunn's Family Medicine, which told you all about what to do if a body was sick or dead. There was a Hymn Book, and a lot of other books. (137)

That there were "a lot of other books" as well would indicate visible wealth on the part of the owners in that day and time, but the rather conventional selection underlines the modest cultural level attained by those owners. The obvious ridicule embedded in the passage is underscored by the fact that the books are "piled up perfectly exact, on each corner of the table," thus illustrating the rigid and risible unnatural neatness of a family that probably does not read much in books so carefully arrayed. As Arthur G. Pettit observes, the irony is augmented by having *Friendship's Offering* "in a family at war" and by the fact that Henry Clay was renowned as a "peacemaker." [3]

Books that make up part of the "truck" Jim and Huck find in the skiff in which they escape from the sinking *Walter Scott* (a boat named for an author, as has often been noted, whose books were held by Twain to be largely "responsible" for the Civil War) [4] serve a somewhat more positive function in providing Huck with superficial knowledge about royalty, "kings, and dukes, and earls, and such" (93). This information serves as the basis for the discussion Huck has with Jim about "Sollermun" and about the "Frenchman" and prepares the reader for the appearance of the king and the duke. It can, in addition, be seen as providing Huck with the facts he refers to in his discourse on kings in chapter 23. Huck muddles the knowledge obtained from books in each case, but his attitude toward it and its application is, for the most part, refreshingly innocent.

That innocence of knowledge gained from books leaves Huck far more flexible than Tom to learn from any source, with only his own common sense as the final arbiter of what is worth retaining or applying. Indeed, in contrast to Tom, Huck seems destined to learn more, and more often, via experience and intuition than through information garnered from book pages. By escaping the influence of the kind of literary "authorities" Tom admires, Huck is also at liberty to grow in the understanding, and toward the practical wisdom, we see him slowly absorbing in the school of hard knocks. If that growth is allowed to continue unabated, the resulting increase in perceptive range promises to lead one day to far more skeptical questioning than he can presently manage with regard to all the "Toms" and their written resources he will encounter. For the moment, Tom and his "book learning" represent only occasional, minor irritations in Huck's life; but, like gravel in one's shoe, they will need at some point to be dealt with.

The references in the novel to Sir Walter Scott and his writings serve, on the other hand, not merely to intimate that Tom is no deeper than what he reads but to point to the more subtle concept that even what books allow to be "known" may in some manner prove disappointing or deceptive. We are given to understand that the knowledge to be gained from such sources may not necessarily offer higher wisdom or, unless properly employed,

serve the greater good. Tom's blurring of the border between factual information and fiction also does little to improve matters. Book dependence is
thus called into question, while the authority it can confer on the pompous
is ridiculed. It is nonetheless indicative of Twain's multilayered approach
to knowledge, and to his characters, that although Huck can be seen to
use the authority he acquires from books to play Tom Sawyer's over-
bearing role toward him in his arguments with Jim,[5] he never uses his
knowledge as a means of domination in the dictatorial and often insulting
fashion of Tom.

In *Huckleberry Finn* the most extreme example of the misuse of the authority conferred by knowledge gained from books is the Evasion sequence
of the novel where Tom's outrageous plan for Jim's escape is based once
again on unrealistic, book-learned, romantic concepts. A typical instance
of the kind of silliness to which such concepts can lead arises when Tom
urges Jim to keep a rattlesnake as a pet and even tame it; he explains that
"every animal is grateful for kindness and petting, and they wouldn't *think*
of hurting a person that pets them. Any book will tell you that" (325).

Twain's treatment of books and their contents represents, however, only
one of the more conspicuous aspects of his portrayal of approaches to how
knowledge is transmitted and received. Actual purveyors of knowledge
come in for criticism every bit as severe as that reserved for printed sources.
In the early stages of the novel, Huck is subjected to the educational influences of the widow Douglas and Miss Watson, as well as of Tom and pap,
and in each case the teacher fails to teach what is aimed at.[6] The widow
loses influence by not permitting Huck to smoke while she herself uses
tobacco in another form (snuff), whereas Miss Watson's "pecking" and traditional Christian conception of heaven also destroy any possible interest
in spelling or religion Huck might otherwise have been able to summon
up. Tom's imagined realm of "adventure" also loses credit with the matter-
of-fact Huck when the dreams fail to produce any material result, and it
does not help pedagogically that Tom levels such words as "numskull,"
"ignorant," and "sap-head" at those like Huck and Ben Rogers who question his authority as a preceptor.

Mark Twain's working notes for his novel contain the entry "Village
school—they haze Huck, the first day—describe Dawson's or Miss N.'s
[Newcomb's] school."[7] Despite what would appear from this note to have

originally been a more ambitious plan on Twain's part for dealing with Huck's formal education, school itself receives only brief mention in the book but provides an exceptional example of teaching that succeeds, despite Huck's weakness at mathematics. It is possible to infer from this that Twain (who reacted proudly to receiving an honorary master's degree from Yale University—only three years following the publication of *Huck*—and in later life to being awarded honorary doctorates from Yale and Oxford) was not at odds with formal education in the way he was with formal religion and the formal restrictions of polite society.[8] But when Twain turns from formal to parental education, we see that pap succeeds no better as a pedagogue than the widow or Miss Watson, who have acted in loco parentis.

Pap declares that he will "learn" the widow "how to meddle" and "learn people to bring up a boy to put on airs over his own father and let on to be better'n what *he* is" (24). In both of these situations Twain slyly has pap say exactly the opposite of what he means. Pap also betrays obvious envy of Huck's ability to read when he knocks Huck's book out of his hand; Huck tells us shortly thereafter that pap then

> took up a little blue and yaller picture of some cows and a boy, and says:
> "What's this?"
> "It's something they give me for learning my lessons good."
> He tore it up, and says—
> "I'll give you something better—I'll give you a cowhide." (24)

In this exchange, the connection between "cows and a boy" at school is not at all what pap has in mind for the boy Huck and the "cowhide." Nor does the picture itself receive the kind of respect from pap for which the school might have hoped. It is indicative of the kind of lesson we are being given that despite his other grammatical errors in the same sentence, Huck uses the word "learning" correctly here, in contrast to pap's misuse of both the word and the idea.[9] Most striking is the paradoxical fact that what pap is actually doing his best to teach Huck amounts to nothing other than to stop learning. And pap, unlike Huck, gives proof of having himself learned this particular lesson only too well since he cannot be taught to learn new ways, whereas Huck cannot be taught not to.

Throughout the book, Twain often shows teaching, even by parents and their proxies, to be a frustrating and frequently disappointed endeavor. This is especially true when the teaching is undertaken for selfish ends, without the best interests at heart of the person taught or when it is done from a do-gooder point of view not based on a clear understanding of human nature.

But failure to educate can also be viewed as frequently stemming from imperfect knowledge on the part of the teacher, all too often combined with a feeling of superiority bestowed by that knowledge. When, for example, Huck takes it upon himself to teach Jim about "kings, and dukes, and earls and such" (93) it doesn't take Jim long to thoroughly confound the boy's simple logic and cause him to throw in the towel with the frustrated exclamation: "I see it warn't no use wasting words—you can't learn a nigger to argue. So I quit" (98). And when Buck Grangerford, who feels confident in spelling Huck's assumed name George Jackson as "Gorge Jaxon," attempts to explain to Huck what a feud is, he haughtily asks, "Why, where was you raised? Don't you know what a feud is?" (146). We are then treated to an amusing display of just how little Buck actually knows or understands about what he feels himself to be teaching competently to the less-informed Huck. Twain shows the reader, in addition, that with the passage of time true knowledge of the origins and details of a feud must be chalked up as one of the fatalities of such long-term foolishness. During Huck's interrogation of Buck, this is underlined at every turn:

> "What was the trouble about, Buck?—land?"
> "I reckon maybe—I don't know."
> "Well, who done the shooting?—was it a Grangerford or a Shepherdson?"
> "Laws, how do *I* know? it was so long ago."
> "Don't anybody know?"
> "Oh, yes, pa knows, I reckon, and some of the other old folks; but they don't know, now, what the row was about in the first place." (146)

Judging from this interchange, it would seem that Buck and Huck meet with similar "success" in their efforts to educate someone they consider to be less knowledgeable than themselves, while the repetition of the word "know" conveys the author's irony.

Buck's question about Huck's "raising" is one that is touched on more than once in *Huckleberry Finn* and not only allows Twain to broach the subject of the extent to which upbringing determines a person's fate but also to comment on the ability of human beings to apply acquired knowledge in changing the style, quality, or direction of their lives. For instance, when Huck saves Jim by lying to slave-hunters about Jim's color, he tells himself, "I see it warn't no use for me to try to learn to do right; a body that don't get *started* right when he's little, ain't got no show—when the pinch comes there ain't nothing to back him up and keep him to his work, and so he gets beat" (127). The same reasoning is applied again in chapter 31, when Huck must once more decide about Jim's fate and concludes, "[I] never thought no more about reforming. I shoved the whole thing out of my head; and said I would take up wickedness again, which was in my line, being brung up to it, and the other warn't" (271). Hence, even if Huck can be seen as having been raised badly by his no-good father to "borrow" whatever he needs, his upbringing has evidently had no serious influence on his decisions concerning Jim, decisions that pap would not have made in anything like the same way as his son. How one is "brung up" is clearly called into question as a valid explanation, or justification, for all of life's later actions.

In this manner, Twain deftly uses the chisel of irony to chip away at the idea that upbringing represents a fatal determining factor in the life of a human being. The point would appear to be that people need not feel condemned by their background, no matter what it might be, and even if shaped by as miserable a rapscallion as pap. Huck can, after all, read and write, and even pap's obvious envy of that ability can never again deprive the young man of the freedom from ignorance and the potential for growth that his newfound knowledge makes possible. In this sense, Huck is his father's son in name only; all other qualities are up to him to develop and fashion in the best way he can and with whatever knowledge he can procure.

On the other hand, Twain has Huck repeatedly express the conviction that a person's upbringing does, indeed, represent a determining and sometimes incapacitating factor in later life; nor does the boy consider that this idea applies exclusively to himself. Huck's long explanation to Jim about the knavish qualities of kings, for example, concludes with, "All I say is kings is kings, and you got to make allowances. Take them all around, they're a mighty ornery lot. It's the way they're raised" (200). While it might seem at first blush that Twain is going counter to what he has indi-

cated elsewhere in his novel, closer observation reveals once again a quiz-
zical smile being directed at any manner of overly simplified attitude regarding the long-term effects of early education.

In the Evasion section, upbringing is also the factor that is at the source
of Huck's amazement at Tom's willingness to help free Jim. Huck reflects
long on the fact that

> Here was a boy that was respectable, and well brung up; and had a character
> to lose; and folks at home that had characters; and he was bright and not
> leather-headed; and knowing and not ignorant; and not mean, but kind; and
> yet here he was, without any more pride, or rightness, or feeling, than to
> stoop to this business, and make himself a shame, and his family a shame,
> before everybody. I *couldn't* understand it, no way at all. It was outrageous,
> and I knowed I ought to just up and tell him so; and so be his true friend,
> and let him quit the thing right where he was, and save himself. And I *did*
> start to tell him; but he shut me up, and says:
>   "Don't you reckon I know what I'm about? Don't I generly know what
> I'm about?" (292)

In view of Tom's later disclosure that Jim was already free at the time Huck
was sweating over what he mistakenly considered to be a problem for Tom,
these words, which pirouette repeatedly around Tom's "knowing," show
that his "superior" upbringing in no way hinders him from taking advantage of Jim for his own fun. Nor does it prevent him from actually "losing"
his "character" in the manner hinted at here but not as yet discerned by
Huck. Once again Twain can be seen to question the wisdom of considering the manner in which a person is reared as a decisive element in defining
his or her character. It would be difficult to imagine a more lucid argument
against a conception of upbringing as a conclusively crippling force and in
favor of the liberating power of an individual's natural instincts.

Many of the questions in Twain's novel that concern how one is raised
are directly connected with Jim's freedom and can be interpreted as addressing, among other things, just how extensively past training and education will come to bear on the attitudes toward former slaves held by post–
Civil War America. It is not unexpected, therefore, to hear Jim himself
utter the most telling analysis of the effects that upbringing can have on a

person's attitude toward those who happen to be subject to the arbitrary dictates of the will of another. In his discussion with Huck about "Sollermun," Jim reacts sharply to being told he doesn't "get" the point:

> "Blame de pint! I reck'n I knows what I knows. En mine you, de *real* pint is down furder—it's down deeper. It lays in de way Sollermun was raised. You take a man dat's got on'y one er two chillen; is dat man gwyne to be waseful o' chillen? No, he ain't; he can't 'ford it. *He* know how to value 'em. But you take a man dat's got 'bout five million chillen runnin' roun' de house, en it's diffunt. *He* as soon chop a chile in two as a cat. Dey's plenty mo'. A chile er two, mo' er less, warn't no consekens to Sollermun, dad fetch him!" (96)

Huck, through the opaque lens of prejudice, sees Jim at this moment less as Jim, his friend and fellow, than as a "nigger" and perceives at this juncture only what he takes to be a seemingly illogical argument. He notes: "I never see such a nigger. If he got a notion in his head once, there warn't no getting it out again. He was the most down on Solomon of any nigger I ever see" (96).[10]

Much more is at stake than Huck realizes, however. Jim can be seen in this discussion as indirectly struggling with a problem that was to face both white and black Americans during the Reconstruction period: the question of whether past upbringing would handicap relations and make whites insensitive to individual blacks and their difficulties. Were the humane qualities often evident in personal human relationships to be forgotten or lost in looking at the former slave population as only an indistinct mass of human beings, each of whom could, nevertheless, be conceived of as one of the "children" of the same "father king"? If considered from this angle, Jim's seemingly "foolish" commentary on "de way Sollermun was raised" can be taken as humane wisdom, equally as profound in its own way as that of Solomon, the sage whose name Jim pronounces in his own way.

In telling Huck "I knows what I knows," Jim also highlights another facet of the novel's many-sided approach to knowledge. The importance that "knowing" carries with it has been noted above, and the verb "to know" figures frequently in *Huckleberry Finn*, beginning with the complicated ambiguity of the first two sentences in the book where Huck apprises the reader of the following facts: "You don't know about me, without you have read a book by the name of 'The Adventures of Tom Sawyer,' but that ain't no matter. That book was made by Mr. Mark Twain, and he told the truth, mainly" (1). What the reader is actually able to *know* about Huck from a writer who only "mainly told the truth" can clearly be considered open to question.[11] Equally puzzling is what the reader can reasonably hope to come to know in the pages that follow, pages that have supposedly been written by a barely literate fourteen year old created by a Mr. Mark Twain who in turn owes his existence to a certain Samuel Clemens.

Following such an enigmatic opening, it does not come as a surprise to find the question of what a person actually "knows" wrestled with repeatedly throughout the rest of the novel. In the following exchange between Huck and Judge Thatcher as it appears in the original manuscript, we can see from the revisions Twain made that he was quite careful about not allowing Huck to display too much reading knowledge at too early a stage in the novel, while at the same time realizing that the boy needed to at least be able to "write a little":

> Then he [Judge Thatcher] wrote something on a paper
>   &handed˄read˄ it over, & says:
>   "Y̶ Read it
>   "There—you see it says 'for a consideration.' That means I have bought
> it of you & paid you for it. Here is a dollar for you. Now, you sign it."
>   I signed it, and left.[12]*

From Twain's painstaking emendations, it is apparent that Huck's protective cloak of ignorance needed to be kept in good condition for the upcoming voyage.

Ignorance also plays a pivotal role in the exchange between Huck and Buck concerning the origins of the Grangerford-Shepherdson feud. Buck's mentioning that no one now knows "what the row was about in the first place" illustrates how a lack of knowledge of the past can contribute to the emptiness and terrible destructiveness of an entire way of life in the present.

Another of Twain's more intricate methods for handling the idea of what a person actually knows entails allowing a character to make a claim to knowledge that at some point is either contradicted by the truth or shown to carry another form of ironic weight. Judith Loftus, we may recall, tells Huck: "You see, you're a run-away 'prentice—that's all. It ain't anything. There ain't any harm in it. You've been treated bad, and you made up your mind to cut" (73). As it turns out, it is precisely this flawed supposition that allows Huck to leave the Loftus place without Mrs. Loftus suspecting any-thing further and return to Jackson's Island in time to save Jim from the threat to his freedom that her husband and his companion represent.

A similar incident transpires when Huck leads the king and the duke to believe that not he but the Wilks girls' slaves have made off with a six-thousand-dollar sack of money. Huck tells us that the king "give me down the banks for not coming and *telling* him I see the niggers come out of his room acting that way—said any fool would a *knowed* some-thing was up" (237). The king's gullible trust of Huck's story permits the boy to avoid the wrath of the two frauds and successfully keep the money out of their clutches, while at the same time the king becomes the butt of humor through his overconfident belief that he *knows* as much as "any fool," although the reader not only knows better but also knows who the real fool is.

To return for a moment to the beginning of the Evasion section, it is Huck's own erroneous assumption that helps lay the groundwork for the final developments of the novel. Neither Huck nor the reader is aware at this moment that Jim is free or that Tom is fully knowledgeable of the fact. Only during a second reading of the book can Huck's mistaken, assumed knowledge take on its full ironic force in the passage where the young man trustingly confides to Tom:

> "All right; but wait a minute. There's one more thing—a thing that *nobody* don't know but me. And that is, there's a nigger here that I'm a trying to steal out of slavery—and his name is *Jim*—old Miss Watson's Jim."
>
> He says:
>
> "What! Why Jim is—"
>
> He stopped, and went to studying. I says:
>
> "*I* know what you'll say. You'll say it's dirty low-down business; but what if it is?—*I*'m low-down; and I'm agoing to steal him, and I want you to keep mum and not let on. Will you?"
>
> His eye lit up, and he says:
>
> "I'll *help* you steal him!" (284)

What Huck presumes to know about how Tom will react takes on an entirely new meaning during a rereading of the novel, and, as a result, those who meander with Huck and Jim more than once are vouchsafed fresh interest and insight through the acquisition of knowledge unavailable prior to completing their first venture on the raft.

In *Huckleberry Finn*, false assumptions are frequently utilized for humorous purposes when contrasted pointedly with what the reader understands to be the truth. To realize just how assumed knowledge serves to produce a smile we need only remember Aunt Sally's belief that the melting butter issuing from under Huck's hat is diseased brains. Similar instances include Uncle Silas's certainty that his horse, which has not made the trip he assumes her to have made, is faster than she is, and Huck, who resorts regularly to lying, being told by Levi Bell, the lawyer, at the Wilks interrogation: "Set down, my boy, I wouldn't strain myself, if I was you. I reckon you ain't used to lying, it don't seem to come handy; what you want is practice. You do it pretty awkward" (253).

Another, more extended example of a humorous situation that depends on mistaken knowledge occurs in the Wilks episode when the duke believes that the king, rather than Huck, has put the orphans' six thousand dollars in the coffin. The mutual ignorance of the two impostors is accentuated by their false suppositions about each other, with "knowing" featuring prominently in the following exchange:

> "Shucks!" says the king, very sarcastic; "but *I* don't know—maybe you was asleep, and didn't know what you was about."
> The duke bristles right up, now, and says:
> "O, let *up* on this cussed nonsense—do you take me for a blame' fool? Don't you reckon *I* know who hid that money in that coffin?"
> "*Yes* sir! I know you *do* know because you done it yourself!"
> "It's a lie!"—and the duke went for him. The king sings out:
> "Take y'r hands off!—leggo my throat!—I take it all back." (262–63)

Under the pressure of the duke's strangling hands, the king finally "owns up" to knowledge that he obviously never had, and Twain, through this dialogue animated by assumptions rather than facts, indicates just how complicated can be the way to true knowledge. Once the two scoundrels have settled into an inebriated sleep, the real truth emerges when Huck tells Jim "everything." Knowledge is thus ironically near to the king and the duke yet, as always, symbolically far from their greedy grasp.

Twain also turns his attention to the critical gap that often exists between what one believes to be the whole truth and what still more complete truth might comprehend. He repeatedly shows the king and the duke, for example, confidently believing that they know more than anyone else. In the Wilks section the king dismisses the possible threat to their schemes posed by the town doctor with the following words: "Cuss the doctor! What do we k'yer for *him*? Hain't we got all the fools in town on our side? and ain't that a big enough majority in any town?" (228). When, to the king's chagrin, the doctor proves instrumental in exposing him and the duke as charlatans, we perceive that, in the final analysis, the king's "knowledge" is insufficient to protect him from his want of common sense.

The duke's belief that he, too, knows everything better than others eventually leads to results fully as dramatic as the king's and even prior to that final denouement causes him to make statements such as the one he utters following the Royal Nonesuch caper, where "knowing" once again receives particular stress: "Greenhorns, flatheads! *I* knew the first house would keep mum and let the rest of the town get roped in; and I knew they'd lay for us the third night, and consider it was *their* turn now. Well, it *is* their turn, and I'd give something to know how much they'd take for it. I *would* just like to know how they're putting in their opportunity" (198). What the duke at this point incorrectly believes he knows comes together at a later stage of the novel with what he does not know and contributes to his and the king's final downfall. The duke's principal worry is that the "nigger" (who never becomes "Jim" to either him or the king) will "blow" on him and his partner and expose the Nonesuch caper. As it turns out, it is, indeed, what Jim knows and shares with Silas Phelps about that "scandalous show" that finally allows the duke to come to know—better than he might have liked—what the "greenhorns" and "flatheads" of Bricksville were thinking about after the third Nonesuch performance in their town.

The duke is also conscious of the fact that he can be betrayed by the king but entertains the mistaken belief that he knows enough to avoid that fate. By not acting on his knowledge, however, he ultimately helps bring about his and the king's tarring and feathering. Huck learns that the foolish, bargain-rate sale of Jim by the king takes place "becuz he's got to go up the river and can't wait" (268), and from the direction the king chooses—"up the river" and thus against the stream and the movement of the raft—it is apparent that he intends to abandon the duke. But there is no indication that the duke is privy to the full story. What the duke does know, on the other hand, is that the king has sold Jim for forty dollars and not divided the money with him. In order to have the king available for the next Royal Nonesuch performance in Pikeville, the duke nevertheless chooses to overlook his associate's underhanded action and fails to act on what he knows. In so doing he tacitly accepts Jim's sale and thereby exposes himself to the fate he most fears.

In treating knowledge and knowing in *Huckleberry Finn*, Twain also concerns himself with the dilemmas in which persons may find themselves if they sacrifice their right to "know what they know." When "Nat, the nigger that fed" Jim at the Phelps plantation first appears, he is portrayed as somewhat ridiculous in holding superstitious beliefs. We are told that he has "a good-natured chuckleheaded face" and that "his wool was all tied up in little bunches with thread. That was to keep witches off" (295). And when Tom, Huck, and even Jim collude in order to make him believe he didn't hear what he actually heard, he not only accepts the affront to his senses but takes it as convincing evidence of what he believes he knows about witches. He "knows," therefore, that his knowledge about witches has been correct all along and states: "But it's awluz jis' so; people dat's *sot*, stays sot; dey won't look into nothn' en fine it out f'r deyselves, en when *you* fine it out en tell um 'bout it, dey doan' b'lieve you" (296–97). In not believing his own sense perceptions he thus exposes himself to extrasensory self-deception.

Jim, too, is victimized in the Evasion section when he entrusts to Tom his right to know what he knows. Huck informs us that "Jim he couldn't see no sense in the most of it, but he allowed we was white folks and knowed better than him; so he was satisfied and said he would do it all just as Tom said" (309). From the suffering Jim goes through, however, it quickly becomes clear just how risky it can be to abdicate one's right to one's own knowledge.

Even Huck is put at risk when he turns over to Tom the right to make most of the decisions on how Jim should be freed, though he tells us, "I went to thinking out a plan, but only just to be doing something; I knowed very well where the right plan was going to come from" (292). When it does, Huck realizes that "it was worth fifteen of mine, for style, and would make Jim just as free a man as mine would, and maybe get us all killed besides" (292). It is evident that Huck possesses the knowledge that Jim's freedom as well as all of their lives may be in jeopardy, but in sacrificing his right to apply this knowledge he effectively allows himself and his friends to become vulnerable to mortal danger, thereby removing this "adventure" from the realm of what can be considered harmless fun.

In a novel that could easily have borne the title *The Education of Huckleberry Finn*, the young protagonist may be seen as obtaining and retaining knowledge in a multiplicity of ways. More than once, for instance, he "remembers" wisdom he has heard from Jim. In recounting that a potato will turn a coin bright he mentions that "I knowed a potato would do that, before, but I had forgot it" (21), and he uses a similar disclaimer about Jim's observation that there is "no high ground around Cairo" (129). In each case, Huck's remark indicates a desire to have a useful piece of practical information acknowledged to be as much his as Jim's, probably in order to participate on equal terms in the wisdom Jim possesses. But whether Huck is truly becoming conscious of this knowledge for the second time, as he claims, can be seen as at least open to doubt.[13]

On other occasions, we are given the impression of actually watching moments of perception take place. After Huck has lived over on the Illinois shore with pap for long enough to become impatient with the whippings and pap's drunken binges, he begins contemplating how to escape. At just the instant during which he is deliberating over the details concerning his planned departure, he seems to awake to an awareness of one way of fleeing when pap asks him whether he "was asleep or drownded" (33). Quiet assimilation of knowledge also occurs in the Grangerford section of the novel when Huck observes Harney Shepherdson "cover" young Buck Grangerford with his rifle but refrain from shooting the boy. Huck understands that this behavior runs counter to what other members of either clan would do and seems to perceive that the pattern has been broken for a reason that has yet to be revealed.

It is, in fact, possible to see Huck as continually in the process of procuring knowledge. During his brief time at school, for instance, he manages to acquire sufficient reading and writing skills to subsequently enable him not only to understand *Pilgrim's Progress* (as well as the note from Sophia to Harney) but also to grasp the content of the books taken from the *Walter Scott* and, though it might seem like somewhat of a "stretcher," to write his own book. In addition, Jim and Judith Loftus both contribute to helping Huck realize how to behave like a girl, and Jim helps the boy slowly learn to regard a person of another color as human. Huck also absorbs knowledge by memorizing "Hamlet's" soliloquy while the duke is teaching it to the king and, on another occasion, comes to realize in wrestling with his conscience that he cannot go against his personal ethics in a direct confrontation with his god. In the latter case, he knows what he should do, according to society's laws, but explains that "deep down in me I knowed it was a lie—and He knowed it" (269). The struggle Huck engages in on this occasion consequently provides him with a perplexing educational encounter rooted in a complex approach to "knowing."

We see Huck learning through formal and informal education, observation, reading, intuition, memory, and many varieties of direct and indirect experience, with knowledge and its origins portrayed in a manner that avoids simplification or moralizing about the superiority of specific categories. Huck displays an openness to imbibing information from any spring, without barriers of prejudice. Even his lack of humor is an asset in that it does not permit him to scorn or lightly dismiss knowledge obtained from what might otherwise be considered unlikely sources. He can learn from the heartless Colonel Sherburn about the psychology and cowardice of crowds, then add to that knowledge through seeing the duke and king tarred and feathered by a crowd and cruelly ridden out of town on a rail. On each of these occasions Huck is an unimpassioned observer who reacts with reflective sadness; neither humor, a taste for vengeance, nor emotion clouds his perceptive faculties. By comparison, we might consider that a Bricksville citizen in the habit of setting dogs on fire for sport would no doubt have reacted quite differently in both of the above situations and learned altogether different lessons.

Huck's sources of knowledge are manifold, as are the means by which he obtains it; but the heart of the issue ultimately lies with the nature of that knowledge. Twain leaves little doubt but that Huck's essential education is in matters humane.[14] Time and again we watch this young man stretch himself to accommodate wider conceptions of tolerance after having experienced negative results from exercising what his surrounding society would regard as acceptable behavior. This means, understandably, that instinctive judgment or knowledge gained from personal experience must take precedence over the lessons society has taught and often precipitate a tense emotional dilemma for the boy as he strives fruitlessly to find a solution that will satisfy all concerned. At such moments, we see Huck's conscience sensing what demands the new experience will place on him, often before he himself becomes aware of it. It constantly constrains him to abide by its dictates, to learn to reject bigotry, to liberate his mind and, more important, his heart from narrow, ignorant responses to life's questions. If Huck as a result appears to consistently find himself in "a tight place," it is because that is where conscience often places us. Twain indicates that all experience and knowledge received must be passed through that selective sieve of conscience before it may be assimilated for longer-term use, and, whatever might be the final disposition of a question under consideration, Huck's sieve allows little to escape unexamined.

What Huck at the end of the day is obviously doing is learning who he is and what he needs to know in order to live something other than an insensitive and less than humane life. He is acquiring the self-knowledge indispensable to transcending both the triviality of Tom's interests as well as the many barriers to enlightenment erected by a society that considers itself already sufficiently enlightened but whose shadows this young adventurer is gradually learning to penetrate. We are only allowed to see Huck at age fourteen (no birthday celebrations for him), but we must nurture the hope that his inborn balkiness of spirit will survive the sandpaper effects of the passing of years, allowing him to evolve into an aware and continuously developing adult. Some of the underlying reasons for the fact that this young man's story speaks so strongly not only to other young people reaching adulthood but also to mature readers, scholars, and writers must, it would seem, be looked for both in the nature of what Huck comes to know in the course of the book as well as in the gradual expansion of his faculty to evaluate, absorb, and apply what he learns.

Huck is not, however, the only character in the novel to be defined by the relative ability to absorb or reject knowledge. Pap, for instance, is un-teachable; Tom, who "knowed how to do everything" (323), is rigid, super-cilious, and closed to Huck's suggestions; all the Grangerfords and Shep-herdsons, save Harney and Sophia, are condemned by their tenacious hold on a crippling ancient idea and their inability to learn any less destructive ones; while Aunt Sally and Uncle Silas are pictured as good-hearted but locked into circumscribed thought patterns that allow no possibility of es-cape. Miss Watson, too, is limited, although her freeing of Jim can be in-terpreted as at least an attempt at learning an important truth.

At the time she makes her decision, Miss Watson is ignorant of the pos-sible long-term repercussions of her action, but in taking that single, and let us hope sincere, step away from what she has been raised to know about slavery and toward freedom for at least one of those human beings directly affected by the system, she allows the possibility to emerge that future gen-erations, inspired by such actions as hers, will possess more progressive attitudes and know a freer world. As A. E. Dyson observes:

> Miss Watson's request in her will is the beginning, maybe, of a challenge to the system of slavery from inside; a moment without which no purer moral protest, however noble, would stand much hope of eventually winning the majority to its side. If we think historically, we shall see that her dying de-cision to free Jim, despite the fact that he has sinned both against herself and against the economic system by escaping, may be as important a land-mark on the road to emancipation as the dangerous quest for freedom on the raft itself. Actual humane progress does come about, whether we like it or not, through muddled insights, muddled kindliness, muddled actions as much as from the straightforward vindication of ideals. Twain's ending draws attention to this, too, and it is also part of the whole truth he has to tell.[15]

Another part of that truth is that, next to Huck, it is Jim who shows himself the most flexible and open of the characters, and despite Huck's description of him as being "the easiest nigger to laugh," Jim is continu-ously seen in the same serious mode as Huck. This seriousness is played upon by Twain early in the novel when Jim is supposedly ridden by witches. Even while the reader chuckles, however, Jim—in a creative manner wor-thy of a fledgling Andrew Carnegie—is cleverly taking advantage of a situation that allows him to exploit his fellow slaves. It is Jim, after all, who creates the witch story and incorporates into it the five-center piece that becomes the focus of wonder for his friends and acquaintances. According to Huck, Jim would claim that "it was a charm the devil give to him with his own hands and told him he could cure anybody with it and fetch witches whenever he wanted to, just by saying something to it" (8). In this manner, Jim astutely applies his own knowledge to a situation that may have initially surprised and interested him but, without his intelligent development of an "explanation," would have remained an unprofitable curiosity. He does this not only by means of the story he creates and keeps adding to—a story that incorporates enough traditional superstition to make it believable to his audience—but also through his management of his five-center-piece asset. Huck informs us that Jim "never told what it was he said to it. Niggers would come from all around there and give Jim anything they had, just for a sight of that five-center piece; but they wouldn't touch it, because the devil had had his hands on it" (8). The "knowledge" Jim appeals to in creating his tale is just as imaginary as the tale itself, but its very existence witnesses to the "reality" it must have for many of its listeners. That Jim's fabricated yarn does not represent an isolated instance of his ability to make a profit from exploiting the superstitions of others, including whites, is evident from his use of the hairball, in combination with some double-talk about white and black angels and light and dark girls, in order to extract payment of a counterfeit quarter from Huck.

Jim possesses other kinds of knowledge as well, as may be seen in the fact that it is he who builds a wigwam and a floor for the raft in order to protect its passengers both from above and below, while Huck tells us that Jim always knows how to formulate a good plan when needed. In addition, Jim is more than once shown to possess useful "natural" knowledge tempered by common sense, humanity, and shrewd perceptive abilities. Even in such scenes as the one where his speculating in "stock" causes him to play the minstrel-show fool to Huck's interlocutor, Jim usually displays unexpected wisdom. In that "stock" scene, Jim does not close the discussion foolishly or in humiliation but with a piercing perception of his value as a human being. Despite the fact that he has just described how he lost all his money in speculation, he claims: "I's rich now, come to look at it. I owns mysef, en I's wuth eight hund'd dollars. I wisht I had the money, I wouldn' want no

mo'" (57). And Jim's capacity for learning quickly, while integrating new
knowledge with what he already knows, is further displayed in his gentle
management of Huck's somewhat unpredictable attitudes with regard to
slavery. Since Huck's hesitation at the wrong moment could prove deci-
sively dangerous for the runaway slave, he can at no point afford to make a
mistake in estimating the current emotional state of the boy.

If we return now for a moment to Jim's discussion with Huck of the
biblical story of Solomon, we can see that Jim does not unreflectingly accept even the most hallowed information without carefully analyzing it according to his own lights prior to incorporating it into a personal system
where he "knows" what he "knows." Considering the manner in which the
Bible served slave owners as a "sivilizing" force among their chattel, Jim's
critical approach to the ideas found in "The Good Book" indicates a tendency that, taken to the extreme, could menace the authority and hence the
effectiveness of that controlling force. Jim dares to challenge the received
"wisdom" of an important biblical figure well known for his wisdom,
thereby compounding the gravity of the act and expanding the potential
for destabilizing the status quo. The fact that this illiterate slave "knows"
what he "knows" is therefore not as uncomplicated a concept as might at
first appear, nor are the possible ramifications of that certainty as circumscribed as might initially be imagined. At the origin of every movement
ever conceived or undertaken in the cause of human dignity and liberty are
roots related to Jim's unshakable conviction concerning what he knows.

Jim understands at the commencement of his quest for liberty that no one
can know in which direction he has fled if he resorts to a means of transportation such as a raft that "don't make no track"; and there is clear evidence in *Huckleberry Finn* that Jim's creator, Mr. Mark Twain, was also
cognizant of the importance of the knowledge to be gained from "tracks."
The first indisputable proof that pap is alive, active, and again in the area
comes, for example, from a tell-tale footprint Huck spots in the snow:
"There was a cross in the left boot-heel made with big nails, to keep off
the devil" (19). Huck, too, creates false tracks in order to cover his flight
from pap and put searchers off his trail. In that instance he makes use of
meal, pap's whetstone, a pig, and a sack of rocks to do just the opposite
of what pap's footprint made possible: to obscure the fact that he is alive

and well. Huck again attempts to conceal his true track when he disposes of the evidence that ties him to Jim's rattlesnake bite: "Then I slid out quiet and throwed the snakes clear away amongst the bushes; for I warn't going to let Jim find out it was all my fault, not if I could help it" (65). The boy also informs us that, shortly after leaving Mrs. Loftus's place, "I doubled on my tracks" in order to keep her from realizing in which direction he was really heading. His next blurring of a track occurs after he safely reaches the island when he creates a diversion for Mrs. Loftus's husband, friend, and dog by starting a fire at the opposite end of the island from where he and Jim are currently lodged. Huck's skill at throwing others off the track is yet again demonstrated at the moment when he first perceives the king and duke running toward the raft and saves the rascals from some pursuing men and dogs by sensibly telling them: "I don't hear the dogs and horses yet; you've got time to crowd through the brush and get up the crick a little ways; then you take to the water and wade down to me and get in—that'll throw the dogs off the scent" (159).

The significance of human tracks is further developed by Twain in the Wilks episode when conclusive evidence as to the identity of the true Wilks brothers is sought from handwriting samples. The threat to the frauds is clear, and the samples do seem to provide confirmation of their lack of legitimacy. The results are nevertheless challenged by the king, who resorts to some quickly conceived excuses, and the confusion is augmented by the fact that the second set of brothers cannot, because of the broken arm of the one who supposedly pens letters for both, provide a current example of "their" handwriting. It is this set of brothers, however, that directs attention at that moment to another track: a possible mark on the dead brother's breast. In the ensuing excitement, the handwriting test is forgotten.

Mark Twain, conceivably beguiled by the opportunity for fun that his first name permits, evinces a continuing interest in marks and tracks that make possible both indisputably genuine as well as imprecise or deceptive knowledge. The notion of proof subject to no uncertainty—true knowledge, in one sense—was a facet of the question that clearly had a special appeal for him, and we will see him make use of one of his age's most recent developments in this field when in *Pudd'nhead Wilson* fingerprints are resorted to in solving a crime. While in *Huck* the king tries to cast doubt on the validity of a test based on a comparison of handwriting, and Twain does not ultimately allow it to bear the weight of condemning the duke and the king, in *Pudd'nhead* a fingerprint comparison becomes the keystone in the edifice of proof convicting Valet de Chambre of murder. Twain's reason for placing more trust in fingerprints than in handwriting becomes clear from Pudd'nhead Wilson's careful description:

> Every human being carries with him from his cradle to his grave certain physical marks which do not change their character, and by which he can always be identified—and that without shade of doubt or question. These marks are his signature, his physiological autograph, so to speak, and this autograph cannot be counter-feited, nor can he disguise it or hide it away, nor can it become illegible by the wear and the mutations of time.[16]

Such marks do away with doubt and provide true and permanent identification, a track not even the most accomplished forger can cover. Is it therefore any wonder that Samuel Clemens, a man who lived much of his life under an alias and needed to learn a new signature as an adult, found this unalterable knowledge concerning individual human beings so engrossing?[17] More than one signature, more than one identity could freely be embraced, while underneath pulsed always and ever the same unchangeable heart. The track would lead home at last. In *Huck* we do not yet get that far; we never learn if the handwriting results were conclusive or if, in fact, there was a mark on the breast of the dead brother. Mark Twain quietly lets those tracks go cold.

Intentionally disseminated disinformation is another complex concept involved with "knowing" that appealed to Mark Twain, and we find him delighting in its myriad possibilities frequently in *Adventures of Huckleberry Finn*. An egregious example of such nonknowledge is the handbill created by the duke that describes Jim and announces a reward for his capture. The description of Jim is exact, but the truth stops there. Although the initial purpose of the handbill is to permit an explanation to outsiders as to why Jim is traveling with Huck, the duke, and the king, once the handbill reaches the public domain it increases the threat to Jim's freedom by making it *known* that he may be around. When Huck learns from a chance meeting with a boy who happens to have seen the handbill that Jim has been sold by the king, he obliquely challenges the credibility of the handbill's offer of a two-hundred-dollar reward with the comment: "Maybe there's something ain't straight about it" (268). Just how easily the printed lie has been swallowed, however, is revealed by the boy's response: "But it *is*, though—straight as a string. I see the handbill myself. It tells all about him, to a dot—paints him like a picture, and tells the plantation he's frum, below Newr*leans*. No-sir-ree-*bob*, they ain't no trouble 'bout *that* speculation, you bet you" (268). The boy's use of the word "speculation" rather than "information" accents the vacuous nature of the "knowledge" on which such unwavering conviction depends. But it is an awkward moment for Huck, since he cannot let it be known that *he* knows for certain that the boy's knowledge is seriously deficient.

Disinformation is also spread, and in a similar manner, by Tom Sawyer with his "nonnamous" letters, supposedly written by a member of a "gang of cutthroats." As with the duke's handbill, the "information" has the ring of truth about it and capitalizes on the limited knowledge available to its recipients. In each case the creator of the bogus document furnishes authenticity through the inclusion of partially genuine information while playing on powerful human motivating factors: the duke appealing primarily to greed; Tom adding fear for good measure.

Huck, too, is at the source of many spurious facts scattered throughout the novel. His descriptions of his life and background change with every telling, but the fictive knowledge usually satisfies the listener's desire to "know." We are thus given to understand that carefully framed falsehoods can often serve in conventional human interaction quite as well as truth, since most of Huck's listeners seem disposed to accept even a minimally plausible tale. In the rare cases where the boy is caught out, he never considers admitting to an untruth but simply shifts gears in order to come up with something more in tune with what the listener seems to expect. Huck is ever chary of sharing factual information about himself, and to keep others from knowing anything essential about him he regularly resorts to imaginative, deflective "knowledge" devoid of much truthful content—a method right down his "line." As he develops toward adulthood, he also continually practices and polishes his skills as a liar. In light of this fact, it would be difficult not to conclude that all that practice (which Levi Bell has suggested he needs) will one day lead to his no longer lying "pretty awkward" but to perfecting the fine art of spreading disinformation. Considering what such perfection could ultimately produce, it would not seem completely out of the question that, in line with Jim's prediction, he might indeed be hung one day "down in de bills."

Mark Twain's deft appeal to the dramatic possibilities inherent in the classic structural device involving what is known or not known, by whom, and at what point adds yet another dimension to his treatment of knowledge in the novel. The fact, for example, that Huck is "dead" for most of the book and that Jim and later Tom are therefore shocked and skeptical about Huck's existence when they meet up with him following his "death" produces tense as well as humorous situations on the basis of the reader's foreknowledge of the actual state of affairs. Each of the major characters in the book, beginning with Huck and including Tom, the king, the duke, and Jim, more than once displays his skills in the art of withholding important information, thereby creating numerous possibilities for suspenseful variations on a theme. Twain, in addition, shows no hesitation about employing this dramatic device, *without* the reader's full awareness of the situation, in scenes such as the one concerned with the supposed tattoo on the body of Peter Wilks. Tension in that case is provided by our not knowing which, if either, set of alleged Wilks brothers knows the truth about the tattoo. It is Twain himself, however, who has the last laugh through failing to provide us with any further knowledge. The issue thus remains unresolved, and we are treated as if we belonged to the unruly cluster of curious citizens who are blinded by the sudden reappearance of the gold while crowding around Wilks's coffin trying to catch a glimpse of the truth. Twain, meanwhile, manages to slip from our grasp with the same agility shown by his hero and escape along with him down the road into the dark, leaving the question forever open.

Another situation where the reader is prepared for a later revelation that never fully materializes ensues when Jim recognizes pap's corpse in the drifting house but reveals the truth neither to Huck nor, via any other conduit, to the reader. If, as Franklin R. Rogers suggests, the denouement of the novel, as originally conceived by Twain, was to coincide with the Shepherdson-Grangerford feud section of the book and probably involve a trial in which Jim was to be accused of the murder of pap,[18] the withholding of Jim's knowledge would have served the purpose of preparing the reader for a highly dramatic revelation at the proper moment. In the novel as published, however, pap's death is revealed at the end of the Evasion section, with much of the original potential for drama sacrificed, since at that point no question of Jim's possible implication in the murder is raised and no trial is threatened. What Twain himself apparently did not know at the time he wrote the drifting-house scene therefore appears to have had major consequences for the novel as we know it, and the author's regular return to the subject of knowing only underlines his sensitivity to the dramatic importance of this theme.

Adventures of Huckleberry Finn can thus serve as a commentary on how knowledge is acquired, effectively processed and applied, or dangerously restricted. Huck, as protagonist, repeatedly finds himself in the presence of others who believe they possess knowledge superior to his yet betray ignorance rooted in arrogance or self-erected barriers to learning or perception. Nor could Twain's novel be as powerful as it is had the boy himself been portrayed as immune to these common failings of humanity. The reader is encouraged in this manner to discover along with Huck that tolerance toward external influences is key to meaningful maturation. And by not having Huck grow up, Mark Twain avoids placing a time limit on how long the doors to education should remain open. The author's subsequent writings illustrate that his own multidimensional engagement with knowledge and knowing did not come to a close with the publication of Huck's novel, while the fundamental questions he consistently posed were ones that have long troubled sentient human beings attempting to establish an unshakable hold on "reality" in a world not always balancing distinctly or predictably between dream and daylight.[19] They are the questions with which a freshly awakened Jim confronts Huck after a bewildering and terrifying night in an impenetrable fog: "Is I *me*, or who *is* I? Is I heah, or whah *is* I? Now dat's what I wants to know" (103).[20]

NOTES

Preface

1. Posner, *Hitler's Children*, 11–24.
2. Ibid., 23.

Introduction

1. Schlesinger, "Schlesinger's Syllabus," 34.
2. Howells, *My Mark Twain*, 101.

1. A New Birth of Freedom

1. Twain, *Adventures of Huckleberry Finn*, ed. Blair and Fischer. Hereafter, page references to this work will appear parenthetically in the text.

2. Hemingway, *Green Hills of Africa*, 22.

3. It is probably impossible to know Twain's intentions as he began to write *Huckleberry Finn*, but mentioning the already widely known and loved earlier novel in the first sentence of the first chapter of his new work and referring shortly thereafter to its conclusion effectively gave the new book a respectable imprimatur and in all likelihood lulled most readers into thinking that what they were getting was simply a sequel to *Tom Sawyer*.

4. On 9 August 1876 Twain informed William Dean Howells that it was "a month ago" when "[I] began another boys' book. . . . It is Huck Finn's Autobiography." (Smith and Gibson, eds., *Mark Twain–Howells Letters*, 1:144. Hereafter this work will be referred to as *MTWH*.) Twain's concern with the appearance of his work found him worrying to Charles L. Webster on 7 May 1884 that the mouth of the boy in one of the illustrations was "a trifle more Irishy than necessary" (Webster, ed., *Mark Twain, Business Man*, 253). Not long thereafter he also complained that "the frontispiece has the usual blemish—an ugly, ill-drawn face. Huck Finn is an exceedingly good-hearted boy, & should carry a good & good-looking face" (24 May 1884, in ibid., 255–56). Twain also permitted his wife, Olivia, to "expergate" the novel, to use the term of their daughter Susy (Clemens, *Papa*, 188), though Bernard DeVoto maintains that Olivia's work did not seriously harm the

book (*Mark Twain at Work*, 82) and allowed Howells to correct the proofs (see Fischer, "Textual Introduction," in Twain, *Adventures of Huckleberry Finn*, ed. Blair and Fischer, 432–514, for a careful explanation of Howells's role). See also Beverly R. David's description of the care Twain accorded the checking and editing of each illustration, being "perfectly aware that what his 'genteel' audience saw in the illustrations would shape their reading of the story and that the illustrations would manipulate the responses of his readers" ("The Pictorial *Huck Finn*," 334).

5. For a discussion of a possible source for Mark Twain's attitude on this subject, see Cummings, "The Commanding Presence of Formerly Enslaved Mary Ann Cord."

6. Everett Carter has claimed that "if Mark Twain has seemed America's most 'national' writer, Huckleberry Finn and his adventures have seemed so indigenous that to understand him and them is to understand Americans" ("The Modernist Ordeal of Huckleberry Finn," 170).

7. See Adams, "The Unity and Coherence of *Huckleberry Finn*," 102. It is my hope that this chapter will contribute to answering Adams's implied question as to the source of "the effect of unity which readers generally feel in *Huckleberry Finn*, but which we are now only beginning to understand and be able to explain" (103) and will provide a partial response to the following observation by Louis J. Budd: "Like other great novels *Huckleberry Finn* has been reinterpreted whenever fashions in ideas have changed. Yet nobody has given a convincing reason why, in spite of many flaws even before the weak ending, it so clearly outshines *Tom Sawyer* as well as their several sequels" (*Mark Twain: Social Philosopher*, 105).

8. Taken from the Lee copy, as quoted in Becker, *The Declaration of Independence*, 175.

9. Ibid., 212–13.

10. Twain, "To the Muscatine *Journal* 4 December 1853, Philadelphia, Pa.," in *Letters: Volume 1*, 30. Twain was seriously interested in the history of the country and visited many of the sites connected with the founding of the United States during his stay in Philadelphia, as his letters and articles sent from there confirm. That the Declaration of Independence and the history surrounding it impressed Twain is indicated by the fact that he mentions Jefferson's document on several different occasions. By February 1854 Twain had moved on to Washington, D.C., where he visited the Patent Office on his second day in the city and viewed "the original Declaration of Independence" (Twain, "To the *Muscatine Journal*," 17–18 February 1854, in ibid., 42).

11. *MTWH*, 1:144.

12. Twain to "Dear Mother Fairbanks," in *Mark Twain to Mrs. Fairbanks*, 199.

13. *MTWH*, 1:140.

14. Ibid., 1 : 141 n. 2. Twain's strong interest in the country's centennial celebrations is also indicated in a letter he sent Mrs. Fairbanks the previous year: "I went to Boston & staid 3 days, at a fearful expense of valuable time, to see the Concord Centennial, but it did not come there—so all *that* was lost" (*Mark Twain to Mrs. Fairbanks*, 191–92).

15. Ibid.

16. Twain to "Dear Mother Fairbanks," in *Mark Twain to Mrs. Fairbanks*, 202.

17. Twain was offering the reader a laugh at an old tradition. Not only had he himself been delivered by a doctor whose first two names were Thomas Jefferson (see explanatory notes 329.9–11 in Twain, *Adventures of Huckleberry Finn*, ed. Blair and Fischer, 421), but he had used the name in humorous travel letters (see Twain, *The Adventures of Thomas Jefferson Snodgrass*, ed. Honce). In the context of the period during which Twain was writing his novel, however, the names take on added significance.

The inverted mention of Benjamin Franklin's name would, in addition, lend support to Richard S. Lowry's contention that "beginning with its characterization of an illiterate boy writing his own 'autobiography,' to use Twain's working title for his novel, . . . the narrative enacts a parody of Benjamin Franklin's *Autobiography* and constitutes Twain's most profound entry in his own autobiography of authorship" (*Littery Man*, 14).

18. Fatout, ed., *Mark Twain Speaking*, 569–71.

19. In *"Huckleberry Finn" as Idol and Target*, Jonathan Arac faults Twain for "omitting treatment of the Fourth of July from *Huckleberry Finn*" (55). My findings demonstrate that his contention is without foundation.

20. "Appendix A" in Twain, *Adventures of Huckleberry Finn*, ed. Blair and Fischer, C-5, 741, 753.

21. Quoted by Budd in "The Recomposition of *Adventures of Huckleberry Finn*," 113–29; reprinted in Champion, ed., *The Critical Response to Mark Twain's "Huckleberry Finn"*, 200.

22. Twain wrote Francis E. Bliss from Vienna on 31 March 1899 that "Mrs. Clemens wants some *more* new copyright matter added—viz., a brief biographical sketch of me. So I stopped writing this letter to jot down a skeleton for it. She wants this skeleton to be handed to my nephew Samuel E. Moffett editor of the New York Journal & she wants him to put it in his own language, & add to it or elaborate it, according to his judgment" (by permission of the Mark Twain House, Hartford, Conn.). At the top of the first page of the manuscript sketch appears the following comment: "[Mrs. Clemens wishes you to ask Sam Moffett, my nephew (editor New York Journal) to write the biographical sketch from these notes, & then she would like to see it before it is printed.] SLC" (by permission of the Berg Collection of

English and American Literature, the New York Public Library, Astor, Lenox and Tilden Foundations). Since corrections on pages 12 and 13 of the manuscript have been attributed to Mrs. Clemens (see Kaplan, *Mr. Clemens and Mark Twain*, 356, 409), Twain's claim that the manuscript was written at his wife's instigation may be genuine. The finished sketch was published under Samuel E. Moffett's name as "Mark Twain: A Biographical Sketch" in *Literary Essays by Mark Twain*, 314–33.

23. In a letter to Moffett dated 25 April 1899, Twain makes clear who will have the final say when he states:

Yes. Use the things you speak of. Also—if you don't mind—I would like to see your MS before you print. I find that I cannot *stand* things which I wrote a quarter of a century ago. They seem to have but two qualities, gush & vulgarity.

You must write the biographical sketch of me, *sure*—as per my recent letter to Bliss on the subject . . .

P.S. I would like *two* type-written copies of the Biographical Sketch—one to return to you revised. (Mark Twain Papers, Moffett Collection, Bancroft Library, University of California, Berkeley)*

24. Moffett, "Mark Twain" 329.

25. Howells, *My Mark Twain*, 101. The idea was picked up many years later by Bernard DeVoto, who further developed Howells's argument in his introduction to *The Portable Mark Twain*, where he stated:

There are striking affinities between Lincoln and Mark Twain. Both spent their boyhoods in a society that was still essentially frontier; both were rivermen. Both absorbed the midcontinental heritage: fiercely equalitarian democracy, hatred of injustice and oppression, the man-to-man individualism of an expanding society. Both were deeply acquainted with melancholy and despair; both were fatalists. On the other hand, both were instinct with the humor of the common life and from their earliest years made fables of it. As humorists, both felt the basic gravity of humor; with both it was an adaptation of the mind, a reflex of the struggle to be sane; both knew, and Mark Twain said, that there is no humor in heaven. It was of such resemblances that William Dean Howells was thinking when he called Mark Twain "the Lincoln of our literature." (5)

DeVoto also felt that "Lincoln expressed a culture and brought a type to climax. Similarly, when that culture found major literary expression it did so from a rich and various, if humble, literary tradition. As always, the literary expression was the later one; the economic, social and political impact was felt much earlier" (4). For Kenneth Lynn,

Twain became the "Lincoln of our literature," in Howells's beautiful phrase, only by transcending the limitations of a sectional outlook without betraying its strengths. His achievement as a literary artist was predicated on his becoming what Howells described as a "de-Southernized" Southerner. Like Lincoln, Twain reached greatness by growing beyond provinciality to a truly national stature—by becoming, in a word, an American. (*Mark Twain and Southwestern Humor*, 143)

26. Gale, *John Hay*, 125.

27. Clymer, *John Hay*, 12.

28. See ibid., 4, and Gale, *John Hay*, 45, in regard to the minor debate on the definitive date of the first meeting of Twain and Hay. It would seem, in this case, that Twain's own claim should be accepted, since Gale has apparently overlooked Clymer's reference to a letter, cited on page 9 of his work, where Twain is purported to have recalled an occasion when he and Hay "had been chatting and laughing and carrying on almost like our earlier selves in '67." For an extensive treatment of the question, see also footnote 3 in *Letters: Volume 4*, 292–93.

29. *MTWH*, 1:308–10. Howells forwarded Twain's letter to Hay, who returned it to Howells, saying, "I wish he and you would come down here and hold the first meeting of three at my house" (Letter of Hay to Howells, 24 May 1880, in *Letters of John Hay and Extracts from Diary*, 2:45).

30. Gale, *John Hay*, 54–55. From Twain's personal notebook for April–August 1885 we also learn that Twain wished John Hay "to write the first notices, to appear, say Dec 3 & Mch 3" for the *Personal Memoirs of U. S. Grant* that Twain was publishing (*Mark Twain's Notebooks and Journals: Volume III*, 160).

31. See footnote 1 in Dennett, *John Hay*, 79. See also Gale, *John Hay*, 54. It is known, in addition, that one of the ballads was of particular interest to Twain. "Jim Bludsoe, of the 'Prairie Bell,'" tells the tale of a brave steamboat captain who, when a fire breaks out, manages to save all on board except himself. Twain is reported to have written to Hay when the poem first appeared in the *New York Tribune* on 5 January 1871, pointing out that only a pilot and not an engineer could have accomplished the task (see Twain, *Letters: Volume 4*, 299–300). Another of Hay's ballads that may have caught Twain's attention is "Banty Tim. Remarks of Sergeant Tilmon Joy to the White Man's Committee of Spunky Point, Illinois," which recounts how Tim, a former Union soldier, stands up for the rights of an ex-slave who had saved his life during the Civil War (*Pike County Ballads and Other Poems*, 17–18).

32. Donald, in his *Lincoln's Herndon*, mentions an interesting sidelight on Twain's personal friendship with Hay. According to Donald, "Mark Twain's firm, Charles L. Webster & Co., publishers of Grant's *Memoirs* and many another historical bestseller, rejected the Herndon-Weik biography because the 'Life of Lincoln, by Gen-

eral Hay and Mr. Nicolay, will give the public all that they wish to know of Lincoln, just at present'" (312). Ironically, the Herndon-Weik biography of Lincoln turned out to be one of the most successful biographies ever published.

33. Douglass, *Life and Times*, 418.

34. Ibid.

35. See explanatory notes 33.33–34.1 in Twain, *Adventures of Huckleberry Finn*, ed. Blair and Fischer, 382; and *Mark Twain's Letters*, arranged with comment by Paine, 1:393–94.

36. In the fourth Lincoln-Douglas debate held on 18 September 1858, Lincoln made the following remarks:

> I will say then that I am not, nor ever have been in favor of bringing about in any way the social and political equality of the white and black races, [applause]—that I am not nor ever have been in favor of making voters or jurors of negroes, nor of qualifying them to hold office, nor to intermarry with white people; and I will say in addition to this that there is a physical difference between the white and black races which I believe will for ever forbid the two races living together on terms of social and political equality. And inasmuch as they cannot so live, while they do remain together there must be the position of superior and inferior, and I as much as any other man am in favor of having the superior position assigned to the white race. (*The Collected Works of Abraham Lincoln*, 3:145–46)

37. That Lincoln could not, however, bring himself to fully accept slavery may be seen in the following remarks also taken from the 18 September 1858 debate:

> I say upon this occasion I do not perceive that because the white man is to have the superior position the negro should be denied everything. I do not understand that because I do not want a negro woman for a slave I must necessarily want her for a wife. [Cheers and laughter.] My understanding is that I can just let her alone. I am now in my fiftieth year, and I certainly never have had a black woman for either a slave or a wife. So it seems to me quite possible for us to get along without making either slaves or wives of negroes. (Ibid., 146)

Lincoln also showed his dissatisfaction with slavery and gave clear indications of the liberal position he would adopt in the Gettysburg Address when on 15 October 1858 he quoted his own words from "more than a year ago" concerning the *Dred Scott* case, during the seventh debate with Douglas; he referred on that occasion to the Declaration of Independence:

> I think the authors of that notable instrument intended to include *all* men, but they did not mean to declare all men equal *in all respects*. They did not mean to say all men were equal in color, size, intellect, moral development or social capacity. They defined with tolerable distinctness in what they did consider all men created equal—equal in certain inalienable rights, among which are life,

liberty and the pursuit of happiness. This they said, and this they meant. They did not mean to assert the obvious untruth, that all were then actually enjoying that equality, nor yet, that they were about to confer it immediately upon them. In fact they had no power to confer such a boon. They meant simply to declare the *right* so that the *enforcement* of it might follow as fast as circumstances should permit.

They meant to set up a standard maxim for free society which should be familiar to all: constantly looked to, constantly approximated and thereby constantly spreading and deepening its influence and augmenting the happiness and value of life to all people, of all colors, everywhere. (Ibid., 301)

The key words here, I feel, are "liberty" and "free." It appears that when the chips were down, Lincoln simply could not avoid coming to grips with these words. Thus it would seem that the grain of sand that Jefferson had placed in the American oyster was irritating Lincoln seriously in 1857, at the time of the Dred Scott affair, and was slowly but surely growing toward the small pearl that would be placed before the world at Gettysburg. In repeating his own earlier comments on the *Dred Scott* decision, Lincoln underlined his deeply felt convictions about what the fathers had actually said as well as the fact that he himself could not escape the logic of their words and ideas.

38. The version used here will be the so-called Bliss copy. According to Mearns and Dunlap, "it represents Lincoln's last-known revision . . . [and] has become accepted as the standard text. . . . The Bliss copy is the only one dated and signed by President Lincoln" (*Long Remembered*, n.p.).

39. Barton, *Lincoln at Gettysburg*, 145.

40. Wills, *Lincoln at Gettysburg*, title page. I am indebted to Wills for the sharply focused argumentation found in his work that I can but point to in this section of my discussion.

41. Ibid., 145–47.

42. Barton, *Lincoln at Gettysburg*, 147.

43. Lowell, "On the Gettysburg Address," 88.

44. Wills, *Lincoln at Gettysburg*, 147.

45. On the title page of the novel Twain wrote: "Time: Forty to Fifty Years Ago." This date was apparently added shortly prior to the time of publication and not when Twain actually commenced writing (see explanatory note liii in Twain, *Adventures of Huckleberry Finn*, ed. Blair and Fischer, 372). The original date "forty years ago," counting backward from 1876, when the author began his book, would situate the action in the period around 1836, at a rather early stage of the antislavery movement. As a point of comparison, we may recall that William Lloyd Garrison began publishing his antislavery journal, the *Liberator*, on New Year's Day of 1831 and joined others in founding the American Anti-Slavery Society in 1833.

46. Rather early in the trip downriver Huck goes through a crisis of conscience before managing to tell two slave hunters that Jim is "white" (126), which would tend to indicate visible, *external* whiteness according to the parameters that those men would be most likely to apply. It takes the experiences that Huck goes through during the rest of the book, however, to bring him to understand Jim's *inner* "whiteness," as close to an open admission of equality as Huck manages in the book (341).

47. Twain emended his original manuscript at this point to include the words "and write just a little" lest the reader doubt Huck's ability to be the author of his own book (*Adventures of Huckleberry Finn*, introduction by Kaplan, foreword and addendum by Doyno, 367–68).

48. See Murphy, "Illiterate's Progress," 367.

49. Clerc's "Sunrise on the River" offers a perceptive exploration of many features of the paragraph describing this experience.

50. That Twain's paralleling of black and white appears to have been intentional may be seen from the fact that the manuscript for the book originally continued at this point with the words "& dressed about the same." The words were subsequently crossed out, probably in order to maintain subtlety. See *Adventures of Huckleberry Finn: A Facsimile*, 2:395 (ms. p. 468). A similar instance of omitted but conscious paralleling of the behavior of black and white is also found in the first portion of Twain's original manuscript where he describes the behavior at the camp meeting of a "fat nigger woman about forty": "Next, down she went in the straw, along with the rest, and wallowed around, clawing dirt and shouting glory hallelujah same as they did" (*Adventures of Huckleberry Finn*, introduction by Kaplan, foreword and addendum by Doyno, 179).

51. In this regard, it is also worth considering the following observations by Betty H. Jones:

> Huck's story springs from Mark Twain's anguished but loving look at his country. As Huck lights out for the Territory, he goes to inhabit a physical space that is but a parallel to his own new and expanded consciousness. The long sojourn on the river with Jim has allowed Huck to move beyond the empty abstraction of the word "nigger" to the recognition of a black man's humanity. Huck's transformation from boy to man, from one who accepts the dictates of a flawed social code to one who triumphantly aligns himself with the values of the natural world, represents Twain's best hope for a country that must give up its prolonged innocence and acknowledge the claims of history. In *Huckleberry Finn*, Twain challenges America to be better, to live up to its shining promise. ("Huck and Jim," 172)

52. Cox touches on this point in *Mark Twain: The Fate of Humor* when he indicates that Huck "is involved in a subversive project which has the reader's complete approval—the freeing of a slave in the Old South, a world which, by virtue of

the Civil War, has been declared morally reprehensible because of the slavery it condoned. Huck's rebellion is therefore being negotiated in a society which the reader's conscience indicts as morally wrong and which history has declared legally wrong" (169).

53. *MTWH*, 2:613.

54. Twain, "The Stupendous Procession," 413.

55. Ibid., 418.

56. Ibid., 419.

57. Ibid., 727.

58. Possible evidence of Twain's interest at the time he was writing *Huckleberry Finn* in more than one facet of Lincoln's thinking may be seen in the fact that one of the books apparently in his possession was McClure, ed., *Anecdotes of Abraham Lincoln and Lincoln's Stories.* See Baender, "Twainiana in Iowa." And that Twain's novel could lend itself—over fifty years following its initial publication—to publicly expressing Lincoln's idealism may be seen in the fact that in the 1939 film version of the book, Hollywood script writers created a new character, Captain Brandy, who openly mentions Lincoln's name in support of abolition and racial tolerance (*Adventures of Huckleberry Finn*, dir. Thorpe).

59. Fatout, *Mark Twain Speaking*, 383.

60. Ibid., 570. Jonathan Arac remarks with regard to the passage:
The very inaccuracies and tendentiousness of Twain's rhetorical gesture are important. He here echoed the New South ideological position that most slaveholders "did not want" their human property but held their slaves only out of responsibility to school and civilize this human "burden" passed on to them by their ancestors, and he still associated the Fourth of July with the freeing of slaves, completely forgetting both the actual date of the Emancipation Proclamation (1 January 1863) and the notorious fact that it did not actually free any slaves, since Emancipation applied only in areas that the Union did not control. (*"Huckleberry Finn" as Idol and Target*, 56)
Arac succumbs here to precisely the kinds of shortcomings he would wish to censure. Twain's associating "the Fourth of July with the freeing of slaves," for example, is legitimated by that date being indelibly linked with the words "all men are created equal," words to which slaves could appeal in their struggle toward ultimate freedom. Arac himself inadvertently substantiates this in recalling William Craft's mention of "the Bible and the Declaration of Independence as the authorities from which they [Craft and his wife] had heard, even as slaves, the principles of human equality that motivated them to resist their status as 'chattels'" (54).

More disturbing is that in charging Twain with "completely forgetting . . . the actual date of the Emancipation Proclamation (1 January 1863)," Arac fails to disclose key information that contradicts his thesis. Twain's speech, celebrating the

"Fourth of July . . . born in Philadelphia on the 4th of July, 1776," treated the Emancipation Proclamation as *generically equivalent* to what he considered to be *other* "Fourths of July" that "England gave to us," including the Magna Carta, the Bill of Rights drawn up "in Charles the First's time," and "that principle . . . no taxation without representation." Since none of those "Fourths" actually took place on a Fourth of July (the Magna Carta, for instance, was signed on 15 June 1215), there is no justification for Arac's accusation. Editing of a similar character occurs at the point where Twain proudly affirms, "We have, however, one Fourth of July which is absolutely our own, and that is the great proclamation issued forty years ago by that great American . . . Abraham Lincoln." Arac suppresses Twain's enthusiasm for Lincoln by expunging the words "that great American" from his citation (56).

What Arac labels a "notorious fact" and would also have Twain "forgetting" is, in reality, a quibble, since one of the purposes of Lincoln's wartime act was to sow doubt in Confederate ranks as to what slaves might do when they came to know that the government in Washington had proclaimed them free. By creating the fear of a threat from the rear, the president hoped to weaken the South's fighting spirit and ultimately produce a Northern victory that could lead to freedom for all persons of African descent. Moreover, as McPherson points out, "The old cliché, that the proclamation did not free a single slave because it applied only to the Confederate states where Lincoln had no power, completely misses the point. The proclamation announced a revolutionary new war aim—the overthrow of slavery by force of arms if and when Union armies conquered the South" (*Abraham Lincoln and the Second American Revolution*, 34). According to Oates, "word of the Proclamation hummed across the slave grapevine in the Confederacy; and as Union armies drew near, more slaves than ever abandoned farms and plantations and (as one said) 'demonstrated with their feet' their desire for freedom. . . . The Proclamation was not some anemic document that in effect freed no slaves. By November, 1864, the Philadelphia *North American* estimated that more than 1,300,000 Negroes had been liberated by Lincoln's Proclamation or 'the events of the war'" (*Abraham Lincoln*, 111–12).

One may challenge the military effectiveness of what Lincoln termed this "fit and necessary war measure for suppressing said rebellion," but his words regarding emancipation were unequivocal and eventually fulfilled, as Mark Twain was certainly not forgetting.

2. Frederick Douglass *in* Huckleberry Finn

1. See footnote 3 in *Letters: Volume 2*, 244. The Reverend Thomas K. Beecher also explained at the memorial service for Langdon that

at a time when opposition to slavery was costly, when it ruled a man not only out of his political party but out of his church and out of good society, and caused his children to be pointed at with a sneer; at a time when his business prospects must needs suffer, and even his personal property be endangered, Mr. Langdon was a pronounced and determined anti-slavery man.

Very few fugitives from slavery have passed through this region without receiving a benefit from him . . . [and when] slavery was abolished, Mr. Langdon's redoubled exertions in behalf of the now freed men were sufficient testimony that his previous zeal had not been a cheap destructiveness, rejoicing in judgments and denunciations, but a true and tender-hearted philanthropy. (*Jervis Langdon*, eulogy delivered on 21 August 1870, 27–28)

A slightly longer version of this quote may be more conveniently found in *Letters: Volume 4*, 182–83 n. 3.

2. According to footnote 2 of *Letters: Volume 3*, Langdon and his wife "had known Douglass since September 1838 when, while living in Millport, New York, they abetted his escape from slavery in Maryland" (428). The editors quote Douglass's 9 November 1870 letter to Olivia Langdon, following Jervis Langdon's death, in which he wrote, "Pardon me the Liberty, but as one who nearly thirty years ago, learned something of the noble character of your lamented Husband, I beg you to allow me to enroll myself among the many who to day hold his name and history in grateful memory. If I had never seen nor heard of Mr. Langdon since the days that you and himself made me welcome under your roof in Millport, I should never have forgotten either of you. Those were times of inefface[a]ble memories with me" (428).

In *The Courtship of Olivia Langdon and Mark Twain* Harris questions the conclusion drawn by Fischer and Frank: "the editors of the Library of America, which is editing both Twain's and Douglass's collected works, contend that Douglass was already lecturing for the abolitionists and that the Langdons put him up during one of his tours (discussion with Hannah Bercovitch, May 30, 1992)" (176 n. 8). Wherever the precise truth may lie, it is clear that the friendship between Douglass and the Langdons was of long duration and that Douglass was appreciative of the treatment he had received. This fact is supported by Harris in quoting Douglass's letter to the Langdons' son Charles recalling "the Millport episode and Olivia Lewis as 'one . . . who was kind and friendly to me when friends were few and foes were many.' Frederick Douglass, letter to Charles Langdon, August 9, 1880, Mark Twain Memorial, Hartford Connecticut" (Ibid.).

In *Lighting Out for the Territory*, Fishkin makes a strong circumstantial case for Twain—who was staying at Susan and Theodore Crane's Quarry Farm in Elmira at the time—being made aware of a visit and lecture by Douglass on 3 August 1880 primarily through newspaper coverage in the *Elmira Daily Advertiser* as well as through possible discussions concerning the event with John Lewis, a tenant-farmer at Quarry Farm and an active participant "in all the Douglass-related festivities" (94–97). Considering the timing of Douglass's letter to Charles Langdon, it is clearly possible that there may have been some connection with this event.

3. Twain, *Letters: Volume 3*, 426–27.

4. Twain to Olivia Langdon, 15 and 16 December 1869, in ibid., 426.

5. Twain to James A. Garfield, 12 January 1881, in *Mark Twain's Letters*, arranged with comment by Paine, 1 : 393–94.

6. See Blair, *Mark Twain and Huck Finn*, 323.

7. Quoted from explanatory notes 33.33–34.1 in Twain, *Adventures of Huckleberry Finn*, ed. Blair and Fischer, 382, which also draws on Baker, "Mark Twain and the Shrewd Ohio Audiences," 17, 28.

8. Fishkin also comes to this conclusion:

The final portion of *Huckleberry Finn* is increasingly coming to be understood as a satirical indictment of the virtual re-enslavement of free blacks in the South during the 1880s. It is quite likely that Frederick Douglass's acidic characterization of this phenomenon influenced Twain. . . . If Mary Ann Cord [the cook at Susan and Theodore Crane's Quarry Farm where Twain was writing his novel] brought the 1840s more clearly into focus with her story of being pulled from her child on the auction block, Frederick Douglass forced Twain to confront the fact that the promise of freedom for black Americans in the South in 1880 was being flagrantly betrayed. . . . As Twain struggled to complete *Huckleberry Finn*, the issues Douglass raised would take on more and more importance. (*Lighting Out for the Territory*, 97)

9. Douglass, *Narrative of the Life of Frederick Douglass*. Page references to this work will appear in the text. See also Douglass, *My Bondage and My Freedom*.

10. Douglass, *Life and Times*. This is the revised version of the work published in 1891, six years after the 1885 publication of *Adventures of Huckleberry Finn*.

11. The context in which this line occurs is strongly supportive of Douglass as a truth-teller, and "a fair specimen of the whole truth" is meant to refer to Douglass's description of the system of slavery itself. One can nevertheless see how a wag like Twain might play with such a line, especially in view of the opening words of *Huck*.

12. Baker, introduction to *Narrative of the Life of Frederick Douglass*, 19.

13. See Foner, introduction to *My Bondage and My Freedom*, viii. The man in question was Dr. James McCune Smith.

14. See explanatory notes 93.26–98.7 in Twain, *Adventures of Huckleberry Finn*, ed. Blair and Fischer, 391.

15. MacKethan, in "Huck Finn and the Slave Narratives," seems to have been the first to note the use of this exact phrase by both Twain and Douglass. MacKethan

expands considerably on Andrews's 1981 study "Mark Twain and James W. C. Pennington" and finds indications of Douglass's influence on *Huckleberry Finn* in chapters 16 (where the small-pox lie occurs), 17, and 31.

16. See "Appendix A," in Twain, *Adventures of Huckleberry Finn*, ed. Blair and Fischer, C-5.

17. In this same connection, MacKethan suggests that

when Huck tricks Buck Grangerford into helping him to remember the alias he invented when he arrived, he employs a strategy that duplicates one that Frederick Douglass devised. When Douglass was trying to get neighborhood children in Baltimore to teach him the alphabet, he would challenge them to spell certain words, and thus he would learn the shapes of letters. Huck tells us that when he woke up at the Grangerfords, "I had forgot what my name was," a predicament he solves easily by saying to Buck "I bet you can't spell my name." ("Huck Finn and the Slave Narratives," 262)

18. For a balanced handling of this subject, see Garvey, "Frederick Douglass's Change of Opinion on the U.S. Constitution." For an explanation by Douglass of his own position at the time, see *My Bondage and My Freedom*, 395–98.

19. Sundquist, "Mark Twain and Homer Plessy," 176–77.

20. Douglass, *My Bondage and My Freedom*, 115–16; Douglass, *Life and Times*, 62–63.

21. The surname Hicks is another used by both Douglass and Twain. Douglass describes a Mrs. Giles Hicks who escapes punishment after murdering a slave girl (*Narrative*, 68), while Twain in *Pudd'nhead Wilson*, his most explicit antislavery novel, mentions a William Hicks with whom he supposedly confers regarding legal issues (1). One may also be permitted to wonder in regard to names where the widow Douglas got hers.

22. Egan, *Mark Twain's "Huckleberry Finn,"* 38–45.

23. Twain, *Letters: Volume 3*, 126.

24. "Appendix A," in Twain, *Adventures of Huckleberry Finn*, ed. Blair and Fischer, A-11, 731.

25. Ibid., C-1, C-4, 751–52.

26. When Douglass revised and expanded his autobiography in 1881 and 1892, he recorded for posterity a more extensive account of the story that Twain related to Olivia. See *Life and Times*, 268–69.

27. Mark Twain, *Adventures of Huckleberry Finn*, introduction by Kaplan, foreword and addendum by Doyno, 167.

28. Ibid.

29. Douglass, "What to the Slave Is the Fourth of July?," 108–30; Andrews's introduction to ibid., 108; Douglass, *My Bondage and My Freedom*, 441–45.

30. Andrews, ed., *Frederick Douglass Reader*, 116.

31. Ibid., 118–19.

32. Ibid., 118.

33. For a helpful discussion of the connection between the forty dollars and Jim's own eight-hundred-dollar value, see Oehlschlaeger, "'Gwyne to Git Hung'," 121–22.

34. Howe also points to a scene in *Life on the Mississippi* that he feels parallels one from Douglass's *Narrative:* "When Bixby lends him [Twain] out to the abusive Brown, the cub's experience imitates the pattern modelled in Frederick Douglass' slave narrative. Twain recalls enduring Brown's abuse by day and dreaming of killing him by night. His antipathy climaxes when Brown's abuse of mud clerk Henry Clemens provokes Twain to intercede violently on his brother's behalf. Like Douglass' physical defiance of Mr. Covey, Twain's throttling of Brown fortifies his evolving personal strength" ("Transcending the Limits of Experience," 425).

3. *"Right" in* Huckleberry Finn

1. Parker, "A Sermon on the Dangers," 333–96. Further references to this work will appear parenthetically in the text.

2. See Chadwick, *A Life for Liberty*, 116; and Conway, *Autobiography, Memoirs and Experience*, 2:295.

3. See Sanborn, "Parker in the John Brown Campaign," 391–448; and Renehan Jr., *The Secret Six.*

4. Evidence of this reason for Lincoln's reticence may be seen in the letter that his law partner, William Herndon, sent to Parker from Springfield, Illinois, on 4 August 1857, in which he explains that "the reason why I wrote to you and said 'private' not long since was on Mr. Lincoln's account, not my own. Base politicians would charge *him* with sending you matter. That was the reason and that alone that made me say 'private'" (William H. Herndon–Theodore Parker Correspondence, Illinois State Historical Library, Springfield, Illinois).

5. See "Theodore Parker's Experience as a Minister," 2:346; Chadwick, *Theodore Parker, Preacher and Reformer*, 274–76; Theodore Parker to James Freeman Clarke, n.d., shelf mark bMS Am 1569.8 (70), Parker Collection, and Theodore Parker to Charles Sumner, 5 March 1854, shelf mark bMS Am 1.14 (4), no. 36, Sumner Collection, both by permission of the Houghton Library, Harvard University.

6. Kaplan, *Mr. Clemens and Mark Twain*, 77.

7. Gribben, *Mark Twain's Library*, 2 vols., 2:526. According to Gribben, the dates in question are "1869 or 1870."

8. Arac makes the claim that "the only person in the book to use the language of

'rights' is pap in his poisonous claims that his rights are violated by a 'govment'"
(*"Huckleberry Finn" as Idol and Target*, 55). By attempting to confine Twain simply
to "the *language* of 'rights'" (emphasis added), Arac effectively but unjustifiably
would ban any of Twain's other methods of treating his themes. However, even
within the unacceptably restrictive parameters Arac wishes to set, his claim proves
to be inaccurate. As my discussion illustrates, Mark Twain's approaches to questions
concerning rights encompass a much broader vision of the subject than Arac has
perceived.

9. Oehlschlaeger, "'Gwyne to Git Hung'," 120.

10. It bears mentioning here that Huck's position is well within the pale of John
Locke's view of natural right, as interpreted by Harry V. Jaffa:

> For example, because I have a right to life, I have a right to kill any man whom
> I have reason to believe might kill me. That is, I have no obligation to respect
> the other man's right to life until he has given me adequate pledges that he
> will not try to kill me. After I have received such a pledge I have an obligation
> to him. But I have this obligation then because, and only because, I have a
> prior concern to preserve myself. (*Crisis of the House Divided*, 324–25)

11. For a thorough treatment of this subject, see Sundquist, "Mark Twain and
Homer Plessy," *Representations*, 102–27.

12. The importance of literacy and writing to Twain's novel receives careful at-
tention from several critics, including the following: Murphy, "'Illiterate's Prog-
ress'"; Gordon, "'Fan-Tods "wid" de Samurai'"; Blakemore, "Huck Finn's Written
World"; Thomas, "Language and Identity in the *Adventures of Huckleberry Finn*";
Krauss, "Playing Double in *Adventures of Huckleberry Finn*"; and Doyno, "Literacy,
Copyright, and Books," in *Writing "Huck Finn"*.

Doyno comes closest to this aspect of my argument—and provides stimulus for
it—when he develops the idea that Twain's personal battle to have effective copyright laws adopted was strongly reflected in his approach to *Huckleberry Finn*.
Doyno maintains that the novel supposedly being written by young Huck, a novice
American author whose rights are constantly being infringed on, in particular by
two self-proclaimed members of European "royalty," makes a subtle but relevant
point about the rights of all authors (including Twain himself) who were not pro-
tected at the time by an encompassing international copyright law. The only safe-
guards available involved a complicated and costly procedure, which Twain was
forced to adopt. But, as Doyno points out, "Only with such a procedure could an
American author protect the 'rights' in what he 'writes' against 'pirates' eager to
steal his individually created 'royalties'" ("Literacy, Copyright, and Books," 189).

13. Jones, "Huck and Jim," 156.

14. Ibid., 159.

15. Wonham remarks in connection with the Raftsmen section of the novel that "Huck proves himself a worthy candidate for inclusion within the community of cultural insiders by nimbly distorting the truth with a yarn spinner's finesse . . . Yet despite his dexterity as a humorist . . . Huck is denied membership in the raftsmen's interpretive circle. . . . Throughout the rest of the novel, Huck never comes closer to a meaningful initiation than in this early episode" (*Mark Twain and the Art of the Tall Tale*, 154). It should be recalled here that the fourteen-year-old Huck, who symbolically arrives at and departs from the scene by immersing himself in the river, is completely naked in the midst of thirteen clothed and fully grown males. Despite his obvious vulnerability in such a situation, the boy coolly manages to hold his own both in tall-tale telling—when he claims to be Charles William Allbright, the subject of one of the raftsmen's wild tales—and in successfully hoodwinking the men into believing a false account of his background. While Huck neither becomes nor seems to wish to become a member of this circle, he nonetheless negotiates a rite of passage connected with survival among rough men. Nor will this be the last such rite in which he will participate. I would thus argue that although, as Wonham indicates, Huck does not join any particular social groupings, he does undergo on-going, meaningful initiation into a world of perceptive and sentient human beings.

16. Johnson, *Mark Twain and the Limits of Power*, 104.

17. As Gabler-Hover observes: "the desire for social change lies at the very heart of Twain's novel. . . . In *Adventures of Huckleberry Finn*, Twain's scrupulous attention to and judgment on the various reasons for deception show a careful social theorist at work trying to explain a culture's weaknesses to itself for the purpose of social change" (*Truth in American Fiction*, 134).

4. *Finishing* Huckleberry Finn

1. See Blair's introduction (xxiii–l), and Fischer, "Textual Introduction" (432–35), in *Adventures of Huckleberry Finn*, ed. Blair and Fischer.

2. See McPherson, *Ordeal by Fire*, 576–77; and Foner, *Reconstruction*, 553–56, 587.

3. Foner, *Reconstruction*, 504–5.

4. Ibid., 532.

5. McPherson, *Ordeal by Fire*, 576.

6. Foner, *Reconstruction*, 533.

7. Stampp, *The Era of Reconstruction, 1865–1877*, 140.

8. Kaplan, *Mr. Clemens and Mark Twain*, 121.

9. Grant told the American people:

The effects of the late civil strife have been to free the slave and make him a citizen. Yet he is not possessed of the civil rights which citizenship should carry with it. This is wrong, and should be corrected. To this correction I stand committed, so far as Executive influence can avail.

Social equality is not a subject to be legislated upon, nor shall I ask that anything be done to advance the social status of the colored man, except to give him a fair chance to develop what there is good in him, give him access to the schools, and when he travels let him feel assured that his conduct will regulate the treatment and fare he will receive. (Grant, "Second Inaugural Address")

10. Adopting a disdainfully didactic tone, Twain made his opinion of Sumner crystal clear to Orion, although the senator was mentioned only in passing:

If you like the idea of changing republican rule into democratic rule, go it! There is something enormously ludicrous about it—to me. Even colossal. To speak of going to hell to avoid our August heats, sounds feeble in its presence. If you will let me make a suggestion, it is this: the present era of incredible rottenness is not democratic, it is not republican, it is *national.* This nation is not reflected in Charles Sumner, but in Henry Ward Beecher, Benjamin Butler, Whitelaw Reid, W^m. M. Tweed. *Politics* are not going to cure moral ulcers like these, nor the decaying body they fester upon. (Clemens to "My Dear Bro," Hartford, 27 March [1875], Mark Twain Papers, Bancroft Library, University of California, Berkeley)*

11. Smith and Gibson, eds., MTWH, 1:144.

12. Letter from Twain to Conway, Elmira, 1 August 1876, in *Mark Twain's Letters to His Publishers, 1867–1894*, 103.

13. MTWH, 1:144.

14. Twain to "Dear Mother," Hartford, 14 September [1876], in *Mark Twain to Mrs. Fairbanks*, 202; MTWH, 1:141 n. 2.

15. Fishkin also reflects on this subject in *Was Huck Black?*, 69–75.

16. McPherson, *Ordeal by Fire*, 595.

17. Williams, *The Life of Rutherford Birchard Hayes*, 1:462.

18. MTWH, 1:142.

19. Ibid., 1:143.

20. Franklin, *Reconstruction after the Civil War*, 202. The downhill slide actually can be seen to have begun at the start of Hayes's administration with his inaugural address, in which he stated:

while in duty bound and fully determined to protect the rights of all by every constitutional means at the disposal of my Administration, I am sincerely anxious to use every legitimate influence in favor of honest and efficient local *self*-government as the true resource of those States for the promotion of the contentment and prosperity of their citizens. In the effort I shall make to accomplish this purpose I ask the cordial cooperation of all who cherish an interest in the welfare of the country, trusting that party ties and the prejudice of race will be freely surrendered in behalf of the great purpose to be accomplished. (Hayes, "Inaugural Address," 4396)

In shifting the responsibility for guaranteeing the rights of ex-slaves away from Washington and onto local governments, Hayes opened wide the door to all those who had an interest in not living up to the trust with which he was seemingly investing them. It is difficult today to imagine "party ties and the prejudice of race" being "freely surrendered" under the circumstances prevailing at the time, and one wonders how many in Hayes's audience managed to suppress a smirk upon hearing the president's words.

21. Twain would finally complete his revisions in April 1884. See Fischer, "Textual Introduction," in Twain, *Adventures of Huckleberry Finn*, ed. Blair and Fischer, 435.

22. *MTWH*, 1:435.

23. Letter from Clemens to Glück, 12 November 1885, cited in Fischer, "Textual Introduction," in Twain, *Adventures of Huckleberry Finn*, ed. Blair and Fischer, 433. This letter is presently located in the Buffalo and Erie County Public Library in Buffalo, New York.

24. Blair, introduction to *Adventures of Huckleberry Finn*, ed. Blair and Fischer.

25. See Fishkin, *Was Huck Black?*

26. According to Foner,

Joseph P. Bradley, whose vote on the Electoral Commission had made Hayes President, wrote the majority opinion, which observed that blacks must cease "to be the special favorite of the laws." The only dissenter was Kentucky's John Marshall Harlan. The United States, he warned, had entered "an era of constitutional law, when the rights of freedom and American citizenship cannot receive from the nation that efficient protection which heretofore was unhesitatingly accorded to slavery." (*Reconstruction*, 587)

27. Foner crystallizes the point by quoting from *The Nation* of 18 October 1883: "The general approval that greeted the decision, observed *The Nation*, revealed 'how completely the extravagant expectations' aroused by the Civil War had 'died out'" (ibid., 587).

28. Budd, *Mark Twain*, 106. Budd also stated as much even earlier in "The Southward Currents under Huck Finn's Raft," 237. Others who have subsequently mentioned or developed aspects of this idea include Brown, "*Huckleberry Finn* for Our Time"; Schmitz, "Twain, *Huckleberry Finn* and the Reconstruction"; Carrington Jr. in his afterword to *The Dramatic Unity of "Huckleberry Finn"*, 189–92; Gollin and Gollin, "*Huckleberry Finn* and the Time of the Evasion"; Nilon, "The Ending

of *Huckleberry Finn*"; Beaver, *Huckleberry Finn*, 37–45; and Fishkin, *Was Huck Black?*.

29. Berkove, however, would not seem to hold out much hope for a successful conclusion to Huck's quest. According to Berkove, "Twain in *Huckleberry Finn* achieves the artistic highpoint in his lifelong appeal to his fellowman to be aware of how desperately far he is from any condition deserving the name of freedom" ("The 'Poor Players' of *Huckleberry Finn*," 310).

30. See ibid. for a thorough treatment of a number of Jim's possible options (307–8).

31. It is also evident that Tom, too, feels this way, for, as Nilon remarks: "Even at the end, Tom shows little concern for what Jim might want to do with his life once he is free, and no regard for him as a person. His assumption that he can simply pay Jim forty dollars for his trouble underscores this" ("The Ending of *Huckleberry Finn*," 27). And Myra Jehlen observes: "When in the end Jim too is freed, this further frees Huck, for Jim's reenslavement would have embroiled his friend in continuing guilt. Freed through no act either of his own or of Huck's, Jim embroils Huck in neither history nor future obligation" ("Banned in Concord," 103). Forrest G. Robinson even goes so far as to make the claim that "it appears that in lighting out Huck is as much in flight from Jim as he is from the civilization that shackles them both," also noting that Huck "makes no place for Jim in his plans for 'the Territory'" (*In Bad Faith*, 118, 181).

32. Brown, "*Huckleberry Finn* for Our Time," 43.

33. Cecil, "The Historical Ending of *Adventures of Huckleberry Finn*," 281–82.

34. Ibid., 282.

35. See Blair, introduction to *Adventures of Huckleberry Finn*, ed. Blair and Fischer, xlv.

36. Twain, *Mark Twain's Notebooks and Journals: Volume III*, 19. As the editors point out, Twain also "described his new enthusiasm to Howells on 20 July 1883" (19 n. 37).

37. Martin Luther King Jr. displayed full awareness of the significance of the double centenary when on 28 August 1963 he stood on the steps of the Lincoln Memorial in Washington, D.C., to deliver his "I Have a Dream" speech. The second sentence of that address echoes the opening of the Gettysburg Address in referring to Lincoln and the Emancipation Proclamation: "Fivescore years ago, a great American, in whose symbolic shadow we stand today, signed the Emancipation Proclamation" ("I Have a Dream," 218). Although King was obliged to recognize that despite Lincoln's efforts "one hundred years later, the Negro still is not free," and that "nineteen sixty-three is not an end, but a beginning," he nonetheless clung to "a dream deeply rooted in the American dream . . . that one day this nation

will rise up and live out the true meaning of its creed, 'We hold these truths to be self-evident, that all men are created equal'" (ibid.).

38. Twain, *Mark Twain's Notebooks and Journals: Volume III*, 88. The editors explain that "Clemens marked with an X passages that refer to or recount anecdotes or that sketch ideas for stories" (65). This passage is marked with a doubled X, one of the three forms used, the others being a single X and #.

39. Ibid.

40. The significance of these two numbers is examined in chapters 7 and 8.

41. Benardette concludes that "apparently, by accepting legal freedom, Jim has implicitly agreed to countenance all other conventions of his society; thus, in exchange for the loss of his time as a free man, he takes money like any wage-slave" ("*Huckleberry Finn* and the Nature of Fiction," 223).

42. In 1896, only a little over a decade following the publication of Twain's novel, the United States Supreme Court would confer on that assumption what amounted in practice to the blessing of legality in writing its decision on "equal but separate accommodations for the white, and colored races" in the case of *Plessy vs. Ferguson* (cited in Lockhart, Kamisar, and Choper, *Constitutional Rights and Liberties*, 828).

43. Gabler-Hover notes that Huck's "emotional honesty is at odds with his intellectual awareness and certainty about the truth of the social codes. . . . When committed to truth, in a world where any action seems to be both a truth and a lie, one's only recourse is inaction" (*Truth in American Fiction*, 147).

44. While I have dealt in this chapter with what I believe were influences exerted on Twain by changes in the political climate during the writing of *Huckleberry Finn*, Robert Sattelmeyer makes a cogent case for the influence on the second half of the novel—beginning with chapter 22—of the ideas of Darwin, Taine, and Lecky. According to Sattelmeyer, these ideas produced "internal change" in Twain's thinking that led to a radical change in his approach to the last half of his work:

> The significant difference between the two halves, then, is that the quest for escape and freedom in the first half was conceived and executed under the influence of mythic analogues that made the quest meaningful and important. Human action and individual responsibility attained weight and significance by acquiring mythic dimensions. In the second half of the novel, however, the system of belief that had undergirded these mythic patterns, and from which the corresponding images had arisen, had been succeeded in Twain's imagination by a kind of despondent materialism that could still see suffering and corruption but could not assign to that suffering or struggle any purpose. . . . If the potential of the Bible and religious tradition to help Huck and Twain impose meaning and order on experience was at best a possibility that was interesting, but tough, the new order of things offered even fewer clues to an

eighteenth-century sensibility projected into the twentieth century, where the world itself didn't say why. ("Interesting, but Tough," 368, 370)

45. It is Henry Nash Smith's view that

In analyzing Huck's debate with his conscience we must take into account yet other feelings that in the 1880s were inevitably called into play for Americans by the topic of slavery. These were related to the complacency that had come to permeate public discourse in the North during the fifteen or twenty years since Appomattox—years during which the articulate spokesmen for the society had developed retroactively a set of war aims and a conception of how the war had been fought, an ideology designed—consciously or unconsciously—to console the victorious section for the half-million casualties it had suffered in the war and for the conspicuous collapse of high-minded Reconstruction policies during the subsequent decade. The emotions clustering around these topics were so strong that an extraordinary effort would have been required to resist their contagion. And Samuel Clemens was not disposed to resist. He surrendered uncritically to the mood of the New England society in which he had chosen to live. (*Democracy and the Novel*, 114)

5. Huck and Jim on the Mississippi

1. Rogers, *Mark Twain's Burlesque Patterns*, 129.

2. Ibid., 135–36.

3. Twain's spelling of Illinois as Illinoi would seem to have at its root the fact that the word is *seen* to be spoken by Jim, and can thus be considered eye dialect. Since the *s* in Illinois is silent, however, there would appear to be no other justification for this misspelling.

4. See Gribben, *Mark Twain's Library*, 1:180–82.

5. In line with the theme of death by water, it is of tangential interest here that the hero of Emmeline Grangerford's poem "Ode to Stephen Dowling Bots, Dec'd" also undergoes death by drowning; in that case, however, the culprit is a well he falls into and not the Mississippi.

6. See explanatory notes 14.24–25 in Twain, *Adventures of Huckleberry Finn*, ed. Blair and Fischer, for Twain's possible source for this belief, as well as for Dr. Alvin Tarlov's statement concerning his observation of the fact that the bodies of "men, women, boys and girls—they all float face down."

7. See ibid., 46.3–4. It is also worth noting that on page C-3 of Mark Twain's working notes for *Huckleberry Finn* ("Appendix A," in Twain, *Adventures of Huckleberry Finn*, ed. Blair and Fischer, 739, 752), there is a clear indication that Twain was fully conscious of the potential of having bread "cast upon the waters" serve a

purpose in his novel: "And bread cast *returns*—which it don't & can't, less'n you heave it upstream—you ~~let~~ ˎcastˎ your bread downstream once, & see. It can't stem the current; so it can't come back no more. But the widow she didn't know no better than to believe it, & it warn't my business to correct my betters. There's a heap of ignorance like that, around." The editors' comment on Twain's note points out: "This note suggests that Mark Twain considered revising or expanding the passage in chapter 8, where Huck eats the bread that has been set afloat to find his corpse and reflects on the efficacy of prayer" (45.27–47.7 [752]). It might be added that from all indications the speaker of the first-quoted passage is clearly Huck.

8. Trilling, introduction to *Adventures of Huckleberry Finn*, xvi.

9. Twain's working notes for his novel reveal other destructive displays he had planned for the river: in the notes for A-6 we find "An overflowed Arkansaw town. River booms up in the night," and on page B-2 we read "(overflowed banks?)" ("Appendix A," in Twain, *Adventures of Huckleberry Finn*, ed. Blair and Fischer, 728, 735).

10. Andrew Solomon suggests in regard to the "Sollermun" debate that Jim's words here are as much an act of mutiny as running away from Miss Watson was, and the penalty could have been, in fact, just as severe. Jim has now started to break his psychological enslavement, just as he had recently broken from physical enslavement; the importance of this break must not be ignored. It could even be argued that the black man's severing of the identification with a Biblical Hebrew, an identification based on their mutual slavery, is in itself his first step toward psychological freedom. ("Jim and Huck," 21)

11. See Oehlschlaeger, "'Gwyne to Git Hung,'" 124–25.

6. *Reflections on* Huckleberry Finn's *Floating House*

1. In Twain's working notes for his novel, we find "Huck's father in floating house—62—64—70" ("Appendix A," *Adventures of Huckleberry Finn*, ed. Blair and Fischer, C-1, 751). The chapter heading for chapter 9 (with which Twain apparently had little to do) reads "The Cave—The Floating House" (lix). The "House of Death," therefore, does not seem to be a designation either used or approved by Twain.

2. See Brown, "*Huckleberry Finn* for Our Time," 45–46; Weaver and Williams, "Mark Twain's Jim"; Cox, "A Hard Book to Take," 391; and Robinson, "The Characterization of Jim in *Huckleberry Finn*," 365.

3. Weaver and Williams, "Mark Twain's Jim," 27; Robinson, "The Characterization of Jim," 369.

4. Murphy, "Illiterate's Progress," 368; quote from Doyno, "Textual Adden-

dum," in Twain, *Adventures of Huckleberry Finn*, introduction by Kaplan, foreword and addendum by Doyno, 376.

5. Page 217 of the original manuscript, located in the Buffalo and Erie County Public Library, Buffalo, N.Y. My thanks to William H. Loos, curator of the Grosvenor Rare Book Room at the Buffalo and Erie County Public Library, for graciously providing access to a photocopy of the original manuscript.

6. See Steinbrink, "Who Wrote *Huckleberry Finn*?," 100.

7. Brown, "*Huckleberry Finn* for Our Time," 45.

8. Doyno, "Textual Addendum," in Twain, *Adventures of Huckleberry Finn*, introduction by Kaplan, foreword and addendum by Doyno, 407.

9. Ibid., 377.

10. This inadvertent windfall of "truck" is all the inheritance Huck will ever receive from his father, but some of the items will prove vitally important for the boy and his companion.

11. Manuscript, 221.

12. T. S. Eliot, introduction to *The Adventures of Huckleberry Finn*, by Mark Twain, xi.

13. Budd, "The Recomposition of *Adventures of Huckleberry Finn*," in *The Critical Response to Mark Twain's "Huckleberry Finn*," 203.

14. A sidelight to this discussion of amputees is the fact that, at a later stage of the novel, Tom Sawyer considers making Jim himself an amputee by cutting off his leg. Fortunately, Tom forgoes that measure, finally deciding that "there ain't necessity enough in this case; and besides, Jim's a nigger and wouldn't understand the reasons for it, and how it's the custom in Europe; so we'll let it go" (300).

15. Manuscript, 221.

7. *The Figure Forty in* Huckleberry Finn

1. Pascal Covici Jr., for example, carefully examines the three appearances of the forty-dollar figure and draws parallels between the novel and Twain's short story "The Man that Corrupted Hadleyburg." Underlining the importance of the link between money and what he terms "sensation," Covici suggests that "the $40,000 in the story of Hadleyburg reminds one in more than simply a numerical way of the ubiquitous $40 in *Huckleberry Finn* . . . The emphasis that Twain puts on these sums of money leads one to contemplate society's love of sensation, to marvel at some people's attempts to substitute cold cash for love, and to recoil in disgust from man's disloyalty to man" (*Mark Twain's Humor*, 208). In Covici's view, it is "no wonder, then, that Twain's characters so often come to grief through a desire for thrills as well as for cash" (212), but he finds Huck distinguished from many of the

other characters in the book through not being "at all eager to exchange silver for sensation" (211). Daniel G. Hoffman preceded Covici in mentioning the three appearances of the forty-dollar figure in connection with loyalty but limited his effort to linking Tom's action in offering Jim forty dollars with the king and duke's earlier sale of Jim. For Hoffman, "All three payments are guilt-money for the betrayal of loyalties. Tom's payment comes last and its meaning is signified by the preceding incidents" (*Form and Fable in American Fiction*, 329 n. 4).

Victor A. Doyno approaches the forty-dollar figure from a markedly different angle, drawing attention to the fact that Twain added the brief section concerning the forty dollars Jim receives from Tom Sawyer only "when revising the *Huck Finn* manuscript for typesetting" ("Over Twain's Shoulder," 3). He offers the following explanation as to "Why 'forty dollars'?":

> This question may best be answered by considering the other uses of forty dollars in the novel. We remember that the two men who were searching for escaped slaves on the river each give Huck twenty dollar gold pieces and that later the Duke and the King get the same amount for Jim.
>
> The placing of these financial dealings reveals one important way in which the novel is structured. Twain created in *Huckleberry Finn* three parallel sequential patterns of action. Each pattern involves first the meeting of Huck with someone who thinks him dead, the formation or renewal of a partnership to free the slave which ends in failure, and finally, the exchange of forty dollars. (3–4)

Doyno's conclusion is that with Tom's gift of forty dollars to Jim "the pattern was completed; the keystone was dropped into place. Since this final payment is both conscience money in substitution for a moral obligation and payment received for an illegal enslavement, the insertion also recapitulates the comparable parts of the previous patterns" (6). And for Doyno, "the form of the work suggests another meaning. The repetition of the pattern . . . indicates that although the struggle to win freedom is ultimately unsuccessful, the attempt is continual, cyclic" (6–7).

Thomas Werge anticipates Doyno's three-step approach in dealing in order of appearance with the slave hunters, the king and the duke, and finally Tom Sawyer as sources of forty-dollar amounts connected with Jim's freedom, but he sees Tom's gift to Jim in quite a different light: "The forty dollars is freely given and freely accepted, and this act of generosity recalls and reaffirms Huck's values while denying those predatory hunters whose lust for money is surpassed only by their absolute moral corruption" ("Huck, Jim and Forty Dollars," 15–16).

Another writer who mentions the three occurrences of the forty-dollar amount is Arthur G. Pettit, who suggests: "Probably the figure became fixed in Mark Twain's mind through repetition, but it happens to coincide with the price Marshall

Clemens got for selling his slave Charley in 1842" (*Mark Twain and the South,* 204 n. 19).

The forty dollars offered for Charley are accorded further attention when Doyno returns to the question in *Writing "Huck Finn,"* 253–54 n. 4. In this work Doyno considers it "within the realm of possibility that at some deep psychological level this novel may have been influenced by memories of the father's action leading to the son's imaginative effort to free the slave and redemptively erase a family shame" (253–54). In addition, Doyno puts forward the novel idea that "in offering Jim, a freedman, "forty dollars for being prisoner for us so patient," Tom has created his own one-sided contract-labor device, perhaps resembling the convict-lease system, to exploit a fugitive/criminal just as whites exploited countless freedmen (254).

2. Others who have emphasized dollars as a recurrent theme in *Huckleberry Finn* include McMahan, "The Money Motif"; Taylor, "*Huckleberry Finn*"; and Slattery, "The Via Dollarosa."

3. Covici points out the Judas reverberation when he states: "First, and most clearly echoed in 'Hadleyburg,' is Huck's attitude toward the 'forty dirty dollars' . . . for which the king sold Jim. Judas' thirty pieces of silver come to mind, and in a sense all the citizens of Hadleyburg are ready to sell out the town's reputation for one thousand times the price of Jim. Huck's use of the word 'dirty' makes this overtone clear" ("The Man," 208).

Spencer Brown also refers to the possible connection with Judas in stating that "the forty dollars echoes the price the Duke and Dauphin sold Jim for—'forty dirty dollars'—marked up from thirty pieces of silver" ("*Huckleberry Finn* for Our Time," 45), and Robert Sattelmeyer adds slightly to the idea in declaring that "this incident would seem to echo the betrayal of Christ by Judas for money (Matthew says it was thirty pieces of silver, though the other evangelists do not specify an amount)" ("Interesting but Tough," 361). For Harold Beaver "it is the repetition of the sum that confirms the symbolic reckoning. It is a Judas sum for an intimate betrayal. First for the king; then from Tom. But Tom, by combining Southern histrionics with Southern treachery, is the ultimate Judas" (*Huckleberry Finn,* 115).

4. Twain, *Adventures of Huckleberry Finn: A Facsimile,* 1:266 (ms. p. 351). Twain also displayed familiarity with Judas (and the correct spelling of his name) in his notebook (#22, Spring 1883–September 1884), where in discussing his history game he suggests, "Judas Iscariot, Guiteau [the assassin of President James Garfield], Whitelaw Reid [the newspaper editor for whom Twain reserved a special distaste] . . . who gets either, loses 3 points. It is called being smirched" (*Mark Twain's Notebooks and Journals: Volume III,* 24). The pun on Judas's last name was very possibly borrowed from the humorist Artemus Ward (Charles Farrar Browne),

who used that precise misspelling twice in a short story called "A High-Handed Outrage at Utica," which appeared, many years prior to *Huckleberry Finn*, in *Artemus Ward His Book*, 34–35.

5. Pettit, *Mark Twain and the South*, 204.

6. See explanatory note liii in Twain, *Adventures of Huckleberry Finn*, ed. Blair and Fischer, 372, and also Fischer, "Textual Introduction," in ibid., 466.

7. In this same connection, it might also be noted that Twain's use of the story of Aladdin in chapter 3 links the figure forty to the book in another context, since according to Keene Abbott, a boyhood friend of Twain, "There was but one copy of the Arabian Nights in the village, and that volume was the property of Squire Clemens, Mark Twain's father. Sam knew all the stories. He could hire us, any day, to help him do his chores by merely a promise that as soon as we were done, he would give us the Forty Thieves or some other yarn" ("Tom Sawyer's Town," *Harper's Weekly* 9 August 1913: 17, as quoted in Twain, *Adventures of Huckleberry Finn*, ed. Blair and Fischer, 380–81).

8. *Adventures of Huckleberry Finn: A Facsimile*, 2 : 558 (ms. p. 632).

9. Ibid., 1 : 395 (ms. p. 468).

10. Twain, *Adventures of Huckleberry Finn*, introduction by Kaplan, foreword and addendum by Doyno, 63, 179, respectively.

11. In Doyno, "Over Twain's Shoulder," 3; and *Writing "Huck Finn,"* 245.

12. *Adventures of Huckleberry Finn: A Facsimile*, 2 : 716 (ms. p. 783).

13. For the English version, see *Adventures of Huckleberry Finn* (1884; London: Penguin, 1966), 368. The English and American versions of the text do not vary at this point.

14. In both "Over Twain's Shoulder" and *Writing "Huck Finn,"* Doyno points out the clearest example of this, which occurs in chapter 8, when Jim talks about the significance of his hairy arms and breast and his belief that he has been rich once and is going to be rich again.

15. See "Appendix A," in Twain, *Adventures of Huckleberry Finn*, ed. Blair and Fischer, C-3, 739, 752. Doyno first draws attention to this crucial piece of evidence in *Writing "Huck Finn,"* 249.

16. The repetition of the number also seems to have had a subconscious influence on the 1939 film version of the novel (starring Mickey Rooney), where mention is made of two of the Wilks brothers not having seen each other for forty years. Twain himself did not employ the number in that instance (*The Adventures of Huckleberry Finn*, dir. Thorpe.)

17. Blair, *Mark Twain & Huck Finn*, 88–89.

18. Twain, "The Facts Concerning the Recent Carnival of Crime," 645.

19. In *Mark Twain: Collected Tales, Sketches, & Essays, 1852–1890*, 661–66. In this

edition it bears the title *[Date, 1601.] Conversation, as It Was by the Social Fireside, in the Time of the Tudors.* See also Turner, "Mark Twain's '1601' through Fifty Editions," 10–15, 21.

20. DeVoto, ed., *Mark Twain in Eruption*, 206.

21. Ibid., 203–11.

22. Ibid., 207.

23. Kaplan, *Mr. Clemens and Mark Twain*, 196.

24. See Lynn, *Mark Twain and Southwestern Humor*, 243; Quirk, "Moses and the Bulrushers"; McCullough, "Uses of the Bible in *Huckleberry Finn*"; and Briden, "Huck's Great Escape."

25. Twain indicates his specific familiarity with this particular line when he cites it (in the abbreviated form "It rained forty days and forty nights") as the final example in a list of descriptions of weather offered for readers to choose from in the appendix to *The American Claimant*, 231.

26. All quotations in this chapter are taken from the King James Version of the Bible.

27. See Quirk, "The Legend of Noah and the Voyage of *Huckleberry Finn*."

28. Davis, "The Veil Rent in Twain," 84.

29. Light, "Paradox, Form, and Despair in *Huckleberry Finn*," 25.

30. Eric Foner explains that in mid-January 1865 General Sherman issued Special Field Order No. 15, setting aside the Sea Islands and a portion of the low country rice coast south of Charleston, extending thirty miles inland, for the exclusive settlement of blacks. Each family would receive forty acres of land, and Sherman later provided that the army could assist them with the loan of mules. (Here, perhaps, lies the origin of the phrase "forty acres and a mule" that would soon echo throughout the South.) (*Reconstruction*, 70–71)

Mark Mayo Boatner III avers that the phrase was a "legend that sprang up among the newly-freed slaves that the Federal government would give them portions of confiscated plantations. It is believed that this came from the division of lands by Sherman's army on the southeast coast in Jan. '65" (*The Civil War Dictionary*, 301). But there may have been an even earlier reason for the freedmen's hopes than Sherman's actions. Herman Belz points out that "the closest Congress came to promising land to the freedmen was the approval by the House in 1864 of a southern homestead bill which proposed to give outright forty or eighty acres of public land to Union soldiers and army laborers irrespective of color" (*Abraham Lincoln*, 156). When in the end neither land nor mule materialized, there was understandably widespread frustration and disappointment.

31. See Goodyear, "Huck Finn's Anachronistic Double Eagles."

32. Doyno, *Writing "Huck Finn,"* 254 n. 4.

33. "Appendix A," in Twain, *Adventures of Huckleberry Finn,* ed. Blair and Fischer, A-1, 714, 725.

34. In chapter 29, the king is described by Huck as "muleheaded," but this seems as close as Twain comes to creating a real mule for the story.

35. "Appendix A," in Twain, *Adventures of Huckleberry Finn,* ed. Blair and Fischer, C-1, 737, 751.

36. Frank Baldanza considers "that without advanced planning, and spurred by momentary impulses, Mark Twain—in all probability unconsciously—constructed whole passages of *Huckleberry Finn* on an aesthetic principle of repetition and variation" ("The Structure of *Huckleberry Finn,*" 350). For further discussion of the question of Twain's intentionality, see Robinson, "An 'Unconscious and Profitable Cerebration,'" which takes strong issue with Wonham's *Mark Twain and the Art of the Tall Tale;* see also the exchange of views between Wonham and Robinson to which Robinson's article gave rise ("Commentary," 137–41).

37. Twain told Charles Webster on 14 April 1884: "[Elisha] Bliss never issued with less than 43,000 orders on hand, except in one instance—& it usually took him 5 or 6 months' canvassing to get them"; he urged Webster to start "canvassing early, & drive it with all your might, with the intent & purpose of issuing on the 10th (or 15th) of next December (the best time in the year to tumble a big pile into the trade)—but if we haven't 40,000 orders then, we simply postpone publication till we've *got* them" (in Webster, ed., *Mark Twain, Business Man,* 248–49). On 23 May of the same year Twain repeated his plan to Webster and added: "Now let's never allow ourselves to *think* of issuing with any *less* than 40,000 while there's the ghost of a show to get them" (255).

The figure of $40,000 will, as noted by Covici (in "The Man"), play an important role in "The Man that Corrupted Hadleyburg." That novella was first published, however, in 1899, about fifteen years after the above exchange took place.

8. The End, Yours Truly Mark Twain

1. In "A Nobler Roman Aspect" Budd wrestles with the question of why Twain would have felt this kind of picture would be an appropriate addition to his book.

2. Webster, ed., *Mark Twain, Business Man,* 275–76.

3. Ibid., 276.

4. Ibid., 277.

5. See Blair, "Was *Huckleberry Finn* Written?," 3.

6. At some point during the creative process Twain apparently removed his own name from what appears, from an examination of the first half of the manuscript, to

have been his original working title for the book, "Huck,leberry, Finn/Reported by/Mark Twain" (see Twain, *Adventures of Huckleberry Finn*, introduction by Kaplan, foreword and addendum by Doyno, 389), a title that, at the very least, would have placed Twain, in Thomas Quirk's words, "in a rather definite relation to his created character" (*Coming to Grips with Huckleberry Finn*, 6). Why Twain altered that original working title is not clear, but whatever may have been his thinking at that moment, several hypotheses might be suggested for consideration. It is conceivable that Twain may have wanted, for obvious advertising reasons, to have the final title of his work (*Adventures of Huckleberry Finn*) more nearly approximate the title of the well-received earlier Tom Sawyer novel (*The Adventures of Tom Sawyer*), or perhaps he wished to add credibility to Huck's claim to being responsible for the writing of the book by removing the direct linkage of his own name with Huck's in the title, thus giving Huck more authority as an author. It may also be worth weighing the thought that among the consequences of preserving the original title would have been the interposing of Twain, as reporter, between himself and the reader. This would have produced an alteration in the speaking "voice" and not only have diminished the immediacy of Huck's narration but, with Huck another step removed from events, could well have resulted in problems with the use of the vernacular, even for the ingenious Twain. There is little room for doubt that an entirely different kind of book would have been the result. From this line of thinking it would follow that Twain rejected the original working title very early on.

7. See Lowenherz, "The Beginning of *Huckleberry Finn*," 201.

8. Budd, "A Nobler Roman Aspect," 31.

9. See Hoffman, "Huck's Ironic Circle," 320.

10. For an interesting account of Twain's concern about his memory and his curiosity in regard to methods for strengthening it, see Walsh and Zlatic, "Mark Twain and the Art of Memory." Kruse, in "Mark Twain's *Nom de Plume*," 26 n. 7, also points out, however, that "the theory that Clemens had a poor memory, a commonplace of Mark Twain scholarship, is increasingly being called into question." Kruse cites as evidence *The Grangerford-Shepherdson Feud by Mark Twain*. Branch and Hirst state, for example, that "Clemens's memory in 1882 of these [feud] details from 1859 is impressive" (51).

9. On Black and White in Huckleberry Finn

1. See Smith, "Huck, Jim, and American Racial Discourse," 6–7.

2. Twain, *Adventures of Huckleberry Finn*, introduction by Kaplan, foreword and addendum by Doyno, 371, 401.

3. See Barksdale, "History, Slavery, and Thematic Irony in *Huckleberry Finn*." As Barksdale explains,

during Twain's lifetime and later, it was an observable fact that poor white trash like the Finns had nothing but hatred and disrespect for blacks. Condemned and reviled as economic and social outcasts by "respectable" society, people like the Finns looked for some inferior group on which to vent their social spleen; and in America's social hierarchy, the only class or group considered to be lower than the Finns and their kin, were black slaves who, after 1865, became the openly reviled black freedmen. (19)

4. Twain, *Pudd'nhead Wilson*, 115.

5. In the view of Steven Mailloux, "Although this is another of those sincere compliments that presupposes racism, it also works on the level of ideological figure to dismantle the opposition upon which that racism is based: Black and white become morally indistinguishable" ("Reading *Huckleberry Finn*," 124–25).

6. See Smith, *Democracy and the Novel*, 110; and Norrman, *The Insecure World of Henry James's Fiction*, 195–96 n. 16. Lawrence Howe draws attention to another such example in regard to the well-known lines: "That book was made by Mr. Mark Twain, and he told the truth, mainly. There was things which he stretched, but mainly he told the truth. That is nothing." According to Howe, "Huck appears to make allowances for the fact that Twain committed a few 'stretchers' as a common human trait, but the dismissive remark 'That is nothing' is ambiguously misplaced; although it appears to refer to the fact that '[t]here was things which he stretched,' it follows the clause 'but mainly he told the truth.' Even as Huck tries to minimize Twain's lapses into falsehood, his language dismissed any credibility Twain may have earned for telling 'mainly . . . the truth'" (*Mark Twain and the Novel*, 85).

7. Gabler-Hover, *Truth in American Fiction*, 154.

8. Crews, "Walker versus Jehlen versus Twain," 521.

9. Shaw argues that "the demand for an unequivocal antislavery commitment from either Mark Twain or Huck Finn amounts to a relatively crude, and . . . unsuccessful enlistment of literature in a cause" (*Recovering American Literature*, 125).

10. One clear possibility is that, as Kenneth Lynn suggests,

Twain chose—for the first and only time in the novel—to violate Huck's point of view in Chapter XXII and speak to the reader through another mask, in order that he might ram home his moral judgment of the society in explicit and unmistakable terms. The mask he chose to assume for this brief moment was a familiar one in Southwestern humor: the mask of a Southern aristocrat. Not, to be sure, the cool and collected Gentleman of the Whig myth, for Colonel Sherburn is self-admittedly a killer. (*Mark Twain and Southwestern Humor*, 238)

11. Quoted in Foner, *Mark Twain, Social Critic*, 218.

12. Williams, "*Adventures of Huckleberry Finn*," 41.

13. Briden, "Kemble's 'Specialty' and the Pictorial Countertext of *Huckleberry Finn*," 8–9.

14. "Appendix A," in Twain, *Adventures of Huckleberry Finn*, ed. Blair and Fischer, C-14.

15. This contention is supported by the fact that, prior to publication, Twain carefully excised from his manuscript the "cadaver story," in which Jim is portrayed as something of a buffoon. Reasons for the deletion may have been that, as Victor Doyno points out, "Jim's fright at the cadaver's 'movements' could be interpreted, unfortunately, by both early and modern audiences as racist—as a depiction of a superstitious, terrified slave," and that "the inclusion of what might be seen as a demeaning racial stereotype of a frightened black male would run counter to the completed novel's story of Huck's individual growth to respect Jim" (Twain, *Adventures of Huckleberry Finn*, introduction by Kaplan, foreword and addendum by Doyno, 374, 375).

16. Arac, *"Huckleberry Finn" as Idol and Target*, 34.

17. Smith, "Huck, Jim, and American Racial Discourse," 6. Joe B. Fulton considers that "in its totality, the novel serves as a grand 'switch' that subjects the reader to an ethico-linguistic 'traumatic event,' causing him or her to enter into the lives of those on the other side of the race and class line. The constant iteration of the word 'nigger' is part of that trauma" (*Mark Twain's Ethical Realism*, 87).

18. Brown, *"Huckleberry Finn* for Our Time," 45.

19. See A-1, "Negro campmeeting & sermon—'See dat sinner how he run.' Swell Sunday costumes of negros"; A-5, "& Uncle Dan, aunt Hanner, & the 90-year blind negress" (the footnote in *Adventures of Huckleberry Finn* for this entry points out that "Uncle Daniel and Aunt Hannah were slaves on the Quarles's farm" and that, according to Twain's autobiography, "We called her 'Aunt' Hannah, southern fashion"); A-7, "Betsy (negro)"; A-9, "po' $??-nigger will set in Heaven wid de $1500 niggers"; C-1, "Miss Watson's nigger Jim"; C-4, "They lynch a free nigger"; C-5, "Takes history class among the niggers?"; C-9, "And themselves as ghosts. Nigger watchman faints"; and C-14, "Nigger-skin (shamoi) for sale as a pat med." ("Appendix A," in Twain, *Adventures of Huckleberry Finn*, ed. Blair and Fischer, 711–57).

20. Brown, *"Huckleberry Finn* for Our Time," 44.

21. One example of this may be found in Jones, where he asserts:
Twain has clearly made a decision for racism. While the middle part of the book celebrates and acknowledges the growing friendship between white boy and black man, in the last part Twain thinks it important that Jim be shoved back into his place. Twain accomplishes this end in two ways as he first makes over Huck's character in such a way that the youngster is made to forget the

warm companionship between boy and slave, and second has Huck support
the certainty of the good white folk of Arkansas that slavery is right, proper,
and just. Put in a slightly different way, Twain opts to make Huck side with
the powerful against the powerless. ("Nigger and Knowledge," 34)

22. Barksdale, "History, Slavery, and Thematic Irony," 20.

23. An example of an approach that achieves the dubious distinction of managing
to combine both of these failures may be found in Smiley, "Say It Ain't So, Huck."
Jocelyn Chadwick-Joshua, in contrast, mounts a balanced defense of the novel in
The Jim Dilemma.

10. "*I Never Seen Anybody but Lied One Time or Another*"

1. Thanks to Alan Gribben's excellent two-volume work *Mark Twain's Library*.

2. Twain, *The Adventures of Tom Sawyer*, 33.

3. Ibid., 237.

4. Twain to John Henry Riley, Buffalo, N.Y., 2 December 1870, in *Letters: Volume 4*, 258–64.

5. Ibid., 261. I have here changed "&" to "and" and omitted words that Twain himself crossed out.

6. Twain, "Lucretia Smith's Soldier," 108.

7. Ibid.

8. Twain, *Roughing It*, xxxi.

9. Ibid.

10. Ibid., 542.

11. Twain and Warner, *The Gilded Age*, v.

12. See Covici, *Mark Twain's Humor*, 127–39.

13. Hawthorne, *The Marble Faun*, vi.

14. Twain and Warner, *The Gilded Age*, v.

15. Ibid.

16. Ibid., v–vi.

17. "The Stolen White Elephant," 199.

18. Ibid.

19. See also Kruse, "Mark Twain's *Nom de Plume*."

20. Twain, *Life on the Mississippi*, 520.

21. Howe, in "Transcending the Limits of Experience," suggests not only that
Twain's explanation of the source of his pseudonym is open to doubt but that

Twain's certification that one might "gamble" that anything written under the
name "Mark Twain" is "petrified truth" guarantees nothing. At the outset of
Part II [of *Life on the Mississippi*], he indicates that he intends to collect picturesque lies, not petrified truth. In *Life on the Mississippi*, the boasts and myths

that give river talk its vitality stand in diametric opposition to the dead facts. Thus the gamble that Twain offers is a sucker's bet. (430–31)

22. Twain, "Luck," in *The Complete Short Stories of Mark Twain*, ed. Neider, 249.

23. Twain, *The Prince and the Pauper*, 45.

24. According to Lin Salamo's introduction to *The Prince and the Pauper*, "The facsimile and transcript of the Latimer letter . . . were reproduced from a volume that Clemens owned—the second part of the *Facsimiles of National Manuscripts from William the Conqueror to Queen Anne*, 'photozincographed . . . by Colonel Sir Henry James'" (ibid., 21).

25. According to Lin Salamo's introduction to *The Prince and the Pauper*, these items were reproduced from engravings in "George L. Craik and Charles Mac-Farlane's multivolume *Pictorial History of England*, first published from 1837 to 1844" (ibid., 20).

26. Ibid., 28–29.

27. Ibid., 29.

28. Schmitz, "Mark Twain's Civil War," 79.

29. As James M. Cox points out, Twain does not, however, directly say that any of these three items are *not* present. See Cox, "A Hard Book to Take," 396.

30. In her article "Playing Double in *Adventures of Huckleberry Finn*," Krauss sees the "Notice" as "situating the work in terms of the European literary tradition from which it emerged and hence from which it claims to deviate. . . . This mandate, which comes before the body of the work, seems to suggest an overall interpretation of *Adventures of Huckleberry Finn* as an examination of American literary form" (22). Krauss also suggests that "Twain's prefatory disclaimer of motive, moral, and plot may be viewed as a defensive apology for his own inability to break out of the confines of a predetermined literary structure (even when focusing on an escape from that structure)" (23–24). Krauss's failure to account for the American contribution to the tradition is an important omission in her otherwise stimulating argument, since Twain was not only conscious of that contribution, as well as of the European one, but was also clearly reacting to it.

31. Carkeet, "The Dialects in *Huckleberry Finn*," 330–31.

32. Katherine Buxbaum is one such skeptic. In commenting on Twain's claims in the "Explanatory" she notes that

it is not unlikely that Mark Twain overestimated his powers as a dialect writer. Indeed, he says of Bret Harte with whom he collaborated in the production of a play, *Ah Sin:* "Of course I had to go over it and get the dialect right. Bret never did know anything about dialect." Although we are disposed to be tolerant of this alleged superiority, we do not quite trust the undeniably inspired but untutored Mark Twain's dictatorship in the matter of dialect writing. ("Mark Twain and American Dialect," 235)

33. Griffith, who believes that Twain "was winking" when he wrote the "Notice," feels similarly about the "Explanatory": "Perhaps . . . one wink begets another. . . . despite doing their utmost not to reveal it, most of the characters do succeed in talking exactly alike. They sound the same because they use words in exactly the same way to encompass a single shared end" (*Achilles and the Tortoise*, 150).

34. In Griffith's view, Carkeet's article is "perhaps . . . too rigorous and solemn for its own good" (ibid., 175 n. 11). While I have only praise for Carkeet's rigor, I would concur with Griffith's observation concerning solemnity.

35. Lowenherz, "The Beginning of *Huckleberry Finn*," 196.

36. Lowenherz's footnote reads, "These words are *sivilize*, one of the few faulty dialect spellings in the novel; *warn't*, used three times; *most*, used twice; and *Bulrushers; somewheres; whippowill; amongst; a-bothering; a-shaking;* and *a-stirring*" (ibid., 197).

37. Lowenherz's footnote reads, "As one might expect, Huck's quoted speech in his conversations with other characters contains more dialect spellings than his narrative speech—actually a little over twice as many dialect spellings. This is but one of the many nuances of language that enhance the novel" (ibid.).

38. Ibid.

39. Ibid., 196.

40. John Seelye laughed along with Twain at the tradition of claiming to tell the truth when he wrote a book-length pastiche of *Huckleberry Finn* for "the crickets." And what better title might he have chosen than the one he did: *The true adventures of Huckleberry Finn*, as told by John Seelye. In the context of the present discussion, attention should be drawn to the fact that Seelye tellingly chooses to cast doubt on the truth of his tale through *not* capitalizing the second and third words of his title. The word "true" is also a final fillip to any claim to truth telling in this reworked fictional narrative.

Jane Smiley, whose "Say It Ain't So, Huck" compares *Huck* unfavorably with *Uncle Tom's Cabin*, reveals a true debt to Twain as well as to Seelye in titling one of her novels *The All-True Travels and Adventures of Lidie Newton*.

41. Camfield, *Sentimental Twain*, 180.

42. Twain, *A Connecticut Yankee*, 45. According to John C. Gerber, Twain twice "softened the preface to make it less offensive to the English, and even told Chatto, his English publisher, he could alter the final version if he wished" (*Mark Twain*, 124). As a result, the devilish second paragraph in which Twain chuckles at "the question as to whether there is such a thing as divine right of kings" does not apparently interest all publishers of the work in merry old England even today.

43. Twain, *A Connecticut Yankee*, 47.

44. *MTWH*, 1:308–10.

45. See, for example, "The Esquimau Maiden's Romance," which begins, "'Yes,

I will tell you anything about my life that you would like to know, Mr. Twain,' she said, in her soft voice, and letting her honest eyes rest placidly upon my face, 'for it is kind and good of you to like me and care to know about me'" (294).

46. Twain, *A Connecticut Yankee*, 49.

47. Ibid., 51.

48. Twain, *Pudd'nhead Wilson*, 1.

49. Ibid., 1–2.

50. Ibid., 2.

51. See Kaplan, *Mr. Clemens and Mark Twain*, 240.

52. Stone Jr., "Mark Twain's *Joan of Arc*," 6–7.

53. Twain, *Personal Recollections of Joan of Arc*, xv.

54. Twain, *What Is Man?*, 124.

55. Cox, *Mark Twain*, 290.

56. See Baender's introduction to *What Is Man?*, 15.

57. See, for example, Vonnegut, *Cat's Cradle*; Eco, *The Name of the Rose*; Galford, *Moll Cutpurse*; Gilchrist, *I Cannot Get You Close Enough*; and Golden, *Memoirs of a Geisha*.

58. Clemens to *William Dean Howells, 21 July 1885*, мтwн, 2:534.

59. In the introduction to the Raftsmen passage in *Life on the Mississippi* Twain tells us that the widow "wishes to make a nice, *truth-telling*, respectable boy" of Huck (emphasis added) (239).

60. Camfield observes: "By tale's end, we trust him [Huck] implicitly, but why? Haven't we let the son of an alcoholic con-man con us? Or haven't we, if we remember the meta-lie of the fictional nature of the story, let Clemens con us into believing in the reality of Huck in the first place?" (*Sentimental Twain*, 180).

Chapter 11. Knowledge and Knowing in Huckleberry Finn

1. See Thomas, "Language and Identity in the *Adventures of Huckleberry Finn*"; Blakemore, "Huck Finn's Written World"; and Doyno, *Writing "Huck Finn*," 174–219, 249–255. Doyno makes a strong case for Twain's distaste stemming from problems derived from the lack of an international copyright law. In the absence of such legislation, cheap European editions were allowed to flood the American market and thus suppress the sales of American books. Doyno argues:

Although Twain at one early point thought that the lack of international copyright laws in America would lead to inexpensive European literature and would help America, he later viewed romanticized stories of nobility as corrupters of American youth.

In consequence, Twain's entire novel deals with the deceptive power of books, and the recently literate narrator often tries advice or "style" from bookish sources only to be disillusioned. (175)

2. Kevin Murphy makes the suggestion that "Joanna's presentation of the dictionary instead of the Bible inadvertently substitutes linguistic facility and display for religious authenticity." And "Huck's willingness to manipulate Joanna's illiteracy, and to belittle her harelip, calibrates his own decline from a spiritually untarnished naiveté to a more corrupt entanglement in the pretensions and abuses of literacy." According to Murphy's negatively nuanced interpretation, "we can, from one perspective, look at Huck's education throughout the novel as a progressive entanglement in literacy; and his willingness here to swear falsely on and through the power of the dictionary marks a significant and sinister shift in Huck's development" ("Illiterate's Progress," 365).

3. Pettit, *Mark Twain and the South*, 89.

4. See Twain, *Life on the Mississippi*, 500–502.

5. See Schonhorn, "Mark Twain's Jim," 10.

6. Blakemore maintains that "Miss Watson and Tom's attempts to 'learn' Huck are often successful, especially when he unconsciously adopts their idioms and talks in a language that expresses their values" ("Huck Finn's Written World," 23). I would argue, however, that what Huck learns and adopts is not "often" what Tom and Miss Watson *wish* to teach. Even if Huck can be seen to speak "in a language that expresses their values," it can be proven neither that he acquired that language specifically from either of them nor that he accepts their values. The entire book would seem to indicate, on the contrary, that Huck generally holds conflicting opinions concerning those values and uses language more than once to subtly mock them. Such is the case, for instance, in Huck's well-known reply to Aunt Sally's question about the supposed accident on the steamboat that Huck claims brought him to Pikesville: "Good gracious! anybody hurt?" asks Aunt Sally, "No'm. Killed a nigger," replies Huck. To interpret this as an expression of prejudice on the part of Huck would be to do both Huck and Twain a grave injustice. See Solomon, "Jim and Huck," 19; Smith, "Huck, Jim and American Racial Discourse," 5; and Nichols, "'A True Book with Some Stretchers'," 15. I would therefore suggest that Huck no more than Twain should be accused of "unconsciously" using language without more convincing evidence than Blakemore offers.

7. See "Appendix A," in Twain, *Adventures of Huckleberry Finn*, ed. Blair and Fischer, 717, 727.

8. For Twain's reactions to his honorary degrees, see Rasmussen, *Mark Twain A to Z*, 520. A useful, if all too brief, overview of the general subject may be found in Robert T. Oliver's "Mark Twain's Views on Education."

9. It is of interest that Huck more than once in the book employs a form of the verb "to learn" in the sense of "to teach," yet never uses it in Pap's skewed fashion.

10. It is possible that Twain at one point intended to exploit this particular "education" vein even further since his working notes for the book contain the line "Takes history class among the niggers?" ("Appendix A," in Twain, *Adventures of Huckleberry Finn*, ed. Blair and Fischer, 741, 753). A somewhat different approach to education could also have developed from the idea expressed in another of the author's working notes: "Teaches Jim to read & write—then uses dog-messenger. Had taught him a little before" (ibid.).

11. See Krauss, "Playing Double in *Adventures of Huckleberry Finn*," 22.

12. This exchange occurs on page 67 of the first half of the original manuscript located in the Buffalo and Erie County Public Library in Buffalo, N.Y. Only on the canceled words in this quotation is copyright claimed for the Mark Twain Foundation.

13. While not subscribing to every feature of Robinson's comments on the counterfeit coin incident, I believe they deserve consideration here, inasmuch as they point to Huck's lack of knowledge (or *memory*, if we accept Huck's story at face value) costing him doubly in this instance:

It is Huck who seeks the advice of the oracle; Jim simply provides what the boy seeks, and in the process relieves him of a counterfeit quarter. The irony is compounded by the fact that Huck regards the quarter as worthless, but offers it to Jim anyway, preferring to "say nothing about the dollar I got from the judge." This rather minor moment of selfish deception, which takes rise from assumptions about Jim's gullibility and genial willingness to be exploited, is abruptly reversed when Jim reveals his plan to use a potato to fix the quarter "so anybody in town would take it in a minute, let alone a hair-ball." The irony grows even deeper when Huck refuses to acknowledge that he has been fooled. . . . We suspect that what Jim has to say about potatoes, true or false, is news to Huck. But by insisting that he forgot what in fact he never knew, the boy submerges the awkward revelation that the tables have been turned on him. Such an acknowledgement so conflicts with the racist prepossessions manifest in his attempt to deceive Jim that he cannot rise to it. Instead, as if to seal the slave's triumph, and to invite its repetition, he clings to the flimsy delusion that Jim has been the easy mark, and not the other way round. ("The Characterization of Jim in *Huckleberry Finn*," 371)

14. Mark Twain's own interest in and sensitivity to matters humane connected with America's minority populations may be ascertained from a letter he sent William Dean Howells on 22 February [1877]—not long after beginning to write *Huck*—upon the election of Rutherford B. Hayes to the presidency of the United States:

Here's a shout for Hayes! . . . I hope he will put Lt. Col. Richard Irwin Dodge (Author of "The Great Plains & their Inhabitants") at the head of the Indian

Department. *There's* a man who knows all about Indians, & yet has some humanity in him—(knowledge of Indians, & humanity, are seldom found in the same individual). Come!—it is high time we were fixing up this cabinet, my boy. (Smith and Gibson, eds., мтwн, 1:172)

Unfortunately for all concerned, Dodge's understanding and humanity did not bring him the appointment (172–73 n. 2).

15. Dyson, "Huckleberry Finn and the Whole Truth," 32. In contrast to Dyson, George C. Carrington, in *The Dramatic Unity of "Huckleberry Finn"*, makes a case for a more selfish motive on the part of Miss Watson, claiming that "the decision to free Jim, like the earlier decision to sell him away from his family, demonstrates her power to control people without limit, and her urge to use that power." Carrington also maintains that "since the slave she is 'freeing' has been gone for months and can be presumed dead or safe up North," her action is only apparent charity. Her estate suffers, but she "achieves the ultimate capitalist triumph of getting something for nothing," since "being dead" she will not be affected by what happens to her worldly goods (129–30).

Carrington's case is only briefly outlined here, but I would suggest that it is one that not only fails to address Dyson's argument but also oversimplifies Twain's multifaceted approach to knowledge and human nature by attempting to set up a good-evil dichotomy in which Miss Watson is neatly slotted into the "malevolent" category. In order to be able to more easily knock over such a deviously evil "capitalist" straw woman (apparently derived more from politicized extrapolation than from anything attributable to Twain's creation), Carrington unfortunately diverges from the perceptive objectivity that serves him so well in the rest of his book.

Nevertheless, in partial support of Carrington's "bad witch" approach may be mentioned the fact that in the original manuscript of Twain's novel the author first described "The widow's big nigger, named Jim" before crossing out "The widow's" and inserting "Miss Watson's" in her place (see Twain, *Adventures of Huckleberry Finn*, introduction by Kaplan, foreword and addendum by Doyno, 392). Twain's emendation results in placing Jim in the possession of the much less flexible Miss Watson and thus allows the more humane widow to live on at the end of the novel while permitting the more rigid sister to expire, albeit on a humane note. It is worth pointing out, however, that at the time when Twain was inserting the Raftsmen scene into *Life on the Mississippi*, his introduction to that scene still mentions Jim as "a slave of the widow's" (239). It would therefore be useful and of interest in this regard to know precisely when Twain penned the working note for his novel that read:

~~Widow Douglas—then who is Miss Watson?"~~

Ah, she's W.D.'s *sister.*—ͺoldͺspinster

("Appendix A," in Twain, *Adventures of Huckleberry Finn*, ed. Blair and Fischer, B2, 734–35).

Also of interest here is Franklin R. Rogers's observation concerning Jim's revelation at the end of the novel that the dead man in the floating house was pap: "In
making this last reference Twain has forgotten or has chosen to ignore the fact that
Jim is not only a runaway slave but an accused murderer with a price on his head.
As a result he credits Miss Watson with a most unprecedented philanthropy when
in her will she sets Jim free" (*Mark Twain's Burlesque Patterns*, 131).

16. Twain, *Pudd'nhead Wilson*, 108. This was not, however, the first time Twain
had made use of the idea of an unchanged print. In *Life on the Mississippi*, published
in 1883 at the time Twain was finishing the writing of *Huck*, the protagonist tells
the tale of Karl Ritter, who employs a print of the "lines in the ball of the thumb"
from the killer of his wife and child to enable him to exact revenge (see Chapter 31,
"A Thumb-Print and What Came of It," 420–32).

17. Given Mark Twain's fascination with new technological developments, he
would assuredly have read with interest Paul Floren's article "The Fingerprint
Could Become the Password of the Future," *International Herald Tribune* 18 November 1997: 18, which describes a device "about as big as a travel clock" that "has
a small screen to read thumbprints." Other biometric methods based on recognition of face, hand, retina, voice, or DNA would also, no doubt, have excited Twain's
curiosity (for accounts of some of these methods, see Gunnerson, "Are You Ready
for Biometrics"; and Sherrid, "You Can't Forget This Password").

18. Rogers, *Mark Twain's Burlesque Patterns*, 135–37.

19. For a quite different treatment of facets of knowing in *Adventures of Huckleberry Finn*, see Boughn, "Rethinking Mark Twain's Skepticism."

20. In drawing attention to the fact that although the fingerprints utilized in
Pudd'nhead Wilson can distinguish between individuals they do not distinguish between races, Susan Gillman observes in reference to Twain's conclusion to his
novel:

> Not even in the world of his own making could he imagine liberation under
> the law or discover a secure basis for knowledge of self and other. Like Aunt
> Patsy Cooper in *Those Extraordinary Twins*, Twain came increasingly to doubt
> whether he could "know—absolutely *know*, independently of anything [oth-
> ers] have told [him]" even that "reality" exists [*Pudd'nhead Wilson*, 152]. The
> tendency in the thoroughly grounded, deeply historical *Pudd'nhead Wilson* to
> question conventional boundaries of racial identity expands in the dream tales
> into challenging the borders of reality itself. (*Dark Twins*, 95)

That challenge had been issued years before in *Adventures of Huckleberry Finn*.

WORKS CITED

Adams, Richard P. "The Unity and Coherence of *Huckleberry Finn*." *Tulane Studies in English* 6 (1956): 87–103.

The Adventures of Huckleberry Finn. Dir. Richard Thorpe, starring Mickey Rooney, Rex Ingram, Walter Connolly, and William Frawley. MGM, 1939.

Andrews, William L. "Mark Twain and James W. C. Pennington: Huckleberry Finn's Small-pox Lie." *Studies in American Fiction* 9 (spring 1981): 103–12.

Arac, Jonathan. *"Huckleberry Finn" as Idol and Target: The Functions of Criticism in Our Time*. Madison: University of Wisconsin Press, 1997.

Baender, Paul. "Twainiana in Iowa." *Mark Twain Circular* 4:7–9 (July–September 1990): 9.

Baker, Houston. Introduction. *Narrative of the Life of Frederick Douglass Written by Himself*. By Frederick Douglass. 1845. Harmondsworth, England: Penguin, 1982. 7–24.

Baker, William. "Mark Twain and the Shrewd Ohio Audiences." *American Literary Realism* 18:1–2 (spring–autumn 1985): 14–30.

Baldanza, Frank. "The Structure of *Huckleberry Finn*." *American Literature* 27 (November 1955): 347–55.

Barksdale, Richard K. "History, Slavery, and Thematic Irony in *Huckleberry Finn*." *Mark Twain Journal* 22:2 (fall 1984): 17–20. Reprinted in James S. Leonard, Thomas A. Tenney, and Thadious M. Davis, eds. *Satire or Evasion?: Black Perspectives on "Huckleberry Finn."* Durham, N.C.: Duke University Press, 1992. 49–55.

Barton, William E. *Lincoln at Gettysburg*. Indianapolis: Bobbs-Merrill, 1930.

Beaver, Harold. *Huckleberry Finn*. London: Allen and Unwin, 1987.

Becker, Carl L. *The Declaration of Independence: A Study in the History of Political Ideas*. New York: Vintage Books, 1942.

Beecher, Thomas K. *Jervis Langdon: 1809–1870*. Eulogy delivered on 21 August 1870. Elmira, N.Y. Pamphlet located in Chemung County Historical Society Library, Elmira, N.Y.

Belz, Herman. *Abraham Lincoln, Constitutionalism and Equal Rights in the Civil War Era*. New York: Fordham University Press, 1998.

Benardette, Jane Johnson. "*Huckleberry Finn* and the Nature of Fiction." *Massachusetts Review* (spring 1968): 209–26.

213

Berkove, Lawrence I. "The 'Poor Players' of *Huckleberry Finn.*" *Papers of the Michigan Academy of Science, Arts, and Letters* 53 (1968): 291–310.

Blair, Walter. *Mark Twain and Huck Finn*. Berkeley: University of California Press, 1960.

———. "Was *Huckleberry Finn* Written?" *Mark Twain Journal* 19 (summer 1979): 1–3. Reprinted in Laurie Champion, ed. *The Critical Response to Mark Twain's "Huckleberry Finn."* Westport, Conn.: Greenwood Press, 1991. 108–12.

Blakemore, Steven. "Huck Finn's Written World." *American Literary Realism 1870–1910* 20:2 (winter 1988): 21–29.

Boatner, Mark Mayo III. *The Civil War Dictionary, Revised Edition*. New York: David McKay, 1988.

Boughn, Michael. "Rethinking Mark Twain's Skepticism: Ways of Knowing and Forms of Freedom in the *Adventures of Huckleberry Finn.*" *Arizona Quarterly* 52:4 (winter 1996): 31–48.

Briden, Earl F. "Huck's Great Escape: Magic and Ritual." *Mark Twain Journal* 21:3 (spring 1983): 17–18.

———. "Kemble's 'Specialty' and the Pictorial Countertext of *Huckleberry Finn.*" *Mark Twain Journal* 26:2 (fall 1988): 2–14.

Brown, Spencer. "*Huckleberry Finn* for Our Time: A Re-Reading of the Concluding Chapters." *Michigan Quarterly Review* 6 (winter 1967): 41–46.

Budd, Louis J. *Mark Twain: Social Philosopher*. Bloomington: Indiana University Press, 1962.

———, ed. *New Essays on "Huckleberry Finn."* Cambridge: Cambridge University Press, 1985.

———. "A Nobler Roman Aspect." In Robert Sattelmeyer and J. Donald Crowley, eds. *One Hundred Years of "Huckleberry Finn": The Boy, His Book, and American Culture*. Centennial Essays. Columbia: University of Missouri Press, 1985. 26–40.

———. "The Recomposition of *Adventures of Huckleberry Finn.*" *Missouri Review* 10 (1987): 113–29. Reprinted in Laurie Champion, ed. *The Critical Response to Mark Twain's "Huckleberry Finn."* Westport, Conn.: Greenwood Press, 1991. 195–206.

———. "The Southward Currents under Huck Finn's Raft." *Mississippi Valley Historical Review* 46:2 (September 1959): 222–37.

Buxbaum, Katherine. "Mark Twain and American Dialect." *American Speech* 2 (February 1927): 233–36.

Camfield, Gregg. *Sentimental Twain: Samuel Clemens in the Maze of Moral Philosophy*. Philadelphia: University of Pennsylvania Press, 1994.

Carkeet, David. "The Dialects in *Huckleberry Finn.*" *American Literature* 51 (November 1979): 315–32. Reprinted in Laurie Champion, ed. *The Critical Response to Mark Twain's "Huckleberry Finn."* Westport, Conn.: Greenwood Press, 1991. 113–25.

Carrington, George C., Jr. *The Dramatic Unity of "Huckleberry Finn."* Columbus: Ohio State University Press, 1976.

Carter, Everett. "The Modernist Ordeal of Huckleberry Finn." *Studies in American Fiction* 13 (autumn 1985): 169–83.

Cecil, L. Moffitt. "The Historical Ending of *Adventures of Huckleberry Finn:* How Nigger Jim Was Set Free." *American Literary Realism* 13:2 (autumn 1980): 280–83.

Chadwick, John White. *A Life for Liberty: Antislavery and Other Letters of Sallie Halley.* New York: Putnam's, 1899.

———. *Theodore Parker, Preacher and Reformer.* Boston: Houghton Mifflin, 1900.

Chadwick-Joshua, Jocelyn. *The Jim Dilemma: Reading Race in "Huckleberry Finn."* Jackson: University Press of Mississippi, 1998.

Champion, Laurie, ed. *The Critical Response to Mark Twain's "Huckleberry Finn."* Westport, Conn.: Greenwood Press, 1991.

Clemens, Susy. *Papa: An Intimate Biography of Mark Twain.* Ed. Charles Neider. Garden City, N.Y.: Doubleday, 1985.

Clerc, Charles. "Sunrise on the River: 'The Whole World' of *Huckleberry Finn.*" *Modern Fiction Studies* 14 (spring 1968): 67–78.

Clymer, Kenton J. *John Hay: The Gentleman as Diplomat.* Ann Arbor: University of Michigan Press, 1975.

Conway, Moncure Daniel. *Autobiography, Memoirs and Experience.* Boston: Houghton Mifflin, 1904. 2 vols.

Covici, Pascal. *Mark Twain's Humor: The Image of a World.* Dallas: Southern Methodist University Press, 1962.

Cox, James M. "A Hard Book to Take." In Robert Sattelmeyer and J. Donald Crowley, eds. *One Hundred Years of "Huckleberry Finn": The Boy, His Book, and American Culture.* Centennial Essays. Columbia: University of Missouri Press, 1985. 386–403. Reprinted in Laurie Champion, ed. *The Critical Response to Mark Twain's "Huckleberry Finn."* Westport, Conn.: Greenwood Press, 1991. 171–86.

———. *Mark Twain: The Fate of Humor.* Princeton, N.J.: Princeton University Press, 1966.

Crews, Frederick. "Walker versus Jehlen versus Twain." In Gerald Graff and James Phelan, eds. *Adventures of Huckleberry Finn: A Case Study in Critical Controversy.* Boston: Bedford Books of St. Martin's Press, 1995. 518–25.

Cummings, Sherwood. "The Commanding Presence of Formerly Enslaved Mary Ann Cord in Mark Twain's Work." *Mark Twain Journal* 34:2 (fall 1996): 22–27.

David, Beverly R. "The Pictorial *Huck Finn:* Mark Twain and His Illustrator, E. W. Kemble." *American Quarterly* 26 (October 1974): 331–51.

Davis, Mary Kemp. "The Veil Rent in Twain." In James S. Leonard, Thomas A. Tenney, and Thadious M. Davis, eds. *Satire or Evasion?: Black Perspectives on "Huckleberry Finn."* Durham, N.C.: Duke University Press, 1992. 77–90.

Dennett, Tyler. *John Hay: From Poetry to Politics.* New York: Dodd, Mead, 1933.

DeVoto, Bernard. Introduction. *The Portable Mark Twain.* Ed. Bernard DeVoto New York: Viking, 1946.

———. *Mark Twain at Work.* 1942. Cambridge, Mass.: Houghton Mifflin, 1967.

———, ed. *Mark Twain in Eruption: Hitherto Unpublished Pages about Men and Events by Mark Twain.* New York: Harper and Brothers, 1940.

Donald, David. *Lincoln's Herndon.* 1948. New York: Da Capo Press, 1989.

Douglass, Frederick. *Life and Times of Frederick Douglass: His Early Life as a Slave, His Escape from Bondage, and His Complete History.* 1892. With a new introduction by Rayford W. Logan. New York: Collier Macmillan, 1962.

———. *My Bondage and My Freedom.* 1855. With a new introduction by Philip S. Foner. New York: Dover, 1969.

———. *Narrative of the Life of Frederick Douglass Written by Himself.* 1845. Harmondsworth, England: Penguin, 1982.

———. "What to the Slave Is the Fourth of July?" 1852. In William L. Andrews, ed. *The Oxford Frederick Douglass Reader.* New York: Oxford University Press, 1996. 108–30.

Doyno, Victor A. "Over Twain's Shoulder: The Composition and Structure of *Huckleberry Finn.*" *Modern Fiction Studies* 14:1 (spring 1968): 3–9.

———. *Writing "Huck Finn": Mark Twain's Creative Process.* Philadelphia: University of Pennsylvania Press, 1991.

Dyson, A. E. "Huckleberry Finn and the Whole Truth." *Critical Quarterly* 3 (spring 1961): 29–40.

Eco, Umberto. *The Name of the Rose.* 1980. London: Martin and Warburg, 1983.

Egan, Michael. *Mark Twain's "Huckleberry Finn": Race, Class and Society.* Atlantic Highlands, N.J.: Humanities Press, 1978.

Eliot, T. S. Introduction. *The Adventures of Huckleberry Finn.* By Mark Twain. London: Cresset Press, 1950. vii–xvi.

Fatout, Paul, ed. *Mark Twain Speaking.* Iowa City: University of Iowa Press, 1976.

Fishkin, Shelley Fisher. *Lighting Out for the Territory: Reflections on Mark Twain and American Culture.* New York: Oxford University Press, 1997.

———. *Was Huck Black? Mark Twain and African-American Voices.* New York: Oxford University Press, 1993.

Floren, Paul. "The Fingerprint Could Become the Password of the Future." *International Herald Tribune* 18 November 1997: 18.

Foner, Eric. *Reconstruction: America's Unfinished Revolution 1863–1877.* New York: Harper and Row, 1988.

Foner, Philip S. Introduction. *My Bondage and My Freedom.* By Frederick Douglass. New York: Dover, 1969. v–xiii.

———. *Mark Twain, Social Critic.* New York: International Publishers, 1958.

Franklin, John Hope. *Reconstruction after the Civil War.* Chicago: University of Chicago Press, 1961.

Fulton, Joe B. *Mark Twain's Ethical Realism: The Aesthetics of Race, Class, and Gender.* Columbia: University of Missouri Press, 1997.

Gabler-Hover, Janet. *Truth in American Fiction.* Athens: University of Georgia Press, 1990.

Gale, Robert L. *John Hay.* Boston: Twayne Publishers, 1978.

Galford, Ellen. *Moll Cutpurse, Her True History.* Ithaca, N.Y.: Firebrand Books, 1985.

Garvey, T. Gregory. "Frederick Douglass's Change of Opinion on the U.S. Constitution: Abolitionism and the 'Elements of Moral Power.'" *ATQ*, Special Issue: *Frederick Douglass* n.s. 9:3 (September 1995): 229–43.

Gerber, John C. *Mark Twain.* Boston: G. K. Hall, 1988.

Gilchrist, Ellen. *I Cannot Get You Close Enough.* Boston: Faber and Faber, 1990.

Gillman, Susan. *Dark Twins: Imposture and Identity in Mark Twain's America.* Chicago: University of Chicago Press, 1989.

Golden, Arthur. *Memoirs of a Geisha.* New York: Alfred A. Knopf, 1997.

Gollin, Richard, and Rita Gollin. "*Huckleberry Finn* and the Time of the Evasion." *Modern Language Studies* 9 (spring 1979): 5–15.

Goodyear, Russell H. "Huck Finn's Anachronistic Double Eagles." *American Notes and Queries* 10 (November 1971): 39.

Gordon, Jan B. "'Fan-Tods "wid" de Samurai': *Huckleberry Finn* in Japan." In Robert Sattelmeyer and J. Donald Crowley, eds. *One Hundred Years of "Huckleberry Finn": The Boy, His Book, and American Culture.* Centennial Essays. Columbia: University of Missouri Press, 1985. 282–96.

Graff, Gerald, and James Phelan, eds. *Adventures of Huckleberry Finn: A Case Study in Critical Controversy.* Boston: Bedford Books of St. Martin's Press, 1995.

Grant, Ulysses S. "Second Inaugural Address." 4 March 1873. In *Messages and Papers of the Presidents.* Vol. 9. New York: Bureau of National Literature, 1897. 4175–77.

Gribben, Alan. *Mark Twain's Library: A Reconstruction.* 2 vols. Boston: G. K. Hall, 1980.

Griffith, Clark. *Achilles and the Tortoise: Mark Twain's Fictions.* Tuscaloosa: University of Alabama Press, 1998.

Gunnerson, Gary. "Are You Ready for Biometrics?" *pc Magazine* 23 February 1999: 160–76.

Harris, Susan K. *The Courtship of Olivia Langdon and Mark Twain.* Cambridge: Cambridge University Press, 1996.

Hawthorne, Nathaniel. *The Marble Faun.* 1859. New York: New American Library, 1961.

Hay, John. *Letters of John Hay and Extracts from Diary.* Vol. 2. New York: Gordian Press, 1969.

———. *Pike County Ballads and Other Poems.* London: George Routledge and Sons, 1891.

Hayes, Rutherford B. "Inaugural Address." 5 March 1877. In *Messages and Papers of the Presidents.* Vol. 9. New York: Bureau of National Literature, 1897. 4396.

Hemingway, Ernest. *Green Hills of Africa.* New York: Charles Scribner's Sons, 1935.

Hoffman, Daniel G. *Form and Fable in American Fiction.* New York: Oxford University Press, 1961.

Hoffman, Michael J. "Huck's Ironic Circle." *Georgia Review* 23:3 (fall 1969): 307–22.

Howe, Lawrence. *Mark Twain and the Novel: The Double-Cross of Authority.* Cambridge: Cambridge University Press, 1998.

———. "Transcending the Limits of Experience: Mark Twain's *Life on the Mississippi.*" *American Literature* 63:3 (September 1991): 420–39.

Howells, William Dean. *My Mark Twain: Reminiscences and Criticisms.* New York: Harper and Brothers, 1910.

Jaffa, Harry V. *Crisis of the House Divided: An Interpretation of the Issues in the Lincoln-Douglas Debates.* 1959. Chicago: University of Chicago Press, 1982.

Jehlen, Myra. "Banned in Concord: *Adventures of Huckleberry Finn* and Classic American Literature." In Forrest G. Robinson, ed. *The Cambridge Companion to Mark Twain.* Cambridge: Cambridge University Press, 1995. 93–115.

Johnson, James L. *Mark Twain and the Limits of Power.* Knoxville: University of Tennessee Press, 1982.

Jones, Betty H. "Huck and Jim: A Reconsideration." In James S. Leonard, Thomas A. Tenney, and Thadious M. Davis, eds. *Satire or Evasion?: Black Perspectives on "Huckleberry Finn."* Durham, N.C.: Duke University Press, 1992. 154–72.

Jones, Rhett S. "Nigger and Knowledge: White Double-Consciousness in *Adventures of Huckleberry Finn.*" *Mark Twain Journal* 22:2 (fall 1984): 28–37. Reprinted in James S. Leonard, Thomas A. Tenney, and Thadious M. Davis, eds. *Satire or Evasion?: Black Perspectives on "Huckleberry Finn."* Durham, N.C.: Duke University Press, 1992. 173–94.

Kaplan, Justin. *Mr. Clemens and Mark Twain.* New York: Simon and Schuster, 1966.

King, Martin Luther, Jr. "I Have a Dream." In *Martin Luther King, Jr.: A Documentary . . . Montgomery to Memphis.* Ed. Flip Schulke. New York: W. W. Norton, 1976. 218.

Krauss, Jennifer. "Playing Double in *Adventures of Huckleberry Finn." Mark Twain Journal* 21:4 (fall 1983): 22–24.

Kruse, Horst. "Mark Twain's *Nom de Plume:* Some Mysteries Resolved." *Mark Twain Journal* 30:1 (spring 1992): 2–32.

Leonard, James S., Thomas A. Tenney, and Thadious M. Davis, eds. *Satire or Evasion?: Black Perspectives on "Huckleberry Finn."* Durham, N.C.: Duke University Press, 1992.

Light, James F. "Paradox, Form, and Despair in *Huckleberry Finn." Mark Twain Journal* 21:4 (fall 1983): 24–25.

Lincoln, Abraham. *The Collected Works of Abraham Lincoln.* Ed. Roy P. Basler et al. Vol. 3. New Brunswick, N.J.: Rutgers University Press, 1953–55. 9 vols.

Lockhart, William B., Yale Kamisar, and Jesse H. Choper. *Constitutional Rights and Liberties: Cases and Materials.* St. Paul, Minn.: West Publishing Co., 1970.

Lowell, Robert. "On the Gettysburg Address." In Allan Nevins, ed. *Lincoln and the Gettysburg Address, Commemorative Papers.* Urbana: University of Illinois Press, 1964. 88–91.

Lowenherz, Robert J. "The Beginning of *Huckleberry Finn." American Speech* 38:3 (October 1963): 196–210.

Lowry, Richard S. *Littery Man: Mark Twain and Modern Authorship.* New York: Oxford University Press, 1996.

Lynn, Kenneth S. *Mark Twain and Southwestern Humor.* Boston: Little, Brown and Co., 1959.

MacKethan, Lucinda H. "Huck Finn and the Slave Narratives: Lighting Out as Design." *Southern Review* 20:2 (April 1984): 247–64.

Mailloux, Steven. "Reading *Huckleberry Finn*: The Rhetoric of Performed Ideology." In Louis J. Budd, ed. *New Essays on "Huckleberry Finn."* Cambridge: Cambridge University Press, 1985. 107–33.

McCullough, Joseph B. "Uses of the Bible in *Huckleberry Finn." Mark Twain Journal* 19:3 (winter 1978–79): 2–3.

McMahan, Elizabeth E. "The Money Motif: Economic Implications in *Huckleberry Finn." Mark Twain Journal* 15:4 (summer 1971): 5–10.

McPherson, James M. *Abraham Lincoln and the Second American Revolution.* New York: Oxford University Press, 1991.

———. *Ordeal by Fire: The Civil War and Reconstruction.* New York: Alfred A. Knopf, 1982.

Mearns, David C., and Lloyd A. Dunlap. *Long Remembered: Facsimiles of the Five*

Versions of the Gettysburg Address in the Handwriting of Abraham Lincoln. Notes and comments on the preparation of the Address by David C. Mearns and Lloyd A. Dunlap. Washington, D.C.: Library of Congress, 1963.

Moffett, Samuel E. "Mark Twain: A Biographical Sketch." In *Literary Essays by Mark Twain.* New York: Harper and Brothers, 1899. 314–33.

Murphy, Kevin. "'Illiterate's Progress': The Descent into Literacy in *Huckleberry Finn.*" *Texas Studies in Literature and Language* 26:4 (winter 1984): 363–87.

Nichols, Charles H. "'A True Book with Some Stretchers': *Huck Finn* Today." *Mark Twain Journal* 22:2 (fall 1984): 13–16. Reprinted in James S. Leonard, Thomas A. Tenney, and Thadious M. Davis, eds. *Satire or Evasion?: Black Perspectives on "Huckleberry Finn."* Durham, N.C.: Duke University Press, 1992. 208–15.

Nilon, Charles H. "The Ending of *Huckleberry Finn*: 'Freeing the Free Negro.'" *Mark Twain Journal* 22:2 (Fall 1984): 21–27. Reprinted in James S. Leonard, Thomas A. Tenney, and Thadious M. Davis, eds. *Satire or Evasion?: Black Perspectives on "Huckleberry Finn."* Durham, N.C.: Duke University Press, 1992. 62–76.

Norrman, Ralf. *The Insecure World of Henry James's Fiction: Intensity and Ambiguity.* London: Macmillan, 1982.

Oates, Stephen B. *Abraham Lincoln: The Man behind the Myths.* New York: Meridian, 1985.

Oehlschlaeger, Fritz. "'Gwyne to Git Hung': The Conclusion of *Huckleberry Finn.*" In Robert Sattelmeyer and J. Donald Crowley, eds. *One Hundred Years of "Huckleberry Finn": The Boy, His Book, and American Culture.* Centennial Essays. Columbia: University of Missouri Press, 1985. 117–27.

Oliver, Robert T. "Mark Twain's Views on Education." *Education* 61 (October 1940): 112–15. Reprinted in Louis J. Budd, ed. *Critical Essays on Mark Twain, 1910–1980.* Boston: G. K. Hall and Co., 1983. 112–15.

Parker, Theodore. "A Sermon on the Dangers which Threaten the Rights of Man in America." In vol. 12 of the Centenary Edition of The Works of Theodore Parker. Boston: American Unitarian Association, 1907–11. 333–96.

———. "Theodore Parker's Experience as a Minister." In *Life and Correspondence of Theodore Parker.* By John Weiss. 2 vols. New York: D. Appleton, 1864. 2:447–513.

Pettit, Arthur G. *Mark Twain and the South.* Lexington: University Press of Kentucky, 1974.

Posner, Gerald. *Hitler's Children: Inside the Families of the Third Reich.* London: Mandarin, 1992.

Quirk, Tom. *Coming to Grips with Huckleberry Finn: Essays on a Book, a Boy, and a Man.* Columbia: University of Missouri Press, 1993.

————. "The Legend of Noah and the Voyage of *Huckleberry Finn.*" *Mark Twain Journal* 21:2 (summer 1982): 21–22.

————. "Moses and the Bulrushers: A Note on *Huckleberry Finn.*" *Mark Twain Journal* 18:4 (summer 1977): 13–14.

Rasmussen, R. Kent. *Mark Twain A to Z: The Essential Reference to His Life and Writings.* New York: Facts on File, 1995.

Renehan, Edward J., Jr. *The Secret Six: The True Tale of the Men Who Conspired with John Brown.* New York: Crown, 1995.

Robinson, Forrest G., ed. *The Cambridge Companion to Mark Twain.* Cambridge: Cambridge University Press, 1995.

————. "The Characterization of Jim in *Huckleberry Finn.*" *Nineteenth Century Literature* 43:3 (December 1988): 361–91. Reprinted in Laurie Champion, ed. *The Critical Response to Mark Twain's "Huckleberry Finn."* Westport, Conn.: Greenwood Press, 1991. 207–25.

————. "An 'Unconscious and Profitable Cerebration': Mark Twain and Literary Intentionality." *Nineteenth Century Literature* 50:3 (December 1995): 357–80.

————. *In Bad Faith: The Dynamics of Deception in Mark Twain's America.* Cambridge, Mass.: Harvard University Press, 1986.

Robinson, Forrest G., and Henry B. Wonham. "Commentary." (An exchange of views.) *Nineteenth Century Literature* 51:1 (June 1996): 137–41.

Rogers, Franklin R. *Mark Twain's Burlesque Patterns: As Seen in the Novels and Narratives 1855–1885.* Dallas: Southern Methodist University Press, 1960.

Sanborn, Franklin. "Parker in the John Brown Campaign." In vol. 14 of the Centenary Edition of The Works of Theodore Parker. Boston: American Unitarian Association, 1907–11. 391–448.

Sattelmeyer, Robert. "Interesting, but Tough: *Huckleberry Finn* and the Problem of Tradition." In Robert Sattelmeyer and J. Donald Crowley, eds. *One Hundred Years of "Huckleberry Finn": The Boy, His Book, and American Culture.* Centennial Essays. Columbia: University of Missouri Press, 1985. 354–70.

Sattelmeyer, Robert, and J. Conald Crowley, eds. *One Hundred Years of "Huckleberry Finn": The Boy, His Book, and American Culture.* Centennial Essays. Columbia: University of Missouri Press, 1985.

Schlesinger, Arthur, Jr. "Schlesinger's Syllabus." *American Heritage* (February–March 1998): 30–38.

Schmitz, Neil. "Mark Twain's Civil War: Humor's Reconstructive Writing." In Forrest G. Robinson, ed. *The Cambridge Companion to Mark Twain.* Cambridge: Cambridge University Press, 1995. 74–92.

————. "Twain, *Huckleberry Finn* and the Reconstruction." *American Studies* (formerly *Midcontinent American Studies Journal*) 12 (spring 1971): 59–67.

Schonhorn, Manuel. "Mark Twain's Jim: Solomon on the Mississippi." *Mark Twain Journal* 14:3 (winter 1968–69): 9–11.

Seelye, John. *The true adventures of Huckleberry Finn.* Evanston: Northwestern University Press, 1970.

Shaw, Peter. *Recovering American Literature.* Chicago: Ivan R. Dee, 1994.

Sherrid, Pamela. "You Can't Forget This Password." *U.S. News and World Report* 17 May 1999: 49.

Slattery, Dennis Patrick. "The Via Dollarosa: Money Matters in *Huckleberry Finn.*" *South Central Review* 5:4 (winter 1988): 29–41.

Smiley, Jane. *The All-True Travels and Adventures of Lidie Newton.* New York: Alfred A. Knopf, 1998.

———. "Say It Ain't So, Huck: Second thoughts on Mark Twain's 'masterpiece.'" *Harper's Magazine* (January 1996): 61–67.

Smith, David L. "Huck, Jim, and American Racial Discourse." *Mark Twain Journal* 22:2 (fall 1984): 4–12. Reprinted in James S. Leonard, Thomas A. Tenney, and Thadious M. Davis, eds. *Satire or Evasion?: Black Perspectives on "Huckleberry Finn."* Durham, N.C.: Duke University Press, 1992. 103–20.

Smith, Henry Nash. *Democracy and the Novel: Popular Resistance to Classic American Writers.* New York: Oxford University Press, 1978.

Smith, Henry Nash, and William M. Gibson, eds., with the assistance of Frederick Anderson. *Mark Twain–Howells Letters: The Correspondence of Samuel L. Clemens and William D. Howells, 1872–1910.* Cambridge, Mass.: Belknap Press of Harvard University Press, 1960. 2 vols.

Solomon, Andrew. "Jim and Huck: Magnificent Misfits." *Mark Twain Journal* 16:3 (winter 1972): 17–24.

Stampp, Kenneth M. *The Era of Reconstruction, 1865–1877.* New York: Alfred A. Knopf, 1965.

Steinbrink, Jeffrey. "Who Wrote *Huckleberry Finn?* Mark Twain's Control of the Early Manuscript." In Robert Sattelmeyer and J. Donald Crowley, eds. *One Hundred Years of "Huckleberry Finn": The Boy, His Book, and American Culture.* Centennial Essays. Columbia: University of Missouri Press, 1985. 85–105.

Stone, Albert E., Jr. "Mark Twain's *Joan of Arc:* The Child as Goddess." *American Literature* 31:1 (March 1959): 1–20.

Sundquist, Eric J. "Mark Twain and Homer Plessy." *Representations* 24 (fall 1988): 102–27. Reprinted in Eric J. Sundquist, ed. *Mark Twain: A Collection of Critical Essays.* Englewood Cliffs, N.J.: Prentice Hall, 1994. 169–83.

———, ed. *Mark Twain: A Collection of Critical Essays.* Englewood Cliffs, N.J.: Prentice Hall, 1994.

Taylor, Paul. "*Huckleberry Finn:* The Education of a Young Capitalist." In Robert Sattelmeyer and J. Donald Crowley, eds. *One Hundred Years of "Huckleberry Finn":*

The Boy, His Book, and American Culture. Centennial Essays. Columbia: University of Missouri Press, 1985. 341–53.

Thomas, Brook. "Language and Identity in the *Adventures of Huckleberry Finn.*" *Mark Twain Journal* 20:3 (winter 1980–81): 17–21.

Trilling, Lionel. Introduction. *Adventures of Huckleberry Finn.* By Mark Twain. New York: Rinehart and Co., 1948. v–xiii.

Turner, Martha Anne. "Mark Twain's '1601' through Fifty Editions." *Mark Twain Journal* 12:4 (summer 1965): 10–15, 21.

Twain, Mark. *Adventures of Huckleberry Finn.* 1884. London: Penguin, 1966.

———. *Adventures of Huckleberry Finn.* Ed. Walter Blair and Victor Fischer, with the assistance of Dahlia Armon and Harriet Elinor Smith. Vol. 8 of The Works of Mark Twain. Berkeley: University of California Press, 1988.

———. *Adventures of Huckleberry Finn.* Introduction by Justin Kaplan, foreword and addendum by Victor Doyno. New York: Random House, 1996.

———. *Adventures of Huckleberry Finn: A Facsimile of the Manuscript.* Introduction by Louis Budd, afterword by William H. Loos. Detroit: Bruccoli Clark, Gale Research Co., 1983. 2 vols.

———. *The Adventures of Thomas Jefferson Snodgrass.* Ed. Charles Honce. Chicago: Pascal Covici, 1928.

———. *The Adventures of Tom Sawyer; Tom Sawyer Abroad; Tom Sawyer, Detective.* Ed. and with an introduction by John C. Gerber, Paul Baender, and Terry Firkins. Vol. 4 of The Works of Mark Twain. Berkeley: University of California Press, 1980.

———. *The American Claimant.* New York: Harper and Brothers, 1899.

———. *A Connecticut Yankee in King Arthur's Court.* Ed. Bernard L. Stein, with an introduction by Henry Nash Smith. Vol. 9 of The Works of Mark Twain. Berkeley: University of California Press, 1979.

———. *[Date, 1601.] Conversation, as It Was by the Social Fireside, in the Time of the Tudors.* In *Mark Twain: Collected Tales, Sketches, Speeches, & Essays, 1852–1890.* Ed. Louis J. Budd. New York: Library of America, 1992. 661–66.

———. "The Esquimau Maiden's Romance." In *The Complete Short Stories of Mark Twain.* Ed. and with an introduction by Charles Neider. 1893. New York: Doubleday and Co., 1957. 294–307.

———. "The Facts Concerning the Recent Carnival of Crime in Connecticut." In *Mark Twain: Collected Tales, Sketches, Speeches, & Essays, 1852–1890.* Ed. Louis J. Budd. New York: Library of America, 1992. 644–60.

———. *The Grangerford-Shepherdson Feud by Mark Twain.* Ed. Edgar Marquess Branch and Robert H. Hirst. Berkeley: Friends of the Bancroft Library, 1985.

———. *Life on the Mississippi.* In *Mark Twain: Mississippi Writings.* New York: Library of America, 1982.

————. "Lucretia Smith's Soldier." In *Mark Twain: Collected Tales, Sketches, Speeches, & Essays, 1852–1890*. Ed. Louis J. Budd. New York: Library of America, 1992. 108–12.

————. *Mark Twain's Letters*. Arranged with comment by Albert Bigelow Paine. New York: Harper Brothers, 1917. 2 vols.

————. *Mark Twain's Letters: Volume 1, 1853–1866*. Ed. Edgar Marquess Branch, Michael B. Frank, and Kenneth M. Sanderson; associate editors Harriet Elinor Smith, Lin Salamo, and Richard Bucci. The Mark Twain Papers, under the general editorship of Robert H. Hirst. Berkeley: University of California Press, 1988.

————. *Mark Twain's Letters: Volume 2, 1867–1868*. Ed. Harriet Elinor Smith and Richard Bucci; associate editor, Lin Salamo. The Mark Twain Papers. Berkeley: University of California Press, 1990.

————. *Mark Twain's Letters: Volume 3, 1869*. Ed. Victor Fischer and Michael B. Frank; associate editor, Dahlia Armon. The Mark Twain Papers. Berkeley: University of California Press, 1992.

————. *Mark Twain's Letters: Volume 4, 1870–1871*. Ed. Victor Fischer and Michael B. Frank; associate editor, Lin Salamo. The Mark Twain Papers. Berkeley: University of California Press, 1995.

————. *Mark Twain's Letters to His Publishers, 1867–1894*. Ed. and with an introduction by Hamlin Hill. The Mark Twain Papers. Berkeley: University of California Press, 1967.

————. *Mark Twain's Notebooks and Journals: Volume I, 1855–1873*. Ed. Frederick Anderson, Michael B. Frank, and Kenneth M. Sanderson. The Mark Twain Papers. Berkeley: University of California Press, 1975.

————. *Mark Twain's Notebooks and Journals: Volume II, 1877–1883*. Ed. Frederick Anderson, Lin Salamo, and Bernard L. Stein. The Mark Twain Papers. Berkeley: University of California Press, 1975.

————. *Mark Twain's Notebooks and Journals: Volume III, 1883–1891*. Ed. Robert Pack Browning, Michael B. Frank, and Lin Salamo. General Editor, Frederick Anderson. The Mark Twain Papers. Berkeley: University of California Press, 1979.

————. *Mark Twain to Mrs. Fairbanks*. Ed. Dixon Wecter. San Marino, Calif.: Huntington Library, 1949.

————. *Personal Recollections of Joan of Arc*. 1896. New York: Harper and Brothers, 1924.

————. *The Prince and the Pauper*. Ed. Victor Fischer and Lin Salamo, with the assistance of Mary Jane Jones. Vol. 6 of The Works of Mark Twain. Berkeley: University of California Press, 1979.

———. *Pudd'nhead Wilson and Those Extraordinary Twins.* 1894. Ed. Sidney E. Berger. New York: W. W. Norton, 1980.

———. *Roughing It.* 1872. Ed. Harriet Elinor Smith and Edgar Marquess Branch; associate editors, Lin Salamo and Robert Pack Browning. Vol. 2 of The Works of Mark Twain. Berkeley: University of California Press, 1993.

———. "The Stolen White Elephant." 1882. In *The Complete Short Stories of Mark Twain.* Ed. and with an introduction by Charles Neider. New York: Doubleday and Co., 1957. 199–216.

———. "The Stupendous Procession." In *Mark Twain's Fables of Man.* Ed. and with an introduction by John S. Tuckey. Text established by Kenneth M. Sanderson and Bernard L. Stein. Series editor, Frederick Anderson. Berkeley: University of California Press, 1972. 403–19.

———. *What Is Man? and Other Philosophical Writings.* Ed. and with an introduction by Paul Baender. Berkeley: University of California Press, 1973.

Twain, Mark, and Charles Dudley Warner. *The Gilded Age, A Tale of To-Day.* Hartford, Conn.: American Publishing Company, 1874.

Vonnegut, Kurt. *Cat's Cradle.* 1963. Harmondsworth, England: Penguin Books, 1965.

Walsh, Thomas M., and Thomas D. Zlatic. "Mark Twain and the Art of Memory." *American Literature* 53:2 (May 1981): 214–31.

Ward, Artemus [Charles Farrar Browne]. *Artemus Ward, His Book.* New York: Carleton, 1862.

Weaver, Thomas, and Merline A. Williams. "Mark Twain's Jim: Identity as an Index to Cultural Attitudes." *American Literary Realism* 13:1 (spring 1980): 19–30.

Webster, Samuel Charles, ed. *Mark Twain, Business Man.* Boston: Little, Brown and Company, 1946.

Werge, Thomas. "Huck, Jim and Forty Dollars." *Mark Twain Journal* 13:1 (winter 1965–66): 15–16.

Williams, Charles R. *The Life of Rutherford Birchard Hayes.* 1914. Boston: Da Capo, 1971. 2 vols.

Williams, Kenny J. "*Adventures of Huckleberry Finn;* or, Mark Twain's Racial Ambiguity." *Mark Twain Journal* 22:2 (fall 1984): 38–42. Reprinted in James S. Leonard, Thomas A. Tenney, and Thadious M. Davis, eds. *Satire or Evasion?: Black Perspectives on "Huckleberry Finn."* Durham, N.C.: Duke University Press, 1992. 228–37.

Wills, Garry. *Lincoln at Gettysburg: The Words That Remade America.* New York: Simon and Schuster, 1992.

Wonham, Henry B. *Mark Twain and the Art of the Tall Tale.* New York: Oxford University Press, 1993.

INDEX

Abbott, Keene, 198n. 7

Abolitionists, 20, 22, 28, 41, 42, 46

Adams, Richard P., 174n. 7

Adult readers, 2; attraction of *Huckleberry Finn* for, 163; in prefatory material, 126

Adventure, 2

Adventures of Huckleberry Finn: admiration for, 2; *Bildungsroman* aspect of, 2; closing section of, 63, 69, 107 (*see also* Evasion section); compared with Douglass's narrative, 21, 22–23, 26–27, 29, 36–37; completion of, 62, 69; English version of, 95, 198n. 13; false assumptions in, 158; film versions of, 181n. 58, 198n. 16; final chapter of, 95; Blair and Fischer edition of, 100; 40,000 orders for, 101, 200n. 37; introduction to, 103; location in time of, 10, 16, 98–99, 179n. 45, 180n. 46; opening of, xv–xvi, 22, 139, 140; original plan for, 70–71; role of slavery in, 32; as sequel to *Tom Sawyer*, 1–2, 173n. 3; sequential patterns of action in, 196n. 1; Twain's commencement of, 57–59, 60, 62, 127; two halves of, 192n. 44; writing of, 62

Adventures of Tom Sawyer, The, 134; advertised in *Huckleberry Finn*, 103; as authority for *Huckleberry Finn*, 22; completion of, 57; conclusion to, 126–27; *Huckleberry Finn* compared with, 1; preface to, 125–26, 133, 136; prefatory material for, 144; publication of, 127

Age: coming of, 147; Huck's, 108, 163; Twain's, 96

Aladdin, story of, 198n. 7

Alden, Jean François (character in *Joan of Arc*), 142

Alden, John, 142

Allbright, Charles William (character in raftsman tale), 77, 188n. 15

America: *Huckleberry Finn* as representing spirit of, xiii–xiv, 19, 174n. 6; soul of, 4

American Anti-Slavery Society, 28, 179n. 45

American dreams, 18

Amputees, 89, 90–91, 195n. 14

Arabian Nights, 198n. 7

Arac, Jonathan, 122, 175n. 19, 181–82n. 60, 186–87n. 8

Aristocracy, and rights of others, 48

Aristocrat, Southern, mask of, 202n. 10. *See also* Southern bias

Audience, for *Huckleberry Finn*, 2

Auld, Sophia, 24, 25–26

Auld brothers (Hugh and Thomas), 24, 25, 31, 34

Authority: of adults, 77; of books, 150; of other authors, 22–23; questionable, 126, 132–33, 135–36; white, 80

Autobiographical sketch, Twain's, 7, 175nn. 22, 23

Baker, Houston A., 22

Baldanza, Frank, 200n. 36

Baptism, reverse, 54

Barksdale, Richard K., 124, 201–2n. 3

Barlow knife, symbolism of, 86, 87–88

Beaver, Harold, 197n. 3

Bell, Levi (character), 52, 158, 169

Belz, Herman, 199n. 30

Folk speech, 134
Foner, Eric, 56, 190nn. 26, 27, 199n. 30
Foner, Philip S., 184n. 13
Food, Huck's attitude toward, 44
Fools, 147, 159
Footnote: "authorizing," 131, 132; Twain's joking with, 130–31
Forty, figure, xv; emphasis on, 68; repeated use of, 94–95, 96, 97–98, 99, 198n. 16; suitability of, 95–96
"Forty acres and a mule," 98, 99, 100–101, 199n. 30
Forty dollars: betrayal associated with, 79, 93, 195–96n. 1; emphasis placed on, 37–38, 195–96n. 1; linked with Jim, 37, 68, 93, 95–96, 98, 100–101; references to, 94; as reminiscent of "forty acres and a mule," 98, 100–101; symbolism of, 197n. 3
"Forty-rod liquor," 90, 94
Fourth of July, 5, 6, 17, 57, 58, 59; Douglass on, 36, 181–82nn. 60. *See also* Independence Day
Franklin, Benjamin, using name of, 4, 175n. 17
Freedmen: land promised for, 199n. 30; openly reviled, 202n. 3; in post-Reconstruction South, 123; rights of, 45; rights to children of, 46; Twain's vision for, 65, 68. *See also* Ex-slaves
Freedom, xiii, 45; desire for, 31–32; for African Americans, 68; idea of, 40; for Huck, 11, 16, 45, 54, 64–65; for Jim, 47, 64, 68, 98, 166. *See also* Birth of freedom, new; Rebirth
Freeland, Betsy, 27
Free whites: Reconstruction and, 63–64; value placed on, 111
"Frenchman" argument, 80, 149
French Revolution, 17

Friendship: and race, 2, 174n. 5; racism and, 203–4n. 21
Frontispiece, plans for, 102, 103, 200n. 1
Fulton, Joe B., 203n. 17
Future: Huck's, 65; Jim's, 65; Twain's musing on, 16, 68–69

Gabler-Hover, Janet, 117, 188n. 17, 192n. 43
Gale, Robert L., 177n. 28
Garfield, President James, 20
Garrison, William Lloyd, 22, 28, 179n. 45
Gerber, John C., 206n. 42
Gerhardt, Karl, 102, 103
Gettysburg Address, 9–10, 18, 41, 43, 67, 178–79nn. 37, 38, 40, 191–92n. 37; and question of rights, 55
Gibson, William M., 4
Gilded Age, The, 129–30
Gillman, Susan, 211n. 20
Good-bad comparisons, associated with white and black, 109
Government: "divine" right of, 40; pap's railing against, 44–45, 186n. 8
Grangerford, Buck (character), 12, 16, 54, 74, 118, 152, 156, 161
Grangerford, Colonel (character), 115, 116
Grangerford, Emmeline (character), 193n. 5
Grangerford, Sophia (character), 12, 26, 76, 164
Grangerford family, 5, 115, 161; lack of knowledge of, 164
Grangerford home, 5, 148
Grangerford-Shepherdson feud. *See* Feud, Grangerford-Shepherdson
Grant, President Ulysses S., 57, 188–89n. 9
Griffith, Clark, 206nn. 33, 34
Guilt-money, 195–96n. 1